D-DAY 1944
THE MAKING OF VICTORY

D-DAY 1944
THE MAKING
OF VICTORY

ANTHONY TUCKER-JONES

The
History
Press

First published 2019

The History Press
The Mill, Brimscombe Port
Stroud, Gloucestershire, GL5 2QG
www.thehistorypress.co.uk

British Library Cataloguing in Publication Data.
A catalogue record for this book is available from the British Library.

ISBN 978 0 7509 8803 2

Typesetting and origination by The History Press
Printed and bound in Great Britain by TJ International Ltd

CONTENTS

Appendices

INTRODUCTION

Half-Man, Half-Beast

The roar of the powerful engines was deafening as the flat-nosed landing craft bludgeoned its way through the choppy waves. On every drop the vessel and its occupants were deluged in fine spray. The overriding smell was of diesel, oil and brine. For delicate stomachs, this and the constant motion was not a good combination. Trying to ignore these conditions, the Royal Marines slithered over their rocking tank carrying out vital last-minute checks. At sea, the five-man crew travelled on the outside just in case of mishap with their struggling vessel.

Every vehicle involved in Operation Overlord on 6 June 1944 had been plastered in a greasy, putty-like substance called Compound 219. This was jammed into all crevices and openings in a desperate effort to keep out seawater when the vehicle waded ashore. On tanks the turret ring and gun muzzle were also sealed with a type of plastic covering. Tankers did not greatly mind the application of the compound as they spent most of their time covered in grease and oil anyway. Seawater, on the other hand, was not welcome as it played havoc with the electrics and the engine. At over 60 tons, no amount of grease would make the Centaur float in deep water.

The Marines were working on their Centaur tank, of which almost a thousand had been built. However, this was specially designed for close support and one of less than 100 armed with a 95mm howitzer destined to see action on D-Day. It was a bunker-buster that could smash open concrete at close range. The driver and co-driver gave the Nuffield-built up-rated Liberty engine one last going over. If it failed to start or stalled when the landing craft ramp went down, then there would be hell to pay.

Although its official speed was about 27mph, with a bit of doctoring it was possible to manage almost twice that. If the driver had his way, he was going to sprint up the beach at full speed, assuming that the obstacles and mines had been cleared by the engineers and the 'Funnies'. The crew had dubbed their tank *Hunter*, and its turret was marked in white with the degrees of the compass in order to bring all the guns of the troop to bear on a target as quickly as possible. The centaur of ancient Greek mythology, half-man half-horse, was often depicted with a bow in its hands, so *Hunter* seemed highly appropriate.

The men, swerving with H Troop, 2nd Battery, 1st Royal Marine Armoured Support Regiment were heading for a beach in Normandy codenamed Gold.[1] Their orders appeared simple enough: provide covering fire from their landing craft, and once they were ashore continue to assist the assaulting infantry and commandos. They had fifty-one rounds for their turret-mounted howitzer, so it was vital they made every shot count.

Amongst the Centaur crews being buffeted by the waves was George Collard. He felt that they looked suitably nautical with their ration boxes and naval hammocks lashed up behind the turret. Also, on the way over, a naval rating had taken pity on one of the crew and 'loaned' them a waterproof oilskin coat that was much more weather-resistant than the sleeveless leather jerkins worn by some of the crews over their overalls, which dated back to the First World War. Looking out to sea, a smile came over his face as he remembered how, earlier in the year, they had pranged the tank before it had even seen combat.

Collard's unit had decamped from Corsham to the estate of Lord Mountbatten near Romsey in Hampshire ready for D-Day. Going through Devizes they had suffered a mishap. 'Our tank, driven by a three-badge Royal artilleryman,' he recalled, 'left the road and promptly crashed through the wall.'[2] The latter was inevitably a write-off, while the tank barely suffered a scratch. Besides, no one cared if the front mudguards got ripped off. It was a funny incident that resulted in much swearing by the troop commander, but such accidents were commonplace. Now, though, was the time to put all their training into practice. Lieutenant-Colonel Peskett, Collard's regimental commander, had pushed them hard, and for good reason.

During the night, the crossing had not been pleasant for the Centaur crews, or anyone else for that matter, because of the rough sea. Thanks to the weight of the tanks, the landing craft rode very low in the water. 'We slung hammocks where we could, sometimes between the tanks,' recalled Collard. 'Many were seasick, including the sailors.'[3] The Royal Marines did not take seasick tablets as 'a point of pride'.[4] Being sick as a Marine was not an option. From experience, Collard had learned that the best preventative measure against feeling nauseous was to fill your stomach with hard-tack biscuits, because it acted 'like concrete in the stomach'.[5]

When they neared the French coast, the Marine gunners and loaders clambered back into the turrets. They quickly rammed a high explosive round into the gun's breech. No one liked the idea of firing a tank from a moving landing craft – least of all the coxswain. The gunners knew they were unlikely to hit anything useful, but their actions added to the general bombardment of the enemy defences nonetheless.

Aboard a tank landing craft, Sub Lieutenant Frank Thomasson, with the Royal Navy Volunteer Reserve, was amazed at how relaxed the Marines were. They had risen early to check their kit and seemed in no haste to disembark. Before marching off they removed their steel helmets, and one man donned a top hat and raised an umbrella. 'This action by the Marines had a calming effect on all,' observed Thomasson.[6] Despite seeing some of his mates killed, Royal Marine Corporal Bernard Slack did not flinch, 'You just get on with your job. This is what you're trained for.'[7]

When Collard's troop finally rolled into the sea off Gold Beach, water rushed into the turret ring and his troop sergeant could not get out of his hatch and was soaked. Collard poked his head out the turret and 'looked with some admiration at the sight of the shells landing on the concrete strongpoints'.[8] The Germans were getting a good 'pasting'.

Directing the sodden driver, they managed to successfully negotiate the anti-invasion obstacles, only to have the left track blown off by a mine. 'A number of wounded and dead were on the beach,' noted Collard, 'including some killed where our own tanks had run over them – pushing – it appeared – the bile in the liver up to their faces.'[9] Having reached the cover of the dunes, his crew managed to repair their lame Centaur and get it back into the fight.

When Sergeant John Clegg's Centaur rolled ashore he became aware of an unwelcome noise above the racket of the engine. 'You can hear possibly bullets,' he said, 'splattering against the side of the landing craft and your tank: pitter-patter, pitter-patter.'[10] In response, he and his crew were soon engaging their assigned targets.

Lieutenant-Colonel Peskett had a total of thirty-two Centaurs and eight Sherman tanks with which to support the landings east of Arromanches.[11] He was not a happy man though, 'Several of my landing craft, being heavily armoured, did not weather the crossing, and either sank or turned back to land on the Isle of White.'[12] From a force of ten Centaurs supporting the attack on Le Hamel, only half reached the beach and these were destroyed straight away.[13]

Peskett's own 'landing was an extremely wet one',[14] with his waterproofed jeep drowning in 4ft of water. His second-in-command, Major Mabbott, was immediately wounded and had to be evacuated. After being rescued by a passing landing craft, Peskett toyed with the idea of taking a Royal Navy bicycle ashore but instead, along with his signaller Sergeant Harris and batman-driver Marine Collis, got a lift in a half-track.

Once inland, he commandeered an abandoned Ford which had been used as a German staff car. This was a choice he was later to regret when it drew the unwanted attention of the RAF. Two days later, one of Peskett's missing lieutenants arrived at his headquarters. When the man was asked where he had been, he responded, 'Bayeux'. A puzzled Peskett pointed out that was impossible as they had not liberated it yet. 'Yes, that's what I discovered,' said the officer nonchalantly.[15]

'Hunter' survived the landings and was photographed on 13 June 1944 rumbling along Normandy's dusty lanes with fumes belching out of its engine. Peskett's Centaurs were supposed to stay in Normandy for a maximum of seven days, but instead they fought for three weeks until they were broken down and had run out of ammunition. Like their mythological predecessors, they died in battle.

The Centaur tank was just one of the many 'mechanical contrivances'[16] that were the making of victory on D-Day. There were far more weird and wonderful contraptions unleashed on Normandy's shores that day. Second Lieutenant Stuart Hills, with the swimming Sherman tanks of the Nottinghamshire Sherwood Rangers, also landed on Gold Beach. He witnessed 'the Centaur close-support tanks …, the flail tanks and the assault vehicles of the Royal Engineers and the underwater obstacle clearance teams from the Engineers and the Royal Navy.'[17] It was these that got them inland.

General Eisenhower, the Allied Supreme Commander, and his staff were in awe of the unparalleled technical innovation shown in support of Operation Overlord. It was problem-solving on an unprecedented scale that helped ensure that D-Day was not a complete and utter bloodbath. Overlord was truly the appliance of science and a battle of the boffins.

1

ABSOLUTE DISASTER

Once Adolf Hitler had made himself master of western Europe, he faced the problem of how to defend 3,000 miles of coastline stretching all the way from Norway to Spain. As early as the end of 1941, when he was preoccupied by the fierce battle for Moscow, Hitler sought to tackle this challenge. He issued orders for the defence of the Atlantic coastline, designed 'ultimately to be built into a "new West Wall", in order that we can be sure of repelling any landing attempt, however strong, with the minimum number of permanently stationed troops'.[1]

He did not give the matter any real further thought until March 1942, when he warned, 'The coastline of Europe will, in the coming months, be exposed to the danger of an enemy landing in force.'[2] He was right, because the British and Canadians were planning their large-scale raid on Dieppe. While his long-winded directive was mainly about command and tactical responsibilities, it did form the basis for the Atlantic Wall. He stated that 'the defence of fortified areas and strongpoints by infantry' was to be treated as a priority.[3] This task fell to Albert Speer and his troublesome deputy, Xaver Dorsch.[4]

General Adolf Kuntzen, commanding LXXXI Corps based in Rouen on the Seine in the summer of 1942, with responsibility for the 302nd and 336th Infantry Divisions, was charged with the defence of Dieppe and the surrounding region. It would fall to Kuntzen's corps, with the assistance of the 10th Panzer Division, to counter any Allied seaborne attacks in the area. Kuntzen was an experienced panzer corps commander, having fought in Poland and on the Eastern Front, and had been sent to take charge in April 1942.

Field Marshal von Rundstedt had ensured that Dieppe was well defended. The port itself was held by Major-General Conrad Hasse's 302nd Division, which included many foreign 'volunteers'. Its equipment also included captured Czech, British and French weapons.[5] The 302nd had a single French tank cemented into the sea wall, and French trucks were used to tow its 75mm anti-tank guns. Hasse's real strength was his artillery and coastal gun batteries on the surrounding headlands. The 1,500m-long beach at Dieppe was hemmed in by two headlands; the western one dubbed *Hindenburg* and the eastern one *Bismarck*. Both had gun emplacements, creating a murderous cross-fire. It was not a good place for the Allies to probe Hitler's defences.

The nearest German armour within striking distance belonged to the 10th Panzer Division, under General Wolfgang Fischer, stationed at Amiens 60 miles away. The 1st SS Panzer Division, under Lieutenant-General Josef 'Sepp' Dietrich, was 80 miles away north-west of Paris. Both divisions had been sent to France for refitting following heavy fighting on the Eastern Front.

Operation Jubilee, conducted on 19 August 1942, was conceived by Admiral Lord Louis Mountbatten, head of British Combined Operations, and his naval advisor, Captain John Hughes-Hallet, as a way of testing German defences prior to reopening the Western Front.[6] It was green-lighted at the most senior levels by Prime Minister Winston Churchill and President Franklin Roosevelt. In addition to frontally assaulting Dieppe, there were to be other landings, including Pourville to the west and Berneval to the east. Tanks would only be involved in the attack on Dieppe itself. Allied preparations and training on the Isle of Wight could not be completely concealed, and by mid-June 1942 Hitler's intelligence was expecting some kind of large-scale assault on the French coast.

Supporting the 5,000 infantry of Major-General J.H. Roberts' Canadian 2nd Division, 1,000 Royal Marine Commandos and fifty US Rangers allocated to the raid, was the Canadian 14th Tank Battalion, Calgary Tank Regiment, equipped with the British Churchill tank. Three flame-thrower tanks were also earmarked for the operation. To make the tanks waterproof up to a depth of 7ft for wading purposes, disposable exhaust and trunking extensions were added.

German exercises at Dieppe proved that it was not good tank ground after the gravel on the beach clogged a panzer's tracks. The leading Canadian tanks were fitted with elementary bobbins with a rolled carpet of hessian and wooden paling strips. Also, to get the Churchills over the shingle, sappers were to unroll 4ft wide and 250ft long bundles of wired wood matting known as chespaling.

The Canadian tankers were not expecting to encounter any panzers; Dieppe was only garrisoned by infantry. However, it was recognised that it was likely to be a one-way trip for some if not all of the Churchill tanks. To that end, each was equipped with nitro-glycerine bombs to prevent them falling into enemy hands intact. Adjutant Austin Stanton of the Calgarys, upon reading that it was planned to re-embark the tanks and troops from in front of Dieppe, remarked drily, 'The only thing they had forgotten to mention was that tea and cakes would be served on the beach.'[7]

This was not the first time the Allies had attacked occupied France. Churchill's first major raids occurred at Bruneval to capture a radar and at St Nazaire to destroy the dry dock in early 1942. While both were successes, the latter saw 185 British troops killed and 200 captured from a raiding force of just 611 men.[8] Things did not bode well for the forthcoming Dieppe raid.

This operation was a lot more ambitious and involved tanks. The Canadian 14th Tank Battalion had been mobilised on 11 February 1941, and by late June was en route to Britain. Initially, the Calgarys were equipped with the British Matilda II tank for training purposes. On 19 November 1941, the battalion's war diary recorded:

> Today the battalion took over its first Mark IV Tanks (Churchills). The Mark IIA Tanks (Matildas) with which the battalion is now equipped are being turned in as Mark IVs become available. Present indications are that the changes will be made quite quickly for more and more Churchills are being made available for issue to regiments.[9]

An inkling of the unit's role in the Dieppe attack was gained on 4 December 1941, when its diary noted, 'A special film called "Combined Operations" was shown to Officers and NCOs [non-commissioned officers] in the 'A' Sqn NAAFI hut. This film showed the various types of landing craft built for assaulting a hostile coast, and also the various ways in which such a coast may be attacked.'[10] As a result, the rumour that the Second Front was about to be opened quickly spread.

Throughout December, the Canadians continued to return their Matildas to the ordnance depots at either Aldershot or Bordon Camp while drawing Churchills to replace them. Taking delivery of the new tanks turned out to be a time-consuming process; not only did each item of equipment have to be checked, but also the greatest care had to be exercised in checking the lubrication, track tension and the remainder of the suspension and hydraulic lines before it could be safely driven away. The manufacturers, Vauxhall, sent its representatives to instruct the Canadians on how to handle the engine. Once fully equipped, planning efforts turned to Dieppe.

On 16 August 1942, the Calgarys transported eighteen Churchill tanks from Seaford to Gosport ready for embarkation; the rest moved to Newhaven under their own power. The following day they were loaded onto the landing ships, and by 0300 hours on the 19th they were 8 miles off Dieppe. The assault fleet comprised eight escort destroyers, nine landing ships, thirty-nine coastal craft and 179 landing craft; in the air, sixty-seven RAF squadrons provided cover, sixty of which were fighters.

While the port was to be stormed by six infantry battalions and an armoured regiment of the Canadian 2nd Infantry Division, No. 3 Commando, led by Lieutenant-Colonel Durnford-Slater, was to silence the German Goebbels battery at Berneval to the east and No. 4 Commando, under Lieutenant-Colonel Lord Lovat, the Hess batteries to the west at Varengeville. Also, on the flanks, the Camerons and South Saskatchewans were to secure Porville and the Royal Regiment's objective was Puits. The Essex Scottish, Fusiliers Mont-Royal and Royal Marines, supported by the Calgary tanks, were to barge their way into Dieppe itself.

Sergeant George Cook of No. 4 Commando, upon hitting the beaches, got over the wire and was relieved to find the German machine-gunners in the pillboxes were firing high. After that their luck was in short supply as a mortar took out four men. Cook remembered:

Sergeant Horne and I had cut some barbed wire. He started cutting, and then I heard an 'Urgh' – and when I looked, there was Sergeant Horne, blood spurting out of his chest. He looked as though he was dead – which was a bit of a shock to me, because he was about the toughest fellow I ever knew, was Geordie Horne. Then I got hit in the face and the shoulder. That was me out of it.[11]

No. 4 Commando scored one of the few successes at Dieppe, destroying the Varengeville battery, though it cost them twelve dead and twenty wounded. In contrast, No. 3 Commando ran into a German convoy on the run-in and only twenty men got ashore. The air cover provided by the RAF also received a rough reception. 'We were taking some Canadians to drop them on a quay at Dieppe,' recalled French seaman Albert Quesnée on the *Bayonne*, 'but of course the Germans were there. That was a bad day, a bad day. I've never seen so many planes come down in the water.'[12]

The Canadian tanks were to attack in four waves; the first with nine tanks supporting the assaulting infantry; the second with twelve tanks; the third with sixteen tanks; and the fourth with the rest of the regiment. Following a preliminary bombardment, the landings started at 0530 hours, though a naval engagement in the Channel followed by an air attack tipped off the Germans that something was going on. During the run-in to Dieppe, the Tank Landing Craft (LCTs) were 15 vital minutes late, leaving the infantry pinned down on the beach.

The first three LCTs, each carrying three tanks and a jeep, were met by heavy fire. Churchills bearing the names *Cougar*, *Cat* and *Cheetah* were landed near the harbour mole, but, wasting more precious time, their cold engines in turn stalled on the ramp. Although the first tank was hit three or four times, the armour withstood the punishment and it kept going, rolling right over the thick belt of barbed wire.

The old French tank armed with a 37mm gun and incorporated into the German defences engaged the Churchill. In a stroke of bad luck, the static tank had been unmanned until a German sentry ducked inside and proceeded to expend 185 rounds against the Canadians. *Cougar* found the sea had conveniently created a pebble ramp up the sea wall, and drove up onto the promenade. Behind it, *Cheetah* frightened the Germans manning a nearby pillbox into flight. *Cat* was finally freed from the landing craft ramp, but in the confusion drove up the beach with a scout car still attached.

In the meantime, the LCT crews were suffering terribly from heavy German mortar bombardment. Bravely, the Canadian machine-gunners exposed on the decks returned fire. However, the sappers and mortar men were unable to deploy. Badly damaged, LCT 2 escaped out to sea; LCT 1, after getting its Churchills – *Company*, *Calgary* and *Chief* – ashore in three minutes, drifted away to sink.

The three flame-throwing tanks on LCT 3 met an equally hot reception, with mortar bombs dropping right on them. 'About 200 yards out a terrific concentration of fire opened up on our craft,' said Captain Dick

Eldred of the Calgarys on LCT 3. 'Most of our gunners were quickly knocked out of action and though their places were immediately taken these too became casualties.'[13]

The first tank, *Boar*, commanded by Captain Bill Purdy, crashed through the ramp and drowned, the LCT passing over it. When the craft hit the beach, the damaged ramp folded under it, leaving a 10ft drop; however, *Bull* and *Beetle* drove ashore, having inadvertently crushed some of their own men. One lost a track on the shoreline and was stranded, while the other tore off the flame-flower fuel container and could only be used as a gun tank.

At 0605 hours the second wave of LCTs, carrying another dozen tanks, arrived. Further Churchill tanks borne by LCT 4, 5 and 6 now came in; although 4 burst into fire 200 yards from the beach and sank, it got tanks *Burns*, *Bolster* and *Backer* ashore. The German defenders, realising they could not pierce the Churchills' impervious armour, switched their fire onto the vulnerable tracks.

In this area of the sea front, unfortunately for the Canadian tankers, the Germans had only recently cleared the shingle from the sea wall using a digger, forcing the tanks to veer side-on. Major Page in *Burns* noted, 'I gave orders to turn to the right and that's when I was hit. I was just on the crest at the top of the trench dug by the excavator and the right track was blown off. The left one went on for a few seconds and kind of pulled me into the trench.'[14]

The other two tanks also lost their tracks before they could clear the beach.

Similarly, after *Buttercup*, *Blossom* and *Bluebell* were landed, LCT 5 was destroyed. LCT 6 took three attempts to land *Bert*, *Bob* and *Bill*. The Canadian infantry and sappers had just as bad a time as the tanks and the casualties were very heavy, with some men refusing to leave their craft. LCT 7 put ashore *Beefy*, *Bellicose* and *Bloody*, followed by LCT 8, 9 and 10. Only ten tanks reached the shore from the third wave, and the fourth wave were not landed, as by 0900 hours it was clear they could achieve little.

RAF Squadron Leader 'Johnny' Johnson of 616 Squadron said:

We could see very little except a bloody great pall of smoke over the town, and lots of shelling going on down below. But we could do nothing about it because the attackers and defenders were all within a hundred yards of each other. We couldn't help the army ... we

knew that the whole thing had been a disaster – but there was nothing we could do to help them.[15]

At 0625 hours, the two German panzer divisions had been put on alert
to move. Some 15 minutes later, the Dieppe German Naval Semaphore
station signalled headquarters, 'The enemy continues to land at Dieppe.
Destroyers making smoke along the coast. Up till now 12 tanks have
been landed, of which one is on fire.'[16] The 10th Panzer headed north
at 0900 but, lacking adequate maps and with worn-out vehicles, its progress was far from proficient, and the Luftwaffe was equally slow off the
mark to react.

At Dieppe, General Hasse's defences were such that the Churchills
found themselves hemmed in and could not penetrate the town, where
they could have created havoc. From a force of twenty-nine tanks landed
during Operation Jubilee, two drowned and twelve never got off the
beach. Although the remaining fifteen got onto the esplanade, they could
not pierce the anti-tank obstacles the Germans had erected.

Bill did attempt to navigate a gap in the Rue de Sygogne, but lost a
track and blocked the approach to the street. *Bellicose* was more successful
in assisting with the attack on the Casino building, though got no further. Frustrated, the men of the Calgarys could only drive up and down,
blazing away until their ammunition ran out. The defenders' 37mm anti-
tank guns had little effect on the Churchills' armour, and 75mm rounds
penetrated only two tanks. According to a subsequent German military
report, twenty-four tanks were put out of action by artillery in the area of
the beach and only five made it to the roadway.

Following the Allies' evacuation order at 1100 hours, the tank crews were
instructed to destroy their vehicles with the nitro-glycerine bombs. The
crews in those tanks trapped on the beach, once they had run out of ammunition, remained inside rather than risk the murderous German fire raking
their hulls. Also, some crews had left these highly dangerous devices behind
or dumped them overboard on the way over. 'I flew over Dieppe four times
on 19 August 1942,' recalled Squadron Leader Johnson, 'but I didn't realise
what an impossible tactical situation it was.'[17] From the Calgarys landed,
only one man got back to Britain. That evening the Luftwaffe chivalrously
dropped photos on the Canadians' barracks at Seaford in Sussex showing
those who had survived.

At 1215 hours, German headquarters issued orders stating, '[T]he 10th Panzer Division, tanks and artillery should immediately go forward. Every weapon available must now contribute to the total destruction of the enemy.'[18] Fischer's panzers arrived at Dieppe just as the survivors were surrendering at 1308 hours. The Germans bombastically noted, 'Our rapid intervention and the powerful aspect of the panzer division made a great impression on the populace.' At 1640, senior panzertruppen were ordered immediately to examine the captured Churchill tanks.[19]

While the Germans were impressed by the Canadians' fighting spirit, their maps and the smokescreen laid on the beach, they were less than impressed by the manufacturing, metallurgical and technical aspects of the Churchill tank. Likewise, they thought the gun, armour and tracks were poor. Their verdict was that the Churchill was easy to fight, and the performance of the German anti-tank gunners was exonerated because they had been firing at long distance.

Kuntzen, Hasse and Rundstedt could not understand why armour had not been used to support the flanking landing at Pourville, nor could they believe that a raid would employ so many tanks. The German Seventh Army headquarters noted:

With the reserves afloat were twenty-eight tanks, certainly of the same type as those landed. Now the employment of altogether fifty-eight similar tanks cannot be connected with a brief sabotage operation. Although operational orders have also fallen into our hands, it is not possible to deduce whether it was a question of an operation of local character, or – in case of success – if it would form the initial stage of 'invasion'.[20]

Many senior German officers assessed that if the Allies had achieved a successful lodgement at Dieppe, it would have heralded a full-scale invasion; though Field Marshal von Rundstedt did not share this view. What the German commanders did not know was where the main weight of the Allied assault, or schwerpunkt, might fall, which meant any initial landings were likely to be considered diversionary. This conclusion was to cloud their thinking when it came to opposing D-Day.

Although the Dieppe Raid provided vital lessons in amphibious warfare and Combined Operations, they were gained at an appallingly high cost.[21] [22] The subsequent successful Allied landings in North Africa were against ill-equipped French forces that were in a state of political disarray, while those on Sicily and the Italian mainland were against the Italian Army, which was largely a spent force. Striking Hitler's Festung Europa was an entirely different matter, even if the German forces were, in some cases, second rate, reconstituting or recuperating.

Lord Lovat blamed the failure of Operation Jubilee on poor planning and intelligence. He said this 'led to slapdash efforts that went astray'.[23]

Peter Young, who served with No. 3 Commando at Dieppe, said it 'showed the planners that the Allies were unlikely to take a port in France on D-Day'.[24] It was clear that any future invasion of France would have to be conducted across open beaches and not against a well-defended port.

Dieppe loomed large in everyone's minds, and despite the Allies' subsequent considerable planning and preparation, there was a very real fear that D-Day might go the same way.

Captain Pat Porteous, who was awarded the Victoria Cross for his role in successfully destroying the Varengeville battery, was scathing of the whole sorry affair:

> My feeling is that it was an absolute disaster. It should never have taken place. A great deal has been made about the lessons learned from the raid which were put into good use for the main landings in Italy and later on in Normandy. But my feeling was that 90 per cent of those lessons could have been learned training in Britain on the beach at Weymouth or anywhere else. But as it was, they had something like 1,000 killed and 2,000 taken prisoner – and what did they achieve? Absolutely nothing.[25]

The most embarrassing aspect of the raid, after the high casualty rate, was the fact that Winston Churchill's namesake tanks lay strewn across the landing beaches like so much junk.[26] Lord Mountbatten, trying to put a gloss on things, informed Prime Minister Churchill that two-thirds of the Dieppe force had escaped. This ignored the inconvenient fact that the bulk of the assault force had never gone ashore.

The failure of Operation Jubilee firmly convinced Hitler that he could easily contain and defeat an Allied amphibious assault on French soil. The shambles at Dieppe was a major propaganda coup for him. Joseph Goebbels, his propaganda minister, was soon claiming they had defeated an Allied invasion and would do so again:

We have fortified the coast of Europe, from North Cape to the Mediterranean, and installed the most deadly weapons that the twentieth century can produce. This is why an enemy attack, even the most powerful and furious possible to imagine, is bound to fail … At Dieppe they held on for nine hours and there was no Wall. If they hold on for nine hours next time they'll do well.[27]

Understandably, after the Dieppe raid the construction of Hitler's Atlantic Wall gained greater urgency. Nonetheless, the Eastern and Italian fronts continued to be the focus of his attention and military resources. Hitler convinced himself that when the Allies opened their Second Front, he would travel to France to take command of his forces personally, a habit he had developed on the Eastern Front. To this end, the Todt Organisation was ordered to build two forward headquarters for the Führer, which inevitably used huge quantities of concrete and hundreds of miles of telephone cable,[28] one of which was dubbed W2 and located between Soissons and Loan.

General Kuntzen's LXXXI Corps' control of an armoured division was short-lived, and by June 1944 its subordinate units consisted of the 245th and 711th Infantry Divisions and the 17th Luftwaffe Field Division. Kuntzen's only effective force was a small combat group from the Panzer Lehr Division.

2

POURING CONCRETE

While the disaster of Dieppe convinced the Allies that seizing an occupied port as a prerequisite for a successful assault on the continent was out of the question, it persuaded Hitler otherwise. 'The first priority had been given to the main port areas,' noted Colonel David Belchem, General Montgomery's planning chief, 'which by 1944 had become virtually impregnable to seaborne assault. Next came the Pas de Calais at the Channel straits, which the Germans considered the most likely area for an Allied invasion attempt. But elsewhere the defences were less formidable.'[1] Building these defences proved to be a nightmare for the man in charge.

Albert Speer found himself in hospital in early 1944 suffering from nervous exhaustion and a possible pulmonary embolism. In the early days he had enjoyed being part of the Nazis' inner circle. He had revelled in being one of the Führer's favourites; thanks to Hitler's patronage, Speer had been elevated into the Nazis' upper ranks as the party's chief architect. As the years wore on though, the constant intrigues and backstabbing had become too much for him. Speer needed time to recuperate and recharge his batteries.

Even in the sanctuary of hospital, he was to find no solace. The deputy leader of the very organisation tasked with building Hitler's Atlantic Wall was plotting against Speer and his loyal supporters even as he lay in his sick bed. Speer's wife called him with regular updates on their children, and that cheered him up. Deep down though, he missed his mentor Fritz Todt, who, in Speer's opinion, had been a good man.

Despite being Hitler's Minister for Armaments and Munitions, Speer felt as if his life was now ruled by concrete. As an architect he was no stranger to the stuff, but as the war progressed the demand for it just seemed to grow and grow. Todt, his predecessor, had also headed up Germany's massive construction industry, so was more of an expert. It was he who had built Germany's autobahns. However, Todt was killed in a plane crash on 8 February 1942 on a flight that Speer had almost taken. 'From that moment on my whole world was changed,' recalled Speer.[2] He had great respect for his former colleague, noting, 'Todt had maintained his personal independence in his relations with Hitler, although he was a loyal party member of the early years.'[3]

Speer inherited not only Todt's job but also the vast Todt Organisation, originally set up to build the Siegfried Line or West Wall, the U-boat shelters along the Atlantic coast and the roads in the occupied territories. As early as the summer of 1940, Hitler tried to get Speer to take over construction of their defences along the Atlantic as Todt was overburdened. Speer declined because he did not want to undermine Todt's authority. Ironically, here he was, four years later, with responsibility for construction of the Atlantic coast defences and just as overburdened as his predecessor had been.[4]

Speer took pride in his achievements with Germany's armaments industries, especially as he had known nothing about them when he started. He recalled with a smile how, just as Hitler was appointing him, Reichsmarschall Hermann Göring arrived, insisting he take charge of the construction industry and the Todt Organisation. Göring was indulging in his usual empire-building, but Speer shuddered to think what would have happened had the head of the Luftwaffe been placed in charge of Germany's static defences. Rebuffed by Hitler, the Reichsmarschall had stomped off, refusing to attend Todt's funeral.[5]

It was easy to see why Göring wanted to get his hands on the Todt Organisation. At its height in 1944, it was the largest employer in Europe, with 336,000 German personnel in charge of a million foreign workers, including 285,000 concentration camp prisoners and prisoners of war.[6] In addition, some 3,000 French armed guards were deployed on the construction sites in France.[7] While the French Resistance took a dim view of such collaboration, it sometimes made it easier to spy on the Germans.

When it came to the Eastern Front, Speer knew that Hitler had a complete aversion to static defences. Time and time again, Hitler refused to give his generals permission to build defences behind which they could regroup their forces. After Hitler's defeat at Stalingrad in 1942–43, the

German General Staff wanted to establish a defensive line on the Dnieper, but Hitler would hear none of it. After the German defeat at Kursk the following summer, it was apparent they needed to do something to strengthen the Eastern Front. In December 1943, Field Marshal Manstein, despite Hitler's dictate, authorised the Todt Organisation to start building fortified positions on the River Bug. At the time this was 125 miles behind German front lines, and when Hitler heard he ordered the work to stop immediately. He simply had no time for such insurance policies. The Western Front, however, was a different matter.

In France, Speer and Xaver Dorsch were infuriated by the activities of French agitators, who seemed to dog their every step with the Atlantic Wall. Spies ensured the Allies were kept well informed. The Todt Organisation's headquarters in the Pas-de-Calais at Audinghen was visited twice by American bombers on 11 November 1943. That same day, they also struck one of the network of new V-weapon launch sites being built in the Cotentin Peninsula at Couville, south-west of Cherbourg. The bombs wrecked the 5m-thick concrete bunker roofs and damaged much of the nearby village. At Audinghen, the first attack flattened the village, while the second hit the Todt headquarters building, scattering frightened staff.

What Speer did not know was that in between the raids at Audinghen, Michel Blot, a French agent, had slipped in and photographed plans for over 100 V-1 flying-bomb sites and stolen secret documents dealing with coastal defences.[8] Controlled from Caen, a network of some 1,500 agents systematically plotted German defences.[9] This included a painter and decorator who managed to steal blueprints from the Todt Organisation.[10]

By the autumn of 1943, thanks to the constant intrigues in the Nazi hierarchy, Speer said, 'I gradually began to feel insecure in my own ministry.'[11] He fell into depression, observing, 'The nearly two years of continuous tension had been taking their toll. Physically, I was nearly worn out at the age of thirty-eight.'[12] On 18 January 1944, he was hospitalised for two months. It was not a good start to the year, especially when he discovered that one of his officials had been plotting against him and members of his ministry. It was none other than Dorsch, Speer's deputy at the Todt Organisation. Speer wanted Dorsch sacked, but the man had Hitler's favour.

Hitler had no desire to dispense with Dorsch's services because he was an experienced fortifications builder. During the late 1930s, Dorsch had been involved in building the 630km West Wall opposite the French Maginot Line. Dorsch's efforts with constructing the Atlantic Wall by April 1944 were faced with an unwanted distraction thanks to Hitler. The Führer had got it in his head that German industry should be moved into six huge shelters to protect them from Allied bombers.

Hitler summoned Dorsch, who pointed out that the Todt Organisation only operated in the occupied territories and not the Reich. Nonetheless, Hitler authorised him to carry out the work and Dorsch promised to finish it by November 1944. Speer was furious that Hitler had sidelined him, especially when he had opposed concentrating their weapons industries, which would make them an even more tempting target for the enemy bombers.

While concrete was being poured all along Europe's coastline to create impregnable bunkers and pillboxes, the intrigue in Berlin continued unabated. Dorsch told General Zeitzler, the Army Chief of Staff, that 'Speer is incurably ill, and will therefore not be coming back.'[13] Speer did not want Dorsch placed in charge of construction in Germany, arguing with Hitler that armaments and construction should be treated as a whole. He suggested that Dorsch's former assistant, Willi Henne, be placed in charge in Germany, with both men reporting to Walter Brugmann, who headed the Todt Organisation in southern Russia. On 25 May 1944, Brugmann, like Todt, was killed in a plane crash. Speer was shaken by this because he suspected that an attempt had been made on his life while hospitalised.

Speer was aghast at the Führer's micromanaging of the Atlantic Wall right down to designing the bunkers. 'Hitler planned these defensive installations down to the smallest details,' noted Speer. 'He even designed the various types of bunkers and pillboxes.' Although Hitler did this late at night, his sketches 'were executed with precision'.[14] Somewhat surprisingly, Hitler's engineers used these plans with few changes.

A major drain on Hitler's efforts to fortify the European coastline, ironically, was the British Channel Islands, which lay to the west of Normandy's Cherbourg Peninsula. It amused Speer that although the Channel Islands were British territory, the French insisted in calling them 'les îles normandes'.[15] Hitler had occupied these in the summer of 1940 and subsequently decided to turn them into an impregnable fortress. He wanted up to 250 strongpoints built on each of the larger islands.[16] Hitler largely took this stance as a matter of prestige, despite the islands being a strategic irrelevance. As a result they soaked up around 10 per cent of all the resources used to build the Atlantic Wall defences.[17]

The German 319th Infantry Division arrived on the islands in July 1941 and remained there until the very end of the war. It was supported by a weak panzer battalion equipped with French tanks.[18] Slave labourers of the Todt Organisation were also sent to start building the numerous gun batteries and bunkers. The showpiece defence in the Channel Islands was the massive Mirus Battery, which consisted of four 305mm naval guns at Le Frie Baton on Guernsey. The emplacements took a year-and-a-half to complete. The weapons had become operational in April 1942 and dominated the Gulf of St Malo.

Most of the Channel Island construction workers were not redirected to the Atlantic Wall until late 1943. In May of that year there were 16,000 labourers on the islands, a number that had fallen by 50 per cent in November 1943.[19] At this stage there were almost two division's worth of troops tied up garrisoning them.[20] By then the Germans were planning 232 concrete installations for Jersey alone; by June 1944, around 182 of these had been completed.[21]

Speer and Dorsch despaired of Hitler's needless obsession with the Channel Islands. At the beginning of 1944, construction of the Atlantic Wall had involved the excavation of a quarter of a million cubic metres of soil and rock. At the same time, almost exactly the same amount was being dug out of the Channel Islands.[22] To many it seemed like wasted effort when digging on the Atlantic Wall could have been doubled. Likewise, while the Atlantic Wall accounted for over six million cubic metres of concrete, the Channel Islands had used almost another half million cubic metres.[23] The garrison had laid 114,000 mines, whereas 18,000 would have sufficed.[24]

By early June 1944, Speer was thoroughly alarmed by the needless consumption of so much concrete, 'in barely two years of intensive building, seventeen million three hundred thousand cubic yards of concrete … In addition the armaments factories were deprived of 1.2 million metric tons of iron.'[25] On top of this, other projects in France, including pens for Hitler's U-boats, gobbled up another six million cubic yards. 'All this expenditure and effort was sheer waste,'[26] lamented Speer.

As far as Speer was concerned, the iron and steel would have been much better used building weapons and munitions. Certainly it could have resulted in more panzers, but these would have been sent to the Eastern

Front, not the northern French coast. After Hitler's defeats at Stalingrad and Kursk, the Russian Front had become a priority. Besides, the Atlantic Wall had initially been a good way to recycle obsolete captured weapons, plus concrete and slave labour was cheap.[27] The problem was not so much with the fixed defences, but devising a strategy with which to complement them.

For the men stationed in Speer's concrete edifices, they found them cold, damp and dark. Like the redundant French Maginot Line, the water seeped in and it was not long before mildew was growing on the walls. During the Phoney War of late 1939 and early 1940, France's media issued photos of naked French soldiers luxuriating under UV lamps as if the Maginot Line was some sort of health spa. Anyone familiar with concrete fortifications knew that this was far from the truth. Soldiers were reduced to troglodytes when confined to their subterranean strongholds. Whilst the bunkers protected their occupants from shrapnel and glancing blows, direct hits were another matter, as was the weather.

German coastal defence units knew from training that the moment they discharged their weapons in the confines of the bunkers, their ears began to ring. Toxic fumes soon mounted, causing eyes to smart and throats to tickle. Some of the larger emplacements had extractor fans and ventilator systems, though these were not terribly reliable. In addition, the generators required to run them, the lights and the ammunition lifts also created fumes. The ventilator shafts inevitably created weak points in the thick concrete. If these were detected by the enemy, then it would not be long before something was hurtling down them. Not only was the noise and smell reflected by the concrete walls, so was the concussion from the guns, which caused dangerous compression of the eardrums and lungs. On some of the bigger guns, the crews wore naval-style flash hoods, but these did little good.

The only thing that alleviated the monotony of garrison duty was the seagulls. They were always attracted to where people were, because it meant rubbish and therefore rich pickings. For some soldiers, after a while the noise made by the birds became particularly bothersome. This was especially so in the mornings and afternoons.

3

A PLEASANT CHATEAU

Field Marshal Gerd von Rundstedt began to enjoy a very civilised existence from March 1942 at his headquarters located in the picturesque Chateau Germain-en-Laye, overlooking the Seine. It did not take him long to settle in and he was soon indulging in regular long lunches at his favourite restaurant, the Côq Hardi in nearby Paris. His predecessor had taken advantage of the comforts of the Louis-Dreyfus mansion, but Rundstedt had opted for the Villa Félicien David on the basis that it was less likely to attract the attentions of Allied bombers.

Germain-en-Laye was dotted with dreary German command bunkers, and during the cold winter months, most of his staff preferred the warmth and other pleasures of the Paris hotels. This was not surprising, as the French winters were reportedly some of the worst, and conditions had been aggravated by fuel shortages.[1] Another reason for Rundstedt's officers wanting to be in Paris was that it gave them access to German female auxiliaries, known as 'Grey Mice' by the Parisians.[2] For both parties, this offered the chance of a welcome diversion from occupation duties.[3] However, Rundstedt did not feel safe in the French capital, especially after the Allies bombed the nearby Renault works.

He had been recalled from retirement for a second time by Hitler and appointed Commander-in-Chief West, which included the defence of Belgium, France and the Netherlands. As Rundstedt observed, this was an enormous task. 'I had over 3,000 miles of coastline to cover from the Italian frontier in the south to the German frontier in the north, and only 60 divisions with which to defend it. Most of them were low-grade divisions and some of them were skeletons.'[4]

Rundstedt had only just taken up his new post when the British carried out a raid on the naval base at St Nazaire. Hitler, highly displeased that the dock was put out of action, ordered the building of yet more defences. The subsequent British and Canadian attack on Dieppe confirmed to Hitler the value of strong coastal fortifications. In contrast, as far as Rundstedt was concerned, Hitler's Atlantic Wall was little more than a 'Propaganda Wall'.[5] Nonetheless, the Führer had also instructed, 'Enemy forces which have landed must be destroyed or thrown back into the sea by immediate counterattack.'[6]

This was fine by Rundstedt, who had greater faith in conventional manoeuvre warfare than in relying on fixed defences. Rundstedt told a reporter in early 1944, 'We Germans do not indulge in the tired Maginot spirit.'[7] From experience, he had no confidence in fixed defences. It was under his command four years earlier that the German Army had shown how France's Maginot Line was a hugely expensive white elephant. His greatest worry was that the Atlantic Wall would prove to be Hitler's white elephant.

What he wanted was a large reserve capable of launching a massive counterattack against any Allied bridgehead. This approach, however, was to bring him to loggerheads with Field Marshal Rommel when the latter arrived as commander of Army Group B. Rommel would be of the opinion that all their forces should be kept as close to the beaches as possible. They were never to be reconciled on this matter.

Rundstedt was not keen on building fixed defences and had a good excuse not to do so. 'The lack of labour troops and material was the main handicap in developing the defences,' he said. 'Most of the men of the Todt labour force, who had been previously available in France, had been drawn off to Germany to repair air raid damage there.'[8] He also reasoned that the infantry divisions were too stretched to conduct the work themselves and that Allied air forces were impeding the supply of building materials. There was another reason for his lack of dynamism. The commander of Panzer Group West, General Geyr von Schweppenburg, said he was simply 'incredibly idle'.[9]

There could be no hiding the slow pace of construction. During the summer of 1943, Rundstedt was instructed to prepare a situation report for Hitler. He submitted it on 30 October and it immediately exposed the shocking weakness of the 'Propaganda Wall'. Rundstedt made no attempt to sugar-coat his findings. The Atlantic Wall had limited value, he said,

'[A]s a rigid German defence was impossible there for any length of time, the outcome of the battle must depend on the use of a mobile and armoured reserve.' Pointedly, he added that the fixed defences were 'indispensable and valuable for battle as well as for propaganda'.[10]

Rundstedt explained that with the units available he could only cover, not defend the Atlantic Wall. Likewise, with the Atlantic Wall south of the Loire he could do little more than keep it under observation. In light of the Allies' successful landings at Sicily and Salerno, Hitler was furious. There was much finger-pointing and excuses were made. The Führer cast about for someone to shake things up. It so happened that Rommel, who had lost out with the commander-in-chief job in Italy, was at a loose end.

When Rommel came on the scene he initially undermined Rundstedt's authority because he answered directly to Hitler. The solution to this was to place Rommel in charge of Army Group B in northern France and General Blaskowitz in command of Army Group G in southern France, with both answering to von Rundstedt. Rommel's staff later claimed that this setup was his solution, 'as the only way of putting his ideas into execution quickly'.[11] Rundstedt was dismissive of Rommel's abilities, saying he was 'not really qualified for high command'.[12] He had this on the highest authority.

Before Rommel's appointment, in order to smooth any ruffled feathers, Hitler sent Field Marshal Wilhelm Keitel, chief of the armed forces high command, to Paris to reassure Rundstedt that his position was secure. He also warned Rundstedt that the 'Desert Fox' could be difficult. 'You'll find Rommel a tiresome person because he doesn't like taking orders from anyone,' explained Keitel. 'In Africa, of course, he very much ran his own show. But the Führer believes you are the one man to whom even a Rommel will show due respect.'[13]

This was not all, as Hitler did not consider Rommel potential commander-in-chief material, because he viewed him as a tactician, not a strategist. 'Should the time ever come for your replacement because of failing health,' Keitel added, 'the Führer wishes you to know that only Field Marshal von Kluge is in the running to succeed you.'[14] Such flattery convinced Rundstedt that he still had the patronage of Hitler and therefore the upper hand with Rommel. Some of the other generals in the West would come to consider Rommel as little more than Hitler's 'inspector'.[15]

Construction of the Atlantic Wall was a complete and largely unwanted diversion for the German Army. In the early part of 1944, German soldiers spent three-quarters of their time working on coastal defences, rather than training.[16] This was a distraction for Rundstedt, who was presiding over a vast military empire. After the Eastern Front, his garrison in Western Europe accounted for the second largest concentration of German divisions. However, they were woefully inadequate.[17] In total he could muster around 1.4 million men, but this included disparate Luftwaffe, Navy and SS personnel, all of whom answered to different masters.

Allied deception plans designed to convince Hitler they intended to invade the Pas de Calais or Norway further muddled Rundstedt's job.[18] 'I expected an invasion in 1943, once we had occupied the whole of France,'[19] he said – because his forces had become so stretched. Despite all his experience, Rundstedt had little knowledge of amphibious warfare or how to counter it. Crucially, he seemed unable to prioritise his defences along the Atlantic Wall. For example, despite the Allies' fiasco at Dieppe, defence of the port in early 1944 was tying up the newly raised 84th Infantry Division, which could have been replaced by a lower-category static unit.

While Hitler needed to defend southern France against potential attack from the Mediterranean, deploying half a dozen new divisions in Brittany defied logic. Although the Allies did toy with the idea of striking Brittany, it was really too distant from England's southern ports; it was also much too far west from Paris and Antwerp. In Brittany, the 77th Division at St Malo could have been replaced by a static garrison, while to the west, the 266th and 353rd Divisions were similarly wasted. Including the 84th Division, these four units alone represented a potential reserve corps of over 40,000 men.

Field Marshal von Rundstedt wanted to create a powerful reserve, and Nazi propaganda spoke grandly of 'Rundstedt's Central Army'.[20] This did not exist, but Rundstedt planned to form such a force by abandoning southern France as far as the Loire. This would have freed up a dozen infantry divisions and up to four panzer divisions. Hitler, though, would not acquiesce to such a request. 'I was not even allowed a free hand with the handful of armoured divisions that were available in France,' grumbled Rundstedt. 'I could not move one of them without Hitler's permission.'[21] He regularly despaired of the German leader, 'Without Hitler's consent I can't even move my own sentry from my front door around to the back!'[22]

Nonetheless, Rundstedt was a shrewd soldier and in October 1943 he highlighted that Normandy, with its major port at Cherbourg, and

Brittany with Brest, should not be ignored as possible points of attack by the Allies. Hitler had come round to his way of thinking by March 1944. Rundstedt, as late as mid-May 1944, was warning that the Allies would need to capture a port in order to maintain their forces once ashore. To this end he emphasised, 'Le Havre and Cherbourg are primarily to be considered for this purpose; Boulogne and the Cotentin peninsula in the first phase would therefore seem very natural.'[23]

Rundstedt later added, 'We thought that any landing in Normandy would be limited to an attempt to capture Cherbourg. The American landing near here was thus less unexpected than the British landing around Caen.'[24] By the end of May 1944, he was assessing that the Allied air attacks on the vital Seine bridges 'may indicate enemy designs on Normandy'.[25] His forecasting of the date for an imminent invasion was not so good. On 4 June 1944, he noted, 'As yet there is no immediate prospect of the invasion.'[26] If the weather had not fouled up the Allies' schedule, they would have invaded the following day.

Looking out of his rain-lashed chateau windows, Rundstedt grew tired of trying to second-guess his enemies. Unfortunately for him, he was not well served by his weathermen; Colonel Professor Walther Stoebe[27] and Major Lettau saw no real danger of the Allies attempting a crossing of the Channel in early June. Lettau, the German deputy chief meteorologist in Paris, 'advised his superiors that invasion after June 4 was impractical because of the stormy weather moving in from the Atlantic'.[28] Stoebe, his boss, predicted Force 7 winds off Cherbourg and Force 6 in the Pas de Calais. The rain would be heavy, with the cloud lingering at 1,800ft.[29]

According to Lettau's assessment, there was to be no let-up for the next few days, and Rundstedt saw no harm in his commanders going on leave or attending scheduled wargames in Rennes. 'The enemy has not already made use of three periods of fine weather for his invasion,' reported Lettau, 'and further periods of fine weather in the coming weeks cannot be reckoned with more accuracy.'[30] All this was relayed to weatherman Major Hermann Mueller, their liaison officer at Rundstedt's headquarters. To Rundstedt and his generals, it seemed the Allies would have to be mad to invade at the end of the first week of June 1944.[31]

Stoebe conferred with Dr Karl Sonntag, his chief in Berlin. They agreed that on the basis of the previous Allied landings in North Africa, Sicily and Italy, unless favourable weather was looming nothing was going to happen. The bottom line was that the Allies wanted clear skies to ensure good air cover. After speaking with Stoebe on the telephone, Mueller wandered along to the office of Rundstedt's Chief of Staff, Major-General Günther Blumentritt. He was relieved because it meant that it was safe for the field marshal to conduct an inspection tour of the Normandy defences in two days' time. Driving in the rain would not be ideal, but at least the enemy-fighter bombers remained firmly on the ground.

In the meantime, Rundstedt was never able to resolve the problem of how best to defend the Atlantic Wall. After the Allied landings became a reality, he lamented, 'I had planned to fight a slow retiring action, exacting a heavy toll for each bit of ground I gave up. I had hoped this might have brought about a political decision that would have saved Germany from complete and utter defeat.'[32] His lack of reserves, however, would mean that he was unable to conduct such an elastic defence or conduct any powerful counterattacks.

4

THE EUROPEAN TOUR

Lance Corporal Herbert Guenther was sorry to be leaving Italy. He liked the weather and the food. It was certainly better than Libya, where the food was poor and sand got into everything. There were few creature comforts in Tripoli and even fewer living in the desert in tents and caravans. In North Africa it had been a real challenge looking after his boss. Being the batman to Field Marshal Erwin Rommel was not always an easy job. Guenther tried to make sure that Rommel ate well – the man had a tendency to overwork himself and as a result suffered regularly from exhaustion and ill-heath. However, Guenther was looking forward to their forthcoming European posting; being in France would certainly be no real hardship. He had heard that life there could be very pleasant.

Guenther had been with Rommel from the start and enjoyed serving the 'Desert Fox'. On the occasions when Rommel's adjutant or aide-de-camp were not available as stand-ins, he had even been granted the privilege of writing to Frau Rommel on his boss's behalf. Not bad for a lowly lance corporal, he thought. Rommel could come across as a rather austere and blunt character, but Guenther had seen another side to the man. He cared deeply about his family and regularly wrote to his wife and young son to reassure them that he was alright. Rommel also had a sense of humour. Guenther chuckled to himself when he recalled how on one occasion he had secured two chickens and managed to persuade his boss they should keep them as mascots.[1]

Before the German defeat in Tunisia, Guenther had accompanied Rommel back to Germany. Once Rommel was given responsibility for securing northern Italy, his headquarters moved to Lake Garda.

Afterwards, Guenther felt that Rommel had been treated shabbily by the Führer. Rommel had been anticipating being appointed Commander-in-Chief for Italy. He was well suited to another Mediterranean command and had great respect for the Italians, having fought shoulder-to-shoulder with them in North Africa. However, at the last moment Hitler changed his mind and appointed Field Marshal Kesselring instead.[2] Guenther wondered if Rommel had not got the post he hoped for because he had been too friendly with the Italians.

At very short notice, Rommel was now tasked to 'improve the defences on the North Sea and Atlantic coasts from Denmark to the Pyrenees'.[3] Guenther packed the field marshal's belongings and accompanied him to Villafranca airfield. He knew from overhearing Captain Alfred Berndt that such an appointment would be a coup for the Nazi propaganda ministry.[4] The 'Desert Fox' was taking charge of Hitler's Atlantic Wall.

Field Marshal Erwin Rommel knew how to play the public relations game. He had done it throughout his military career. Rommel appreciated that his friendship with Propaganda Ministry representative Captain Berndt, who had been on his staff since North Africa, was a major asset. Berndt always portrayed Rommel in a very positive light in his reporting to Nazi Propaganda Minister Joseph Goebbels. The latter liked Rommel very much, and this was useful in deflecting criticism over Germany's shameful defeat in Tunisia.

Blame very firmly rested at the feet of the joint German-Italian Commander-in-Chief Field Marshal Kesselring and Reichsmarschall Göring. However, Rommel's name had been associated with the campaign in North Africa for so long that it was hard for his reputation not to be tarnished. The British and American press were able to make much capital out of how the 'Desert Fox' had finally been defeated, when in reality he was not even there.

After their departure from North Africa, Rommel and Berndt had paid their respects in Berlin to Goebbels, who was still trying to manage the fallout from the even more catastrophic German defeat at Stalingrad. Inevitably their meeting was photographed, and the warm smiles on the men's faces seemed very genuine. As the minister and field marshal shook hands, Berndt could not conceal his look of adoration for Rommel.[5]

Goebbels was keen to find Rommel a new job as quickly as possible, especially one that would have great propaganda value. He even considered suggesting that Rommel resurrect the Sixth Army which had been lost at

Stalingrad. Such a move would have actually been a demotion, as Rommel had been expecting to take over an army group in Africa. In the end Goebbels concluded that, 'The Führer is keeping him in reserve for a greater task.'[6] Rommel found himself flying from Italy to France on 21 November 1943 to take charge of the Atlantic Wall defences and the divisions of Army Group B.[7] This was a posting that Goebbels could capitalise on.

Rommel was always good at rising to a challenge. Problem-solving was what he did best. In North Africa he had excelled in leading the Afrika Korps against the British. The back-and-forth war fought along the North African coast had been like a giant chess game. His shrewd and fast-thinking abilities had ensured that the Germans had scored some remarkable victories and then survived complete defeat until the very last. Beefing up Hitler's defences in France was exactly the type of challenge Rommel relished. To some it might have been a truly terrifying task – ensuring the defeat of the long-awaited Allies' Second Front.

Despite the quite considerable German forces deployed across France, Belgium and the Netherlands, Germany could not afford to fight a two-front war. It had tried that in 1914 and had ended in humiliating defeat. Whatever happened, the Americans and British had to be defeated swiftly and decisively. Rommel's job was to ensure his forces achieved a much larger Dieppe victory. To Rommel, the most logical place for an Allied attack would be somewhere between Dieppe and Rotterdam.

Looking at his situation maps, Boulogne and Calais offered the shortest possible crossing points for the Allies, so it seemed prudent to keep the bulk of Army Group B's forces north of the River Seine. Nonetheless, Rommel appreciated he could not ignore the coastline running between Cherbourg and Le Havre. In particular, Cherbourg's Cotentin Peninsula offered a tempting landing point, though he reasoned it would be easy to bottle up an invasion force should their initial goal be Cherbourg.

Rommel threw himself into his new task wholeheartedly. He liked to keep busy, and this new posting was certainly a major challenge. It was good to put North Africa and Italy behind him. Rommel had been appalled at how the German forces and their Italian allies had been left to their fate in Tunisia. Likewise, although Italy's defection had been headed off with the partition of the country, it had saddened him to see their old ally occupied and disarmed.

Amongst the many lessons Rommel had learned in North Africa were that Allied air superiority greatly hampered the movement of troops and supplies, and that the Allies seemed to have limitless resources. He had seen how easily the American Army had simply shrugged off the loss of so much equipment after their setback at Kasserine. This experience was to bring him into conflict with Rundstedt, who had no faith in static fortifications and favoured keeping back a mobile reserve ready to counterattack when the Allies landed.

In sharp contrast, Rommel was to come to the conclusion that the Allies must be denied a beachhead at all costs. This could only be achieved by hitting them the moment they came ashore with every available unit. Bringing up reserves would invite air attack and take precious time. Rommel argued that the Allies must not be allowed to consolidate a foothold should they achieve one.

From the very start, Rommel did not make himself popular with Hitler. Shortly after his appointment, Rommel saw the Führer and was forthright with his views. 'We must repulse the enemy at his first landing site. The pillboxes around the ports don't do the trick,' he warned. 'Only primitive but effective barriers and obstacles all along the coast can make the landing so difficult that our countermeasures will be effective.'[8] Yet Hitler was convinced that the Allies would have to capture a large port to land supplies, otherwise they would be unable to withstand a counterattack. Rommel pointed out that Allied bombers would hamper any counterattacks. 'If we don't manage to throw them back at once,' he warned firmly, 'the invasion will succeed in spite of the Atlantic Wall.'[9] Albert Speer, who witnessed this exchange, recalled that a displeased Hitler 'curtly bade Rommel good-by [sic]'.[10]

The first thing Rommel did was to undertake a major tour of the anti-invasion defences, starting in the north. Rommel, who had spent over two years living in fly-infested and windblown caravans and tents in North Africa, soon discovered that his colleagues on occupation duties had all gone soft. The army and corps commanders, and indeed some of the divisional commanders, had requisitioned impressive-looking chateaus and the surrounding estates as their headquarters. Housed in luxury, they were able to indulge themselves in fine dining, hunting, shooting and fishing.

Arriving at Munich railway station on 1 December 1943, Rommel and his staff, including engineer General Wilhelm Meise and Lieutenant Hammermann, his new adjutant, boarded a special train. They spent two weeks visiting the Danish coast.[11] He and the accompanying generals and staff officers were regularly photographed. Rommel, in his leather trench coat with a thoughtful expression, looked every bit a field marshal come to take charge.

Rommel wrote to his wife Lucie, 'We're back from the capital [Copenhagen] … You can still buy everything you want here in Denmark. Of course the Danes will only sell to their own compatriots. I've bought a few things for Christmas.'[12]

Although they were impressed by the ready availability of food, the weather was foul, which gave the trip an air of melancholy. Rommel was not impressed by what he found. The main defence lines were too far from the coast, and the coastal defences consisted of isolated gun batteries. Rommel, nonetheless, was reassured that the Allies were unlikely to invade Denmark because of the strength of the Luftwaffe in the region. Despite Rommel's views, the western Danish coast facing the North Sea was still mined very extensively.[13]

Afterwards, he took a few days' leave and flew down to Bavaria in mid-December with General Meise.[14] Staring out of the windows of their aircraft, Rommel began to formulate his ideas based on what he had just seen and his experiences in North Africa and Italy. 'When the invasion begins,' he warned loudly to Meise above the din of the engines, 'our own supply lines won't be able to bring forward any aircraft, gasoline, rockets, tanks, guns or shells because of enemy attacks.' Glancing at the sunlight, he added, 'That alone will rule out any sweeping land battles. Our only possible defence will be at the beaches – that's where the enemy is always weakest.'[15]

Rommel then became preoccupied with mines, saying, 'I want anti-personnel mines, anti-tank mines, anti-paratroop mines – I want mines to sink ships and mines to sink landing craft.'[16] Meise was impressed by Rommel and subsequently recorded, 'Quite apart from Rommel's greatness as a soldier, in my view he was the greatest engineer of the Second World War. There was nothing I could teach him. He was my master.'[17]

Shortly after, Rommel arrived back in France for the first time since 1940. Succumbing to the spoils of the victors, he took an immediate liking to his ostentatious headquarters located in a chateau at Fontainebleau outside Paris.[18] He paid a courtesy call on Field Marshal von Rundstedt, CinC West, who at 68 was now well past his prime. After lunch, Rundstedt concluded his briefing by saying, '[T]hings look black.'[19] This was hardly very encouraging.

Rundstedt recalled how the previous summer, Hitler had insisted he host a delegation of senior Turkish military officials, who were visiting both the Eastern and Western Fronts. Rundstedt had been instructed to give the Turks a favourable impression by showing them only the strongest defences in the Atlantic Wall – 'He had been given orders from Führer HQ not to spoil the impression the Turks had been given at the Panzer-division manoeuvres on the Eastern Front.'[20]

His visitors were duly taken to the very impressive Todt battery on Cap Gris Nez in the Pas de Calais, the nearest point to England.[21] They were kept well away from the batteries equipped with ancient guns plundered from across the occupied territories.[22] Rundstedt had not been impressed by Hitler's smoke and mirrors act, but the Turks had gone away suitably captivated by the massive guns.

The following day, Rommel set out to see General von Salmuth, commander of Fifteenth Army defending the coast from Le Havre to Rotterdam, whose headquarters were located in a chateau near Tourcoing. Together, with reporters in attendance, they toured the fortified ports and the motor torpedo boat bunkers at Dunkirk. German propagandists had a field day photographing him in front of the Todt Organisation's formidable-looking concrete structures, including the Todt battery. He was also taken to the top secret V-weapon launch sites which were almost operational. These would soon be raining down flying-bombs on London.

On the whole, Rommel was not happy with what he found: the defences were far from complete, and there was a lack of manpower and resources. All the corps and divisional commanders told him the same thing: their units were armed with old weapons and were not up to strength. In the area of the Allies' proposed landings, and indeed elsewhere, the defences were manned, he noted, by 'ill-equipped and badly armed infantry divisions'.[23] Occasionally he would managed a smile, though his expression was more one of surprise when he inspected the Free Indian Legion stationed south of Bordeaux.[24]

In late December 1943, Rommel sat down and wrote a detailed report for Hitler. He concluded that the Allies would want to capture the area from where the Germans were about to start launching their V-1 flying bombs. Rommel assessed, 'It is most likely that the enemy will make his main effort against the sector between Boulogne and the Somme estuary and on either side of Calais', which would provide 'the shortest sea-route for the assault and for bringing up supplies'.[25]

In addition, the field marshal assessed that the Allies would want to get their hands on a port as quickly as possible. Rommel thought that they would use their airborne forces to capture the launch areas of Hitler's 'long-range missiles'.[26] He was uncertain of when the Allied landings would start, but felt confident the Allies would seek to pre-empt Hitler's long-range attack on Britain.

It was clear to Rommel that the crust of their Atlantic defences was simply not thick enough. The minefields in particular were inadequate and he had no faith they would hold the enemy for long. His recommendation was that the coast should have a fortified and mined zone extending up to 6 miles inland. 'We have learnt in our engagements with the British that large minefields with isolated strongpoints dispersed within them (field positions) are extremely difficult to take,' he wrote. 'Moreover, mined zones of this kind lend themselves particularly well to garrisoning by auxiliary troops or reserve formations.'[27]

Rommel's extensive plans envisaged the use of up to 200 million mines.[28] He also advised that the number of foreshore and air-landing obstacles should be increased and improved.[29] In the new year, Rommel remained fixated on his minefields, which he seemed to view as a panacea to all his defensive problems. During a visit by General Jodl, Chief of the Operations Staff of the Armed Forces High Command (OKW), on 13 January 1944, Rommel stated that he needed two million mines a month. Three days later, Rommel fell out with General Salmuth when he demanded their sappers lay twenty mines a day, twice the current rate. 'When the battle begins,' grumbled Salmuth, 'I want fresh, well-trained soldiers, not physical wrecks.'[30] He was a veteran of the Eastern Front and disliked intensely being told how to do his job.

Rommel accused Salmuth of insubordination, and when the latter argued it would take a year to complete Rommel's mine-laying, an ugly shouting match followed. As a red-faced Salmuth drove away, he knew it was unwise to pick a fight with Hitler's 'inspector'. Rommel's parting shot to those around him was, 'That's the only language he understands.'[31] Rommel was infuriated by the intransigence and lethargy that surrounded him. 'The job's being very frustrating,' he said to his wife. 'Time and again one comes up against bureaucratic and ossified individuals who resist everything new and progressive.' Then, on a brighter note, he added, 'but we'll manage it all the same'.[32]

Rommel's next port of call was Le Mans and the headquarters of General Dollmann's Seventh Army. He went for a briefing prior to visiting the defences in Brittany. In light of the distances involved, Rommel told Dollmann that he thought Salmuth would bear the brunt of the Allied attack. The 62-year-old Dollmann did not like answering to a man who was a former junior. Nevertheless, he tried to warn Rommel about the advantages Normandy could offer an invader – not least the opportunities for airborne assault and the desirability of the port of Cherbourg. In Brittany, he cautioned that one division was holding 180 miles while another was responsible for 150 miles.

At the end of the month, Rommel finally set off to visit Normandy. In the coastal area, unbeknown to him, selected by the Allies as their invasion point, he found four infantry divisions which were part of General Dollmann's command.[33] Upon visiting its headquarters in Caen, to Rommel's dismay he discovered that the 716th Infantry Division had responsibility for the entire area stretching from the Orne estuary to Carentan.[34] Things only improved when the 352nd Infantry Division under General Dietrich Kraiss was deployed east of Carentan.

Even then, the chain of command became muddled with the two divisions intermingled. Three of the 716th's battalions (at Bayeux, Grandcamp and Isigny) were placed under the operational control of Kraiss. East of the Orne was the 711th Infantry Division, while on the western flank, north of Carentan, was the 709th. Kraiss' command was the best of the bunch. Little did Rommel know that just elements of three divisions would be able to resist on the Allies' five invasion beaches.[35]

He then drove down to Saint Lô to visit General Erich Marcks, the LXXXIV Corps commander. He was another old war dog who had orchestrated the invasion of the Soviet Union and lost a leg during the campaign. Rommel tried to instil a sense of urgency into Marcks over the ongoing construction of the coastal defences. Marcks liked what he heard, and wrote to his son Manfred saying:

> Rommel's the same age as me but looks older – perhaps because Africa and its many trials have left their mark on him. He's very frank and earnest. He's not just a flash-in-the-pan, he's a real warlord. It's a good thing that A.H. [Adolf Hitler] thinks a lot of him, for all his bluntness, and gives him these important jobs.[36]

Marcks also noted, 'If there's something he doesn't like, then all his Swabian pig-headed rudeness comes out.'[37]

Rommel made no apology for his bluntness. Writing to his son shortly after, he said, 'People get lazy and self-satisfied when things are quiet … I'm out on the move a lot and raising plenty of dust wherever I go.'[38] Whilst Rommel was desperately trying to problem-solve, so were the Allies on the other side of the Channel.

5

THE FANATIC

By mid-February 1944, Hitler had a hunch that the Allies would want to capture Cherbourg, which inevitably meant an invasion in Normandy and quite possibly Brittany as well. Hitler repeated this suspicion at a conference with his generals on 4 March, and this was promulgated to the various commands, 'The Führer ... considers Normandy and Brittany to be particularly threatened by invasion, because they are very suitable for the creation of beachheads.'[1]

As if he did not have enough on his hands, Hitler insisted that Rommel review the progress being made with the Normandy defences. Two days later, he found himself once again heading for the Bay of the Seine. Rommel was in a foul mood because he knew exactly what he wanted to achieve, but felt constantly thwarted at every turn by a paucity of resources and a lack of cooperation from his generals. He was not blind to fact that many of the combat veterans felt they knew what was best and, more importantly, achievable. Most were blooded on the Eastern Front, so their experiences were very different to those of his in North Africa and Italy.

Rommel, and indeed his fellow commanders, had every reason to be gloomy as the war was unrelentingly going against Germany. On the Eastern Front, since Hitler's defeats at Stalingrad and Kursk his hold on the occupied territories was continually contracting. In the air, the Allies had attained superiority and were relentlessly bombing Germany's industries day and night. At sea, the U-boat offensive had been defeated. Only in Italy had Hitler's forces managed to hold the Allies at bay.

Rommel collected General Marcks, whom he felt was at least supportive of the endeavours to beef up Normandy's defences. 'These visits are very strenuous because Rommel is a fanatic,' grumbled Marcks behind the field marshal's back, 'and it's impossible to do too much on the schemes he's thought up, like the gigantic minefields.'[2]

Together, they then descended on the headquarters of the 711th and 716th Infantry Divisions. The latter was at 83 rue de Goole in Caen, a city that had turned into a rest and recreation centre for German troops posted across Normandy. Admiral Friedrich Ruge, who was with Rommel's entourage, recalled, 'We toured the coast and gunsites almost as far as the Orne estuary, and then to Trouville. Beach obstacles are now being built everywhere. Pile-driving with water jets is working first class.'[3]

Rommel's humour was not improved when he discovered an unauthorised trial had been conducted using a captured British landing craft. Embarrassingly, it had crashed through his stake obstacles with ease. In a bad mood, he went to bed early. 'Rommel is cantankerous and frequently blows his top,' observed Marcks. 'He scares the daylights out of his commanders.'[4]

The following day, Rommel and his party headed west to the River Vire, from where they witnessed all the flooded areas. Further up the coast they arrived at Quineville, which lay to the north-west of the Americans' proposed Utah invasion beach. This region was defended by the 709th Infantry Division, which lacked combat experience. Here, roller-trestle obstacles had been built to block a 5-mile section of the beach. On this occasion Rommel was genuinely pleased and he instructed Marcks to send his thanks to the men involved.[5] Admiring these obstacles and the numerous 'Achtung Minen' signs, Rommel remarked with some satisfaction, 'The enemy won't get through here.'[6]

It transpired that this praise was not entirely deserved, as the area commander had duped Rommel. He lacked mines, so in many cases his minefields consisted solely of the warning signs. As Rommel's temper was well known, rather than own up, the officer felt it best the field marshal saw what he wanted to see. Afterwards, 'The local commander wiped his sweating forehead and turned to his subordinates with a sigh of relief,' wrote American reporter Clark Lee. 'They shared with him the knowledge that along the coast only a handful of mines had been planted.'[7]

While the laying of dummy minefields was a regular practice to mislead the Allies and to make up for shortages, in this instance it does appear that the man simply lied to Rommel. It is quite possible that this type of deception was commonplace all along the Atlantic Wall. Senior officers, keen to please and avoid a public dressing down, simply made it up. On 9 March, Rommel returned to his Army Group B headquarters at La Roche-Guyon halfway down the Seine.

The area selected for Omaha Beach, stretching from Vierville sur Mer in the west to Ste Honorine, is crescent-shaped. Rommel understandably ensured that his strongest defences were designed to block the main exits leading to Colleville and Vierville. Major Werner Pluskat and his subordinates, Captain Ludz Wilkening and Lieutenant Fritz Theen of the 352nd Division, were largely responsible for the defence of the eastern half of Omaha Beach. Colonel Goth was in charge of the western half, commanding the fortifications on the Pointe et Raz de la Percée, which overlooked the Vierville sur Mer end of the shore.

Pluskat commanded twenty guns, divided into four batteries deployed about half a mile from the coast, from his headquarters at Etreham some 4 miles from the sea. He also had a forward command post in a bunker 100ft up in the cliffs near Ste Honorine, which placed him roughly in the centre of the Allies' proposed Normandy bridgehead. Effectively, Pluskat was destined to have a grandstand seat for D-Day. His observation post offered a clear view across the whole of the Seine Bay, from Le Havre in the east to the top of the Cherbourg Peninsula in the west.

Allied intelligence wrongly assessed the 352nd was new to the Omaha defences[8] and had only arrived to conduct an exercise, whereas some units had actually been there for over two months. Pluskat's batteries had been deployed since March. Nonetheless, even two days before D-Day, Allied intelligence indicated that the division was over 20 miles away, holding positions around St Lô. They believed that Omaha was held by the much inferior 716th Infantry Division.

Although the 352nd Division was up to strength and had its full complement of weapons, it still had critical shortages. While Pluskat's guns were new Krupps of varying calibres, he had a slight problem in that he only had enough ammunition for 24 hours. 'If an invasion ever does come in your area,' General Marcks, the LXXXIV Corps commander, had reassured him, 'you'll get more ammunition than you can fire.'[9]

The division's artillery regiment had around 300 tons of shells,[10] but these were not all stored alongside the guns. As a whole, the division suffered shortages of ammunition which meant they only did live firing three times and threw just two hand grenades in the early part of the year. Fuel shortages had also hampered driver training.

During his tour, Rommel visited the fortifications overlooking the Colleville exit known as Widerstandsnest 62, or WN62.[11] There he found a lieutenant in charge of twenty teenage soldiers, who included the fresh-faced 18-year-old Private Franz Gockel. The positions included two concrete casemates with 75mm and 50mm guns. During this inspection, Gockel heard Rommel telling his lieutenant that the Allies would land at high, not low tide.[12]

In his letters home, Rommel's optimism seemed to be rising. Notably, Speer's Todt Organisation kept pleasing the field marshal by presenting him with dogs.[13] 'I saw plenty to cheer me here yesterday,' Rommel wrote to his wife at the end of March. 'Although we've still a lot of weaknesses, we're looking forward full of confidence to what's coming.'[14]

When Rommel visited the high ground to the north-east of the city of Caen, a new 35-acre defensive site about a mile inland to the east was under construction. At the beginning of 1944, the Todt Organisation contacted the French building company Enterprise Rittman, based in Houlgate, and instructed them to start work immediately on a new gun battery. Rommel's engineers ensured that the port of Ouistreham was well fortified as it guarded the entrance to the Orne River that flows through Caen. Early in the year they had decided to strengthen the coastal defences to the east of the port on the far bank of the Orne estuary at a place called Merville.

Construction of this new battery was an unwelcome development for the Allies as it overlooked the left flank of their proposed landing zone. RAF reconnaissance units kept a close eye on the progress of the Merville Battery. Despite the best delaying tactics of the French workers, by the end of March 1944, aerial photographs showed that two of the four concrete gun emplacements had been completed. British intelligence, on the basis of the size of the large bunkers or casemates, calculated they were to be equipped with 150mm guns capable of throwing up to four 96lb shells out to a range of 14,600 yards at a rate of three to four rounds every minute.[15] By the end of the following month, the work had been largely completed but there was no sign of the heavy guns.

It was at this point that Lieutenant Raimund Steiner found himself in charge of the battery.[16] He was serving with the 1716th Artillery Regiment, part of the 716th Infantry Division, but his unit was only equipped with old First World War vintage Czechoslovakian 100mm light howitzers.[17] Steiner had only got the job by default after his commanding officer, Captain Karl-Heinrich Wolter, was killed in an air raid whilst with his mistress.[18] Whatever type of gun the Germans installed at Merville, it was evident from the positioning of the casemates that they would be firing toward the beaches and not out to sea.

Rommel had no idea that this entire area would be the target of a major Allied airborne operation. He had little interest in Merville as it was just one of many such batteries along the Atlantic Wall. His real concern was in the high ground either side of Caen. He knew if the Allies came ashore in Normandy and got inland, it would be here that he would have to hold them. Yes, thought Rommel to himself, Caen could be the shield with which to prevent the Allies reaching the Seine and Paris. That, though, would be a last resort.

In Rommel's mind, there was only one real strategy for defeating an Allies invasion of occupied France. In April he reissued an order first sent out in February that made his aim perfectly clear, 'The enemy must be annihilated before he reaches our main battlefield. We must stop him in the water, not only delaying him but destroying all his equipment while it is still afloat.'[19] He could not have been any clearer.

Rommel was pleased to hear in May that the 709th Infantry were being reinforced by General Wilhelm Falley's newly raised 91st Airlanding Division. This was to be deployed behind Ste-Mére-Église to the west of Utah Beach. However, General Dollmann was exasperated to learn from his quartermaster that much of the division's artillery was useless as it employed a type of ammunition not compatible with standard field guns.[20] When Falley set up his headquarters to the north of Picauville, he knew that his command had little combat power and was really no more than a weak security division.

When Rommel revisited the sector in mid-May, he was annoyed to discover that his proposed anti-airborne landing defences, instead of being completed, were only just being started. The intention was to set up poles, which would be extensively mined to obstruct gliders and paratroops. These were later dubbed 'Rommel's Asparagus'. When he demanded to know what was going on in his customary manner, he was advised that the 13,000 shells needed had not been delivered.[21]

Further east, Rommel found General Kraiss was still grumbling about the lack of civilian labour to help with the construction work.[22] This meant his soldiers were having to cut timber in the Cerisy Forest just west of Balleroy and transport it the 11 miles to the coast. They were then having to take the stakes out onto the beach and hammer them in themselves.[23] According to Lieutenant-Colonel Fritz Ziegelmann, the divisional Chief of Staff, their men were spending 9 hours a day on construction work and just 3 hours training.[24] Kraiss also complained that his 30-mile front needed ten million mines, of which he had received just a tenth.[25] Furthermore, it transpired that in the 352nd Division's sector, only 15 per cent of its installations were bombproof; the rest were almost completely unprotected. Rommel discovered the situation in the sectors held by the 711th and 716th Divisions to be even worse.

While WN62 was designed to be bomb and shellproof, Private Gockel almost got himself killed whilst outside the bunker. Shortly after Rommel's visit, he was in the nearby house that his unit used to prepare meals with the aid of a local Frenchwoman. At midday they were subjected to an air raid and ten bombs exploded just 50 metres from the building. Thanks to low cloud, they did not see their attackers approaching and the first two explosions took out the windows, showering glass everywhere. He and his comrades then made a dash for the trenches. The shock waves from the subsequent bombs threw Gockel and the cook back into the kitchen before they could reach shelter. Afterwards, having dusted himself off, he remarked, 'We'd all been really lucky.'[26] Despite this ordeal, Gockel wrote home to his family in good humour, saying, '"Tommy" obviously wanted to salt our lunch.'[27]

At Cherbourg, it was apparent that the defences were designed to repel invasion from the sea. The old ring of forts around the city were outdated. The Todt Organisation had built two new outer fortifications, Westeck and Osteck, but again they offered little defence against attack from the landward side. During an exercise on 1 May 1944, General Marcks had shown that there was a weak spot between strongpoints 422 and 426, and an assault battalion had broken through.[28]

Rommel's problems continued as he vainly sought to get the units of General Schweppenburg's Panzergruppe West moved closer to the coast. He argued that because of Allied air power it was vital they be brought into action in the very first few hours. All that happened was an unwieldy compromise and a muddled chain of command that would inevitably cause a delay in getting German tanks committed to the battle. In North Africa, Rommel had been the master of mobile warfare, but he knew that Allied air power would curtail his freedom to manoeuvre their forces in France.

Fed up with the bickering between his generals in France, Hitler sent General Heinz Guderian, his inspector general of armoured forces, to broker a solution. Upon studying their plans, Guderian realised that if, as Rommel wanted, the panzer divisions were deployed near the coast, it would make it difficult to redeploy them quickly should the Allies land at multiple sites. When he pointed this out to Hitler, the Führer rather surprisingly made it clear he did not want to countermand Rommel's strategy.

Guderian visited Rundstedt's chateau in April 1944 to discuss the disposition of their reserves, and then with General Schweppenburg drove down to La Roche Guyon to talk with Rommel. The latter told the pair of them where to go in no uncertain terms. Guderian had been friends with Rommel and knew his character well. 'I was therefore not surprised by Rommel's highly temperamental and strongly expressed refusal,' said Guderian, 'when I suggested that our armour be withdrawn from the coastal areas.'[29] There was no point in arguing the point any further. Rommel also expressed the view that he was convinced that the Allies would attack north of the Somme.

As Lieutenant-Colonel Peter Young, commander of the British No. 3 Commando destined for Sword Beach, commented, 'Von Rundstedt continued to sit on his mobile reserves, while Rommel sped up and down the coast, inspecting units and fortresses, siting guns, inventing obstacles and gingering up the defenders with his considerable powers of leadership.'[30]

When Rommel inspected the all-important 21st Panzer Division, he was photographed looking extremely grim-faced. For a start, its headquarters was 30km south-east of Caen at St Pierre-sur-Dives. Units were scattered between Caen and all the way down to Falaise. This division had once been one of his premier armoured divisions in North Africa, and after being lost in Tunisia had since been rebuilt from scratch.

He found it to be in poor shape. In light of this being the nearest tank division to Normandy, he was not pleased to find its armour included antiquated French tanks and bodge-job, self-propelled guns converted from tracked French carriers.[31] Although the division's old tanks were being replaced, it lacked ammunition, including tank rounds.[32] Likewise, the only panzer units defending the Cherbourg Peninsula were two very weak battalions of second-hand French tanks.[33]

Out of necessity, Rommel had wed himself to a static defence along the Atlantic coast. While his plans were ambitious and vast, they were also labour-intensive and material-consuming. The effectiveness of his troops suffered as their training schedules were disrupted by the need to help work on the defences. 'I telephoned to the Führer for the first time a couple of days ago,' noted Rommel on 19 May. 'He was in the best of humours and did not spare his praise of the work we've done in the West. I now hope to get on a little faster than we have been doing.'[34]

Time was running out for Rommel, and ultimately his defensive plans were unachievable. Crucially, by the end of the month in Dollmann's area just 18 per cent of Rommel's measures had been implemented, while in Salmuth's sector things were immeasurably better, with 68 per cent completed.[35] When Rommel met General Wolfgang Pickert, commander of the Luftwaffe's III Flak Corps, he had warned, 'Unless we succeed in throwing the enemy back into the sea in 24 or, at the latest, in 48 hours, then the entire West will be lost to us.'[36]

Fatefully, on the morning of 4 June 1944, reassured that the tides were 'unfavourable' for an invasion, Rommel left La Roche Guyon to see Hitler.[37] He intended to request more resources for Normandy[38] and to get home, near Ulm on the Danube, in time for his wife's birthday. As far as Rommel was concerned, there was nothing that 'had given the slightest indication that a landing was imminent'.[39] [40]

He climbed into the back of his staff car and sighed. It would be good to get some rest and recreation, as the stresses and strains of the last few weeks were beginning to take their toll. He was feeling weary. Rommel pulled his overcoat tightly round himself. The constant wet weather was almost making him miss the desert. It was going to be a long drive, but it would be worth it. He was looking forward to seeing Lu and his son, Manfred.

6

GET MONTY

Lieutenant-General Sir Frederick Morgan was appointed Chief of Staff to the Supreme Allied Commander, or COSSAC, in early 1943, in preparation for the appointment of an Allied Supreme Commander. It was a vital and extremely stressful job. Morgan's deputy was an American, Brigadier-General Ray Barker. Their enormous assignment was to start planning for the opening of a Second Front. It was a thankless task, with a million and one things to consider.[1]

Morgan first learned of his new posting purely by accident thanks to a chance encounter on 12 March 1943. He was at the Combined Operations headquarters in New Scotland Yard, going up in the lift, when Admiral Mountbatten hopped in. Mountbatten then proceeded to congratulate a very surprised Morgan, in front of everyone else, about his new job. Mountbatten had inadvertently let the proverbial 'cat out of the bag' prematurely. Morgan's orders appointing him did not arrive until 1 April, and were not confirmed for another two weeks.

General Alan Brooke, Chief of the Imperial General Staff (CIGS), had recommended Morgan for the post. However, Prime Minister Churchill, before giving his approval, had checked Morgan's ancient Staff College records. They stated, 'Character: strong and exceptional personality. Professional knowledge: good and backed by considerable experience. Mental and physical characteristics: quick and above average, possessing originality combined with soundness; energetic and active.' Churchill must have smiled when he got to the end and read, 'a keen but kindly sense of humour which should prove a great asset to him.'[2]

'The prospect of launching an invasion out of England was little short of appalling,' observed Morgan. 'There was no precedent in all history for such a thing on the scale that must of necessity be achieved.'[3] He also soon realised that far from just heading a planning staff, they were also 'the embryo Supreme Headquarters Staff'.[4]

The problems facing Churchill over opening the Second Front in Europe were simply enormous. The Allied planning staffs had to prepare for every eventually. Lives would be lost, but the planning was designed to ensure the success of the landings and minimise losses. These problems were never far from his mind, especially when Joseph Stalin was constantly lobbying him and Roosevelt to attack the Germans in France to alleviate the pressure on the Red Army on the Eastern Front. As far as Stalin was concerned, issues over Allied troop build-ups, availability of landing craft and tides were trivia. When Stalin wanted something done in his own country, he made it happen. Stalin, quite understandably, remained exasperated by Churchill and Roosevelt constantly delaying the opening of the Second Front. Stalin, though, never really understood the enormous task that faced his allies.

Winston Churchill was a man of incredible drive and energy, quite often fuelled, it has to be said, by the prodigious consumption of cigars and alcohol. Thanks to his upbringing and early career, he had melded himself into a polymath. He had become a decisive decision maker on a plethora of subjects, and it was this ability that made him Britain's greatest wartime leader.

Winston enjoyed the intellectual challenge of solving strategic and even tactical questions. If he had learned one thing from his experiences in the trenches in the First World War, it was that preparation and decisiveness achieved military victories. Preparing for D-Day was one of the biggest wartime challenges he ever faced. An incredible amount of planning was needed, including tact and diplomacy when it came to agreeing these plans with the Americans. Choosing General Morgan was a good start.

While Morgan helped ensure that COSSAC functioned as a highly effective brains trust, there were inevitably severe stresses and strains. These, however, were largely not on national lines, but rather differing opinions amongst the experts. However, one thing the Americans did not like was the British habit of doing everything by committee. Morgan sensibly reviewed the twenty-nine committees that were meeting at Norfolk House and kept just four.[5]

In light of the Germans having fortified all the occupied Channel ports, Brigadier-General Barker and chief British planner Major-General Sinclair concluded that one of the best places to invade would be the beaches either side of the Contentin Peninsula and in the Caen coastal area. The beaches also needed to be sheltered to facilitate the landing of supplies before a port could be captured, so this ruled out those in Belgium, which were too overlooked in any case. Dutch beaches were beyond fighter cover, lacked enough exits and were exposed. Likewise, in France the Pas-de-Calais area was exposed to prevailing winds and over-looked by considerable German defences.[6]

The Normandy coast was found to be suitable in every respect. Its wide flat beaches were sheltered from the westerly winds. Also, Caen hosted airfields that the Allied air forces needed in order to deploy to the conti-nent. Nonetheless, initially a dispute arose between the Americans, who favoured Normandy, and the British, who wanted to assault the Pas-de-Calais. During the summer of 1943, final agreement was reached that they would go for Normandy and an outline plan was delivered.

'This, the first acid test of our work … was good for us all,' said Morgan. 'When one has lived by day and by night, slept, woken, eaten, drunk with one idea, breathed it in and talked it out for months, there is a danger that one may lose judgement and balance.'[7] Later, when he arrived on the scene, Colonel David Belchem, who was head of Monty's Operations and Planning Staff, commiserated about the enormity of it all. 'The need for such design, technical development and industrial production tasks had been foreseen and to some extent initiated by COSSAC,' he observed, 'but it still took time for people involved to grasp the sheer size of the task that lay ahead.'[8]

It was not until the end of the year that Churchill and Roosevelt agreed that an American general, Dwight D. Eisenhower, would be Supreme Commander. This was logical, as Eisenhower (or Ike, as he was known) had commanded the American-led landings in North Africa. He had first arrived in London in 1942 to act as the US theatre commander. One of his biggest challenges with North Africa had been navigating the labyrinthine French politics, which were a shifting sea of conflicting loyalties. Eyebrows were raised in some quarters at the idea of Eisenhower being in charge of Operation Overlord and D-Day. While Ike was a very good diplomat and staff officer, he lacked actual combat experience. Arguably, his subordinate commanders more than made up for this.

Eisenhower's deputy would be British, Air Chief Marshal Sir Arthur Tedder, and their Chief of Staff another American, General Walter Bedell Smith. Allied naval and air forces would be placed under two other British commanders, Admiral Bertram Ramsay, RN, and Air Chief Marshal Sir Trafford Leigh-Mallory, RAF. Perhaps rather foolishly, no corresponding overall ground forces commander was appointed. Although Montgomery was placed in charge of planning and implementing D-Day, he would remain senior ground forces commander only until such time as American ground forces outnumbered the British. In the meantime, this inevitably left General Omar Bradley, the US ground forces commander, rather out on a limb.

Montgomery departed Italy in December 1943, flying back to England via Morocco, stopping off to see Churchill who was convalescing there. Understandably, the pair wanted to discuss future plans. In particular Churchill was secretly seeking to derail Operation Anvil, the proposed Allied invasion of the French Riviera, which was supposed to coincide with Overlord.

Churchill always felt that Hitler should be defeated via the Mediterranean and up through Italy. While he was not keen on Overlord, the prospect of Anvil was a complete anathema to him. In Churchill's mind, any expansion of Overlord would eat away at resources for Anvil, which was a good thing, as this would prevent any further weakening of the Allied campaign being fought in Italy. However, while Stalin kept lobbying for the opening of the Second Front as soon as possible, the Soviet leader also wanted Anvil to take place in order to keep the Allies out of the Balkans.[9]

'It is most undesirable that Monty should be given an opportunity of criticising the plan,' warned General Sir Hastings Ismay, Churchill's military secretary, 'before he has discussed it with the people who are preparing it.'[10] Ismay knew such a move would inevitably be seen as a snub by Morgan, Barker and Sinclair. Churchill took no heed of such concerns and showed Montgomery the plans, asking for his 'first impressions'.[11] Predictably, Monty drafted a quick critique for Churchill.

Morgan's plan, which was always very much a work in progress, envisaged three assault divisions landing between the Vire and Orne rivers, followed by four further divisions. Within the week, it was hoped to have a total of nine divisions ashore. Monty was not happy, remarking, 'The initial landing is on too narrow a front … the present plan is impractical.'[12]

Eisenhower, who was on his way to the United States to see President Roosevelt before taking up his role of Supreme Commander, also stopped off in Marrakesh. A few days earlier, in Algiers, Eisenhower had tipped off Monty that the plan 'did not look too good'.[13] Eisenhower was later to claim that he and his Chief of Staff, General Bedell Smith, 'decided, off the cuff, that a five-division attack was far more desirable'.[14]

Predictably, Montgomery's calls for greater resources to be committed to D-Day impacted elsewhere, most notably on the Italian campaign. 'In the operations in Italy I lost seven divisions,' complained Field Marshal Alexander, commander-in-chief of Allied forces in Italy, 'four American and three British – to the landings in Normandy. And Operation "Dragoon" [formerly Anvil in the Riviera] was to entail the switch of another five of my divisions.'[15] These redeployments consequently hampered the Allied advance up the Po Valley, and Alexander held Eisenhower responsible for this sorry state of affairs.

Eisenhower asked Montgomery to act as his representative in London until he returned from America. In Washington, he found Roosevelt confined to bed with flu. 'He asked me whether I liked the new title "Supreme Commander",' recalled Ike, 'and I acknowledged that it had the ring of importance, something like "Sultan".'[16] Fortunately for all involved, Eisenhower was not to act like one.

Monty was also given authority to revise the Overlord plans ready for Ike's arrival in mid-January 1944. While in Morocco, Montgomery went for a picnic lunch with Churchill and Clementine, his wife. 'In all the operations in which I had had a share so far, changes in the plan had been necessary and there had been all too little time e.g. Husky in May 1943 [the Allied in vasion of Sicily], and now Overlord which did not look good,'[17] warned Montgomery.

When Eisenhower got to England and was briefed, he truly appreciated the enormous challenge they faced:

Behind the dunes and low cliffs the Nazis had through four years been fortifying beaches and ports. These were supported by mobile reserves who could be rushed to any point we might choose to assault, concentrating masses of armor and infantry against the relatively small numbers we could land by sea or from the air. Our lines of support, on the other hand, would be subject to fatal interruptions by stormy weather, by undersea attack, and it was rumoured, by assault from new projectiles whose range and speed would change the nature of war.[18]

Major-General Freddie de Guingand, Monty's Chief of Staff, had gone on ahead to London to liaise with Bedell Smith and be briefed by COSSAC. 'General "Freddie" Morgan and his staff had certainly thought of most things,'[19] noted de Guingand. The first thing Montgomery did when he arrived was to expand the landing area west of the Vire, as this would speed up the drive north to capture Cherbourg. As Rommel had flooded much of this area, he would not be expecting airborne forces. It was also decided that the area east of the Orne was suitable for another airborne assault, thereby securing both flanks of the invasion area. It also soon became apparent that 1 May 1944 for 'D' day was not achievable, despite an undertaking given to Stalin.

From the start, one of the biggest challenges after the landings was to prevent Rommel from impeding the American drive on Cherbourg. Colonel Belchem appreciated Monty was going to have a tough time, 'While First US Army was battling in two directions, and until Cherbourg had fallen and the peninsula was cleared, Second British Army *had* to attract, and hold, the greater part of the German offensive divisions.'[20] Such a strategy was going to lead to major controversy. While it was a very sound policy to ensure the Americans were not subjected to any sizeable counterattacks as they fought north and south, it meant Monty would face a bloody slogging match.

Despite this approach, Monty told his staff that he was confident that the Allies would be on the Seine by D+90. One day in London, Belchem and his American colleagues were informed that a phase line map was required for US briefing purposes to indicate progress in Normandy and Brittany. While this was a quite reasonable request, Belchem was resistant to this on the basis it would be pure speculation.

Bradley's staff would not be detracted, and instead produced their own which was shown to Belchem by his American deputy. Belchem, knowing his boss's feelings on this matter, undertook to show it to Monty. The following Sunday, on a warm afternoon, he visited Montgomery's flat located near his headquarters' offices in St Paul's School. Belchem unpacked his paperwork, and recalled, 'I showed him the map and asked him what to do about it … Montgomery gave me back the map and said … I should make it quite clear that he did not wish to be associated with such guesswork.'[21]

Belchem returned to his American colleague and diplomatically said Monty's position should be relayed to Bradley. What Montgomery, de Guingand and Belchem did not know was that the map had not been produced at Bradley's behest. It was the air force planners working on his staff who wanted some idea of when they would capture enemy airfields ready for their move onto the continent.

This map came back to haunt Montgomery on 7 April when he held a plans presentation in the lecture hall at St Paul's School. This was for the benefit of all the senior air, ground and naval commanders, as well as Churchill. Ramsay and Leigh-Mallory both conducted briefings on their side of things. De Guingand recalled, 'I think the Army's contribution consisted of a "Phase line" map.'[22]

Monty outlined the plan for Bradley's US First Army to assault astride the Vire, where once established they would capture Cherbourg, then east of Carentan strike south towards St Lô. After this, the goal was Rennes. The British Second Army would hit the beaches west of the Orne, then push south and south-east to capture airfields and safeguard the Americans' eastern flank. They would be followed by Lieutenant-General Crerar's Canadian First Army, which would fight alongside the British, and the US Third Army, tasked with clearing Brittany and protecting the southern flank. 'Montgomery made a big impression that day,' recalled de Guingand, 'especially amongst some who were still not quite convinced of his true ability.'[23]

'Having got an agreed plan (or so I thought at the time!),' observed Montgomery, 'I left the details to de Guingand and his staff and devoted my main efforts to ensuring that the weapon we were to use would be fit for battle.'[24] The use of the phase line map gave de Guingand some cause for concern, and he later cautioned, 'A phase line does in no way imply a guarantee that we shall reach such and such a position by a certain date.'[25]

However, the damage was done; Monty was to be held hostage to fortune by these phase lines. 'Montgomery's retention of the forecast maps – borne out of his overriding concern that the air force planners should not block acceptance of the invasion plan,' said Belchem, 'led almost inevitably to a serious misunderstanding between Bradley and Montgomery.' This bad blood would mar their relationship throughout the entire campaign fought in north-west Europe.[26] It was never to be resolved.

While planning to get the invasion forces safely across the Channel, at the same time a supporting air campaign needed to be devised. Logic dictated that Rundstedt's armed forces in France should slowly be cut off from the outside world. In wartime, though, things are rarely that easy. Morgan was soon to discover, along with Tedder, that the bomber barons had their own very set views on how to defeat Nazi Germany and how this translated into helping D-Day. This led to friction between the commanders of the different strategic and tactical air forces.

The seeds of this discord were laid in 1943 with the instigation of Operation Pointblank, which conceived a strategic bombing campaign designed to destroy Hitler's war-fighting cabilities by attacking his weapon factories. The result was that Air Chief Marshal Sir Arthur Harris, in charge of RAF Bomber Command, and General Carl Spaatz, commander of the United States Strategic Air Force in Europe, saw any diversion of effort toward France as an unwanted drain on their resources. They were respectively engaged in intensive night and day bombing raids against Germany, which they were convinced would defeat Hitler irrespective of the ground war.

Tedder was to favour Leigh-Mallory's tactically focused plans, which envisaged gaining air superiority and concentrating on destroying Hitler's lines of communication,[27] both of which would greatly support the opening phase of the invasion. However, Spaatz and Harris refused to co-operate with Leigh-Mallory. Harris made it perfectly clear that he had no faith in such a plan. 'Tedder brought a genuinely scientific mind, with all the detachment of the scientist,' remarked Harris with faintly damning praise. He then pointed out, 'Railways are extraordinary difficult and unrewarding targets for air attack.'[28] Spaatz's only concession was to target Germany's oil supplies, which would affect not only German industries, but also the Army and Luftwaffe.[29] Spaatz and Harris were only forced to cooperate once Eisenhower had approved Leigh-Mallory's recommendations.

Churchill and Air Chief Marshal Sir Charles Portal, Chief of the Air Staff, did not help matters by trying to insist that only part of Bomber Command should be placed at Eisenhower's disposal. 'Just when Ike thinks he has the problem of air command licked, as he put it today, "someone else's feelings are hurt and I have another problem to settle",' noted Captain Harry Butcher, Eisenhower's naval aide.[30] A highly exasperated Eisenhower told Churchill that if the British bombers were not committed he would 'simply have to go home'.[31]

Inevitably, it was Tedder who bore the brunt of Ike's mounting fury over the squabbling air commanders when he finally lost his temper. 'I am

tired of dealing with a lot of prima donnas,' Eisenhower shouted down
the phone at Tedder on 6 March 1944. 'By God, you tell that bunch that
if they can't get together and stop quarrelling like children, I will tell the
Prime Minister to get someone else to run this damn war.'[32]

Until Eisenhower was granted authority over them in mid-April
1944, the bomber barons answered to the Combined Chiefs of Staff in
Washington. Even then, thanks to the clash of personalities, Harris, Leigh-
Mallory and Spaatz reported to Eisenhower independently of each other.[33]
'The complications of Allied command were intriguing,' Eisenhower later
wrote with the greatest of tact. 'It's just as well; otherwise they might have
been infuriating.'[34] He also added with some pragmatism, 'Nevertheless, in
the meetings, tension and anxiety were inescapable.'[35]

These three separate commands were supposedly coordinated by Air
Chief Marshal Tedder in his role as Deputy Supreme Commander. 'It will,
I think, be a considerable time before anybody will be able to set down
in the form of an organizational diagram,' said a frankly baffled General
Morgan, 'the channels through which General Eisenhower's orders
reached his aircraft.'[36]

Coordinating with Stalin was never easy, especially as he was growing
angry over the constant delay in opening the Second Front. By the spring it
was becoming increasingly necessary to commit to a firm date for D-Day.
High-level talks amongst the Allies meant such a commitment could no
longer be avoided. On 8 April 1944, Captain Butcher wrote, 'The time has
come to inform the Russians of the D date for Overlord so they can carry
through with Stalin's commitment to Roosevelt and Churchill at Tehran to
launch a large-scale offensive on the Eastern Front which would contain
the maximum number of German troops and thus assist our invasion.'[37]

The plan was that D-Day would be two or three days either side of
1 June 1944, depending on the tides and the weather. In Moscow,
Lieutenant-General Burrows of the British Military Mission warned that
Stalin would never forgive the Allies if Overlord were postponed. Even so,
'Stalin, I understand, took the news extremely well,'[38] noted Brigadier de
Guingand with some relief.

The Allies were soon alerted to the difference Rommel was making
along the French coast. Colonel Belchem reported:

When we had started planning in January, the Normandy coast
defences had not been as well developed as those elsewhere, but

when Rommel took over, the Germans immediately stepped up the installation of obstacles, particularly of the underwater type. Rommel also ordered anti-landing devices to be placed on potential dropping and landing areas and as these indications reached us by analysis of aerial photography, they naturally caused us some anxiety.[39]

Allied intelligence and photo-reconnaissance monitored with interest every innovation that Rommel introduced along the length of the Atlantic Wall. 'Pictures were studied and one of the most disturbing things these continued to show was the growing profusion of beach obstacles,' said Eisenhower, 'most of them under water at high tide.'[40] This clearly suggested the Germans expected a high-tide assault.

Rommel's engineers did everything they could to enhance the effectiveness of their mines. Some were rigged so they would all explode simultaneously. They also sowed them across broad areas of the sea bed that included the high-tide point. Just before D-Day, Allied air force operations accidently highlighted this development. 'On 23 April in an air attack against a coastal battery one bomb fell wide of the underwater obstacles,' reported Australian war correspondent Chester Wilmot. 'The instantaneous photograph of the bomb-fall showed fourteen explosions – sympathetic detonations which told planners that the Germans had now laid mines below high-water mark.'[41] This further convinced Eisenhower and his commanders that a low-tide attack was the best option.

While Hitler's Atlantic Wall looked to be a truly formidable barrier, there could be no hiding a very basic shortcoming in Rommel's defences. He lacked manpower, which meant that his divisions were stretched too thinly. Allied intelligence was aware of this, as Colonel Belchem noted their 'density was thus less than one division per 80 kilometres. Even with modern weaponry, the classic defence scale is of the order of one first-line division deployed in depth per ten kilometres.'[42]

The Allies assessed that Rommel could counter their five assault divisions with seven of his own. Nonetheless, most of these lacked mobility. The real question was how quickly Rommel could reinforce his defences once the Allies were ashore. German responsiveness hung, in part, on the success of the Allied deception plans to convince Hitler the Pas de Calais was the true objective, and the effectiveness of the Allies' tactical air force and the French Resistance.

Worryingly, it was expected that Rommel would be able to contain the Allies with some twenty divisions (including eight panzer divisions) by D+6. This was why a rapid Allied build-up was so crucial. To start with, though, Colonel Belchem said 'it was anticipated that on D-Day the German garrison would amount to three coast defence divisions (243, 709 and 716); two first-line infantry divisions (91 and 352) and one Panzer formation (21).'[43]

The Allies also knew that they had another initial advantage over Rommel. 'There was no centralized control of the three German services on the Western Front,' noted Belchem, 'each service had its own chain of command back to Berlin.'[44] Ridiculously, the coastal batteries, when firing out to sea, answered to the Navy, but if they fired on the beaches then they were the responsibility of the Army. Likewise, Panzergruppe West, which controlled most of the tank divisions, answered to Rundstedt and Hitler, not Rommel.

While Rommel was confident that his comprehensive coastal radar system would give him warning of an Allied invasion, he had little hope of the Luftwaffe or navy acting as his eyes and ears. Naval forces consisted of only 'a few destroyers and torpedo vessels, together with a number of motor torpedo boats and patrol craft'.[45] By the end of May 1944, the poor weather had largely grounded his reconnaissance aircraft and confined the Navy to its bases. It was this bad weather that lulled Rommel into a false sense of security.

7

WEIRD & WONDERFUL

In 1944, Major-General Percy Cleghorn Stanley Hobart was in command of the most unique armoured division in the history of the British Army. Its job was to ensure that all the terrible errors committed during the Dieppe raid were not repeated. Speed was of the essence: enemy defences had to be overcome as quickly as possible, as any delays could be fatal. To that end, the division had been equipped with swimming tanks, bunker-busting tanks and mine-clearing tanks.[1] Hobart was in his element, and had much to be thankful for. However, his command was not to fight as a division. It was with some reluctance in March 1944 that he assigned his units to the formations that they were to support in the opening assault.

Back in late 1940, Lance Corporal Hobart, of the Home Guard, found himself being interviewed by Sir John Dill, the CIGS. Hobart had asked irritably whether he should attend in civilian clothes, as a lance corporal or, more pointedly, in his former major-general's uniform.[2] He was reassured that he was wanted back as a divisional commander, in particular an armoured division. It mattered little what he wore, as whatever his attire he always looked like a very grouchy headmaster. His round glasses and moustache gave him the appearance of an academic rather than a fighting man.

Much to Hobart's irritation, he thought he was going to have to sit out the war in enforced retirement. The problem was that he suffered from 'attitude'. As a close friend put it, 'he had a fascinating and forceful mind'.[3] The truth of the matter was that Hobart did not suffer fools gladly, could be highly intolerant and incredibly rude. This naturally did not endear him to his superiors. Just before the war broke out, Hobart was sent to Egypt with the challenging task of creating a fully mobile division with which to challenge the Italians should they side with Hitler. His abilities shone out as he melded very disparate units into a highly efficient divisional force.[4]

Despite this achievement, Hobart's abrasive nature resulted in him being sacked, though some of his men were genuinely sorry to see him go and many of his officers felt he had been badly treated. Hobart's immediate superior, Major-General 'Jumbo' Wilson, had complained to General Archibald Wavell, CinC Middle East, that his 'tactical ideas are based on the invincibility and invulnerability of the tank'.[5] To some this may have been seen as forward thinking, but Wavell had little choice, saying, 'Hobart was not trusted as a commander either by his superiors or many of his subordinates.'[6]

Returning home, Hobart retired from the Army and offered his services to the Home Guard. However, although Hobart had made many enemies, he also had some powerful connections. For a start, his former brother-in-law was Montgomery – his sister had died in the late 1930s. More importantly, Hobart's sterling efforts in Egypt had caught the eye of Churchill, who wanted to capitalise on his experience. It was Churchill who had called Dill.[7]

Churchill was of the opinion that Hobart was 'of strong personality and original view … and also the vision'.[8] Hobart was asked to form and train the new 11th Armoured Division. This he did until it became operational, but he was then relieved of command on medical grounds. In September 1942 he was sent to Leeds to train another new formation, the 79th Armoured Division.[9] The month before, Dieppe had shown just how badly an armoured landing could go. Not long after, Hobart was instructed that his division was to be converted to a specialised assault role. His armoured vehicles were to be dubbed unofficially the 'Funnies', a title that Hobart hated.[10]

Major-General de Guingand, now Chief of Staff of Montgomery's Twenty-first Army Group, was delighted about 'Hobo' Hobart's appointment; it was his drive and personality that was largely responsible for the success of the project. 'Some of the staff under me would become terrified when they knew General Hobo was about,' recalled de Guingand with some amusement. 'He was such a go getter that they never really knew until he had left what new commitment they had been persuaded to accept.'[11] However, not everyone was impressed by Churchill's generosity with second chances. Lieutenant-Colonel Stuart Macrae observed wryly that Hobart was 'said to be the only general to be twice bowler-hatted and who had been brought back by the PM'.[12]

'To implement this charter an astonishing variety of devices were examined and tried out,' said Brigadier (later Major-General) Nigel Duncan, 'either to be included in the division's armoury or to be rejected. Many of these devices and techniques were evolved from suggestions put forward by members of the division.'[13] Hobart spent much of the second half of 1943 and early 1944 at Orford in Suffolk and Linney Head in South Wales. Thanks to intelligence from the French Resistance, exact replicas of German defences were built on the heathlands of Orford so that his men could practice their assault operations. At Linney Head, dummy defences were also created to enable large exercises in August and September 1943. He also kept an eye on the development of swimming tanks at a number of secret locations, including Stokes Bay near Gosport and Studland Bay opposite Poole.[14]

When it came to Operation Overlord, nothing could be left to chance. Eisenhower was very impressed by British thoroughness. 'At a secluded spot in eastern England,' he recalled, 'the British Army constructed every type of tactical obstacle that the German[s] might use in defending against our attack.'[15] These included anti-tank ditches, pillboxes, sea walls, barbed-wire entanglements, minefields and steel obstacles.

The safety of the crews of these swimming, or DD (for Duplex Drive) tanks as they were known, was made a priority.[16] 'We had to go through a lot of swimming exercises,' grumbled Trooper Peter Davies of the 1st East Riding Yeomanry. 'I couldn't [swim] as it happened.'[17] He spent a month learning with his unit during the winter in soaked tanker's denims. They were also taught to swim underwater using breathing equipment.[18]

This culminated with escape drills from a flooded tank. The crew had to sit in it while the concrete holding tank was filled to a depth of 20ft. 'We had ten seconds to get the escape equipment on,' said Davies, 'then wait until the hull and turret were full and get out.'[19] He and his crew had to do the drill three times after several false starts. Like Davies, Trooper M.E Mawson with the 13th/18th Hussars, recalled, 'Originally [we] were seated in an old tank turret at the bottom of a deep pit and thousands of gallons of water were poured on top of us. We had just a few seconds to don apparatus and surface.'[20]

Second Lieutenant Stuart Hills, of the Nottinghamshire Sherwood Rangers Yeomanry, went through the drills and remembered, 'Some men

found the whole business very disconcerting, especially the non-swim-
mers, and several flatly refused to enter the tank in spite of direct orders
and threats of all kinds.'[21] To the alarm of the mutineers, the regimental second-in-command, Major Michael Laycock, was summoned. As he
was variously nicknamed Black Mike and Sweeney Todd,[22] it was clear
that things did not bode well for them. After berating the men, Laycock
decided to lead by example and promptly almost drowned himself coming
to the surface.

Afterwards, Captain John Semken noted, 'Like all mutinies the thing was
smoothed over and the chaps became reconciled to it.'[23] On the whole,
though, the authorities were sympathetic to those who simply could not
face the underwater ordeal. 'My own driver, Geoff Storey,' said Lieutenant
Hills, 'had only joined my crew because his predecessor was one of those
who had refused to use this apparatus, something he found highly stressful.'[24]

Drowning was not the only danger. Trooper Ronald Mole, of the
4th/7th Dragoon Guards, experienced the perils of a night exercise in
Stokes Bay. He and his fellow crewmen found themselves knee-deep in
water, 'and the poor old driver down below was getting electric shocks
because he had a twelve-volt battery by his elbow'.[25] Simple things like
paying attention were also vital. 'Once, a driver misheard an order to form
line abreast as one to deflate,' recalled Hills. 'The tank sank in the middle of
the lake, although all the crew escaped.'[26]

The value of this intensive training was driven home when, on 4 April
1944, an exercise in Studland Bay ended in tragedy when six tanks sank,
drowning six crewmen.[27] 'On one occasion,' recalled Lieutenant Hills,
'I received orders from the squadron leader by radio to launch in conditions I deemed suicidal.'[28] Luckily good sense prevailed.

Hobart's task of overseeing effective training of the swimming tank
units was greatly hampered by the authorities backing the wrong horse
when it came to the selection of tank. Hobart ended up with around 650[29]
Valentine swimming tanks, mainly armed with 40mm and 57mm guns,
which by 1943 were simply not adequate tank weapons. In particular, the
40mm gun was little more than a pop-gun.

The Valentine first appeared in mid-1941 and had been of value in
North Africa, but even by late 1942 it was considered obsolete. Crucially,
its turret was too small to take a larger gun and it was not fast enough.
However, moves were underway to rearm the Valentine with a 75mm
gun by converting the 57mm. The Valentine DD tank was kept afloat by

inflated canvas screens, but these could only be raised with the turret facing backwards. This meant that the Valentine could not land fighting. All these shortcomings proved that it was simply not suitable for combat conditions and the crews trained in a tank that was not the one they would go into action with on D-Day.

The handling properties of the M4 Sherman DD were completely different, because the Valentine weighed about 40 tons whereas the latter was 65 tons. Both, though, just bludgeoned their way through the water. Trooper Ronald Mole, with the 4th/7th Royal Dragoons, was alarmed by the Valentine DD, saying, '[T]hey didn't ride the wave, they just bumped into it.'[30] Brigadier Duncan noted rather diplomatically, 'They had proved seaworthy and difficult targets to hit when afloat.'[31]

Importantly, as the Sherman DD tank approached the beach, the front screen could be dropped to allow use of the gun. Also, when swimming, its tracks were in motion as the rear idler wheel powered the twin propellers. This meant the tank could drive straight onto the beach, firing at enemy targets. Duncan viewed the Sherman DD as an improvement as it had 'a more robust propeller drive, a better screen, and above all a better gun in the shape of the 75mm for use when the enemy shore had been reached'.[32]

Trooper Mawson remembered weight was always a problem:

There was much need to experiment with tank stability because of the necessity of loading as much ammunition as possible, plus a variety of supplies to contribute to our well-being. I even had a small shelf welded in my turret for Penguin books. Waterproof pocket escape kits became the fashion and Admiral Ramsay (who commanded the whole show) had a brainwave that each tank should have an inflatable rubber dinghy – and to this I owe my D-Day life, as I am a non-swimmer.[33]

To try and stop the DD tanks taking on too much water, they were fitted with a bilge pump that was manually operated by the co-driver. For safety reasons, only the driver tended to stay inside; the crew rode on top. They were not idle, though, because they had to maintain the flotation screen and bail out water using their helmets.

One major issue Hobart had was getting sufficient Sherman DD tanks converted in time to equip his units.[34] While initial trials in May 1942 had employed the Valentine, the following year the decision was taken to use the American Sherman, as it was by then the backbone of the Allied tank fleets. Hobart hoped that he would get 900 Sherman DD tanks[35] and that each tank regiment assigned to an amphibious role would convert all three of its squadrons; however, this was reduced to two squadrons, indicating a shortage.[36] Inevitably, conversion of the later-model Valentines to DD tanks impacted on the Sherman programme.[37]

Part of the delay was due to obstruction by the Royal Navy and the Ministry of Supply, who were highly sceptical of the whole enterprise. 'Naval experts had declared that these tanks would never be able to swim in the open sea, and could not be launched from landing craft,' noted war correspondent Chester Wilmot.[38]

Fortunately for Hobart, at the end of January 1944, Eisenhower saw the Sherman DD tank in action and set American factories to producing them. Due to problems with British deliveries, the Americans agreed to transfer eighty DD tanks.[39] In February 1944, the East Riding Yeomanry gave up its DD tanks due to a shortage of equipment. However, its place was taken by the Nottinghamshire Yeomanry.[40] By April, some 300 Shermans had been converted and were shipped to England.[41]

Hobart also had responsibility for training the American and Canadian crews. This fell to his B Wing on the Solent at Stokes Bay, where training was taken disembarking from the Landing Ship Tank (LST) and the smaller Landing Craft Tank (LCT). To his horror, the whole thing had been a complete shambles. It took two whole hours for five tanks to be launched, and two of those sank. 'Yet within a week,' recalled Brigadier Duncan, 'an LCT was regularly discharging its seven tanks in two minutes.'[42]

Once Hobart's DD tank brigade[43] had finished its training, it was the turn of two Canadian tank regiments, followed by three American tank battalions.[44] The American tankers suffered the same trials and tribulations as their British counterparts. 'We trained in the water in the swimming pool in case something happened to the tank,' recalled Corporal Wardell Hopper of the 741st Tank Battalion. 'We trained in the pools on what to do if our tanks went down. They threw us into the water and we inflated our Mae Wests [life jackets] with capsules.'[45]

Staff Sergeant Gibson with the 70th Tank Battalion, after arriving in England, initially trained on the Sherman: 'Then we moved to Portsmouth, where we trained on the British Valentine DD (duplex drive) tank ... After this we moved to Torcross, England on the channel shore and were issued with M4 DD tanks.'[46]

Lieutenant-Colonel Allan Younger and his 26th Assault Squadron, Royal Engineers, were equipped with new bunker-busters based on the Churchill tank known as the Armoured Vehicle Royal Engineers, or AVRE. He was in awe of its firepower:

> It had a thing called a 'Petard', which was a codename for a Spigot Mortar that fired a charge of about 25 pounds of explosive a limited distance, I think about 50 yards was the maximum range. The object of this was to break up concrete so that if, for instance, you met a wall and you couldn't get over it any other way, you could smash it down.[47]

Like the DD tanks, the rehearsals with this type of tank did not always go according to plan. 'Most of these were pretty catastrophic exercises,' said Younger, 'all sorts of things went wrong, but we were learning.'[48] Again, people inevitably got injured. 'I remember one tank … turned upside down and I think a couple of chaps got quite badly hurt.'[49]

Brigadier Duncan and his 30th Armoured Brigade were assigned to Hobart in November 1943 with the job of being minesweepers. This was news to Major Ian Hammerton, with the 2nd County of London Yeomanry, when Hobart personally announced their new job. Hammerton was completely baffled, 'We had a visit from Major-General Percy Hobart … He gathered everybody round him and said, "I have some news for you … You are going to be mine clearers. Flails." None of us had ever heard of them.'[50]

Numerous other specialised armoured vehicles were developed for the coming invasion. 'Naturally, we had contributed to his collection, notably with a rocket-operated tank bridge,' said Lieutenant-Colonel Macrae, deputy head of a specialist military research department. 'We also had tank ploughs and a few other pieces of equipment on the stocks.'[51]

Brigadier Duncan set about training his crews to use the flail tanks, called Sherman Crabs.[52] Bouncing around in his Humber scout car, he watched as the tanks, fitted with rotating drums covered in chains, detonated mines in front of them, thereby clearing a safe path. Hammerton remembered how nothing was left to chance:

> To find out how these things worked, I was sent back to my old battalion in Suffolk, who were experimenting with flails, Snakes

and Scorpions and all the other strange menagerie of things, in the Orford training area, a part of Suffolk that was sealed off, highly secret. Some of the villages were evacuated, boarded up and there they'd built replicas of the Atlantic Wall – pillboxes, bunkers, walls, minefields, wire, anti-tank ditches, the lot, full-sized and we practiced breaching them.[53]

Brigadier Duncan found the mock German defences at Orford immensely helpful:

They were assaulted from every angle and the results were analysed and dissected to finalize the technique for the assault between flails, AVREs and the infantry battalions who came to the area in increasing numbers for training. This was the fruition of the work done at Linney Head and here procedure was finally settled.[54]

Duncan grew to respect Hobart, whom he found inspiring:

He was utterly fearless, a devoted patriot and a man of high principles with a great sense of urgency. His divisions admired him, respected him, and either feared or loved him. He was a constant inspiration, and irritation, to all his subordinates; a fount of new ideas and new thoughts and a leader who drove those under him as fast and furious as he drove himself.[55]

However, not everyone warmed to Hobart. Lieutenant-Colonel Macrae thought he was 'a great martinet'.[56] Macrae also discovered that Hobart was a stickler for protocol:

One day, General Hobart elected to visit Whitchurch to talk to [Brigadier] Millis [Jefferis] and inspect some of our 'funnies'. His cavalcade arrived late and he was in a bad temper. Generals were now ten a penny so far as I was concerned, so had made no special arrangements for his reception … and a bad time was had by all.[57]

Hobart was furious and angrily rounded on Jefferis for disrespecting a major-general. To make sure this did not happen again, Jefferis was promoted to major-general, probably much to Hobart's annoyance.

To get Duncan's tanks onto the beaches required even more specialised equipment that could overcome Rommel's defences. This was a job for the Royal Navy's assault groups. Lieutenant-Commander Hugh Irwin was one such man allotted this task:

> Our landing craft were fitted with twenty-four 60-pound spigot bombs and the object was to blow up the beach obstacles at half-tide, clearing a passage for the LCTs that were carrying tanks with flails. The flails would clear any mines that were left and then the troops could go in.[58]

In addition, added Irwin, they were 'to blow up the beach obstacles before the Duplex Drive tanks touched down'.[59] They had a third job, 'placing sticky bombs on top of Teller mines on top of beach obstacles'.[60]

As well as punching through the sea defences, Hobart's forces were tasked with helping to deal with the various man-made obstacles that obstructed the shoreline. The best methods devised were to blow them up with demolition charges or simply drag them out of the way. 'I paid a visit to see these activities,' said General de Guingand, 'and returned feeling that yet another "horror" had been laid low.'[61]

Montgomery reportedly took a close interest in Hobart's work.[62] 'Montgomery,' recalled Hobart, 'was most inquisitive. After thorough tests … he said in effect "I'll have this and this and this; but I don't want that or that".'[63] The first formal rehearsals involving the 'Funnies' were conducted at Studland in front of a very senior audience, including King George VI, Montgomery, Ramsay and Eisenhower.

'To me, the most exciting new gadget demonstrated is a Sherman tank which has been made amphibious,' said Captain Harry Butcher. 'Ike went aboard one of these when it was launched and steered it during its amphibious run.'[64] Butcher called the DD tank 'one of the surprising innovations of the war'.[65]

Eisenhower was shown 'transportable bridges to span tank ditches, flame-throwing anti-tanks, and flails, ploughs, and heavy rollers for destroying mine[s]'.[66] He was very keen and less discerning than Montgomery, saying, 'We'll take everything you can give us.' Bradley, though, was non-committal, replying, 'I'll have to consult my staff.'[67]

De Guingand was involved in a meeting on the train back to London.

He recalled from this meeting:

It was agreed at this conference that the DD tanks would be the first
to land, and that the self-propelled artillery would be positioned in
the rear, firing over the leading waves. Naval ships would support
the assault from the flanks. No fixed rule was made for the different
gun devices [i.e. the Funnies]. A 'menu' would be selected to suit the
problem presented by the particular beach in question. This arrange-
ment worked very well.[68]

Major Peter Sutton recalled, 'I was in command of a breaching squadron
of eighteen assorted specialised armour, flail tanks for mine destroying,
assault vehicles Royal Engineers for destroying concrete pill-boxes, laying
mats across mud, and even one tank carrying a 30-foot bridge.'[69] These
were transported by three LCTs.

Although Montgomery ordered Hobart to offer a third of his equipment to the Americans, in the event, Bradley only requested DD tanks.
Bradley's staff thanked Hobart for his offer of help, but explained there was
simply not time to get American tanks crews proficient with the Churchill
tank. However, the rejection of the Crab, based on the Sherman, betrayed
Bradley's very evident scepticism of Hobart's specialised armour.

8

SEND THE ENGINEERS

The coastline of rural North Devon proved to be of great value to Hobart's men. Trials with the early carpet-laying AVRE 'Bobbins' and bridgelayers, DD tanks and flails were conducted at Braunton beach (Saunton Sands), Instow and Westward Ho! These were filmed by the Combined Operations Experimental Establishment, which was based at the latter, for further analysis. But the 'Funnies' were not the only specialised D-Day equipment that was experimented with in North Devon.

The pipeline under the ocean (or PLUTO) was another vital piece of kit conjured up by the boffins. It was designed to pump fuel from southern England across the Channel to the troops once ashore in Normandy. Testing of the underwater pipeline was carried out in the Bristol Channel in 1942. Fitted with an engine, a former Thames sailing barge, *Oceanic*, practiced at Westward Ho! The great coils of cabling were loaded at Bank End Shipyard in Bideford.[1]

Some innovations proved to be a dead end, though they might have served to deceive Rommel. Testing of the bizarre Great Panjandrum may have helped convince the Germans that the Allied landings were to take place in the Calais area. In early 1944, what was essentially a giant Catherine wheel carrying 4,000lb of explosives, was let loose on Instow beach. It was designed to blow up sea walls, which indicated it was to be used at Calais. In the event, the trials were not successful and the idea was quietly shelved.

North Devon also hosted the 'Boom Commandos', who were to clear the way for Hobart's 'Funnies'. These demolition frogmen were taught at HMS Appledore[2] to blow up Rommel's elaborate beach obstacles.[3]

Amongst them was Sergeant Keith Briggs, a Royal Marine from Dorking, Surrey. He and his team were billeted on local families, and he soon made good friends with his hosts.

The sheltered tidal estuary between Appledore and Instow was an ideal place to train. As was the beach and dunes at Instow. Sergeant Briggs fell in love with the place. He and his men learned how to cut 8ft-high obstacles down to 10in so that landing craft could pass over them unscathed. Briggs, who recalled his unit's morale was very good, was to serve with the landing craft obstruction clearance units alongside the Canadians.[4] They were very well prepared, Briggs recalled, 'We knew all about those [obstacles] because people had been to different places in France and we'd got all their photographs of the beach defences.'[5]

A total of 120[6] frogmen were trained to destroy obstacles obstructing the British and Canadian invasion beaches. They would have just 20 minutes to carry out their allotted tasks before the first landing craft arrived. Briggs' colleagues included other Royal Marines such as Sergeant Peter Henry Jones, but the demolition teams were also drawn from Royal Navy frogmen, including Lieutenant John B. Taylor,[7] who was to later remark that, 'This bloody job is impossible.'[8]

Equally important for D-Day, the Americans came to Devon. Two officers, Colonel Paul W. Thompson and Lieutenant-Colonel Frank Holmes, arrived in London in early 1943 with the task of thoroughly preparing the US Army for D-Day. The American armed forces had gained considerable experiences during the landings conducted in the Mediterranean and the Pacific, so had developed their own amphibious tactics.[9] Training for D-Day, however, was another matter.

US Engineer Colonel Thompson and his staff were posted to a hotel overlooking the picturesque beach at Woolacombe in North Devon. He had been given the unique job of creating an assault training centre for the US Army from scratch. He was well qualified for this challenge because he was familiar with German defensive tactics. During the mid-1930s, he had served as the military attaché in Berlin and had spent time with a German engineer battalion.

However, when Thompson's assault training centre was activated in early April 1943, it still only existed on paper. The following month, he hosted a conference to discuss amphibious tactics with all the experts, including the acerbic Major-General Hobart.[10] It was not until 17 August

1943 that Thompson, with 100 staff, left London for their new headquarters in Woolacombe.[11][12]

Inevitably there were tragedies. The US 743rd Tank Battalion and the US Navy suffered unfortunate fatalities on 18 December 1943 during a training exercise off Woolacombe beach, when three landing craft carrying tanks capsized after turning parallel to the waves. Major Allan Pixton, who was in charge of amphibious training, recalled:

There were fourteen men killed that day … nine … tank crewmen and five Navy landing craft crewmen. I personally pulled nine drowned tank crewmen out through the turrets of the three tanks … To my knowledge that was the single most costly training accident we ever had at the training center.[13]

A few days earlier an artillery round had fallen short and killed four men and wounded another six.[14] Lieutenant Wesley Ross, with the US 146th Engineer Combat Battalion, remembered a number of such deaths, 'I saw two men killed when an 81mm mortar round blew up in the tube.'[15] He also recalled, 'During one exercise Melvin Vest from Boat Team 8 was killed when a quarter pound block of TNT exploded in his hand … he died of shock about four hours later.'[16] The unfortunate private lost an arm and a leg in the blast, as well as being horribly burned.

On another occasion the lieutenant's team accidently killed a sleeping infantryman. 'We were unaware that he was in the restricted area,' said Ross, 'and blew the practice steel obstacles per plan.'[17] Despite these unfortunate losses during training, Ross was philosophical, noting that 'the confidence gained saved many lives'.[18] Understandably, if the men trained hard, they also played hard. There was inevitably rivalry between units, which sometimes led to punch-ups. Men of the 146th teased a tank unit by yelling 'Quack, quack' at the passing crews. In response they were accused of being 'sons of bitches'. When they met in Barnstaple that night, a fight broke out. Sergeant Roy Holmes recalled, 'What a brawl!'[19]

For obvious reasons, the Assault Training Centre proved very popular and hosted a steady stream of visitors.[20] Notably, these included Major-General Raymond Barton and Brigadier-General Theodore Roosevelt of the US 4th Infantry Division.

Around the same time, Lieutenant-Colonel Holmes found himself on the way to sleepy Bideford in North Devon. His role was to set up an ordnance experimental station, known as Depot O-617, that was to develop waterproofing techniques for vehicles and other equipment.[21] Despite all the specialist work conducted with the 'Funnies', they and every other Allied vehicle faced a fundamental problem: how do you prevent water from flooding the engine compartment when going ashore? Behind the scenes, steps were being taken to remedy this.

Mr F.J. Slee was sitting in his office in Cecil Chambers, the Strand, London, in early 1943, happily minding his own business. His role as Manager responsible for Industrial and Marine Lubricants for Shell Mex and BP had brought him enough headaches thanks to wartime restrictions and the demands of Britain's weapons factories. The last thing he wanted was another problem to solve, when his secretary announced that there was an American Transportation Corps captain waiting to see him.

The captain was shown in and Slee offered him a seat. His visitor smiled and explained, 'The British and ourselves are making wading tests off the west coast of Britain. Every vehicle we have must be able to wade ashore from a landing craft, in any depth of water, so long as the driver's head is clear.'[22] Slee's ears pricked up at the words 'landing craft'. This sounded like a challenge rather than a problem; evidently something big was brewing. The captain went on to explain that he needed to come up with a way of making an engine compartment watertight. Clearly, as Slee had 35 years in the business of lubricants he was the right man to talk to.

Slee agreed to see what he could do. He then spoke to his assistant manager, Mr H.W. Clark, and they decided they needed to get Mr H.W. Humberstone, manager of their Manchester Barton Installation, down to London. Humberstone was one of the country's foremost specialists in grease. Once they got together, they decided the sealant had to be soldier-proof, in that it would have to be extremely easy to apply and remove. Furthermore, '[T]he material would not only have to be waterproof, but have good electrical insulation properties and be heat-resisting.'[23]

What Slee, Clark and Humberstone came up with was a combination of grease and asbestos fibres, which was dubbed Compound 219. Tests showed it to be highly successful, but they needed to subject it to proper field conditions. Samples were flown to North Africa and put through prolonged field trials, and it was used operationally for the first time in the invasion of Sicily in 1943. Back in England, tests off the North Devon coast showed that vehicles could wade for 6 minutes without ill-effects.[24]

Humberstone was given the green light to mass produce the compound, and by D-Day 10,000 tons were ready thanks to Barton.[25] Once it and other waterproofing techniques had been refined, Lieutenant-Colonel Holmes' unit became responsible for training American instructors in the seas off North Devon.[26]

'I remember seeing all these enormous tins,' recalled Sergeant Anthony Bashford, of the 44th Royal Tank Regiment, 'enormous piles of Compound 219 … a bit like putty – which you applied around any particular crack or crevice in the Sherman tank to make it waterproof.'[27] This also involved smearing it into the joins in the escape hatch in the bottom of the tank and the engine doors.

Trooper Peter Davies, of the 1st East Riding Yeomanry, remembered:

We had to seal every part of the hatches where the driver and gunner get in, and where the guns come out. They had to be sealed and covered in rubberized canvas and stuck with Bostic glue. The turret flaps and turret ring had to be sealed, and the exhaust at the back was covered with a metal box affair.[28]

Sapper William Dunn, an AVRE driver with the 26th Assault Squadron who went through the same laborious process, recalled, 'We had to go round with a black compound all round the tank and this compound dried into a very hard sealing.'[29] This posed problems for the turret because it meant that it, the gun mantlet and the gun barrel ended up rigid, which was not ideal for combat.

Once again everything was thought of. Bashford said, 'The gunner or the crew inside could activate these charges and blow away the water-proofing membranes so that the turret would be able to rotate freely.'[30] Likewise, the extended exhausts were rigged for quick removal. '[T]here was a small explosive charge coupled to the turret,' said Dunn, 'and the tank commander just pressed a button and blew these things off.'[31] Doing all this in the heat of battle, however, was another matter.

In the meantime, many soldiers grew weary of testing out the compound, as it meant constantly risking a soaking. 'If there was a hole or a gravel pit in the south of England with water in it,' said Lance-Bombardier Stanley Morgan, 'we went through it in our waterproofed vehicles.'[32]

Another American officer who arrived in North Devon in early January 1944 was Lieutenant Colonel Irvin H. Sonne, commanding the

US 313th Station Hospital, along with his staff officers under Major Ervin Hinds. His unit took over a US military hospital at Fremington. Their role was to provide much-needed medical facilities to support the troops going through the Assault Training Centre and then to handle causalities evacuated after D-Day.

Although Sonne was impressed by the officers' quarters in the rather grand-looking Fremington House, he was not happy with what he found had been left by the preceding unit that had set up the camp. An inspection tour discovered that poor drainage was resulting in muddy water contaminating not only the administrative buildings but also the wards. His first order of the day was to remedy this, as he did not want medical staff traipsing mud everywhere.[33]

The British were relying on a combination of the 79th Armoured Division, sappers and marines to initially secure the beaches and clear the way, whereas for the Americans this role fell to three spearhead engineer brigades.[34] These units started arriving in England in late 1943 to conduct training.

Colonel Thompson took command of 6th Engineer Special Brigade in early 1944 and made sure it was put through its paces at the assault training centre. 'Was there ever a unit so meticulously put together, so precisely engineered for a specific mission as this?' he later said of these brigades.[35] Notably, nearly 25 per cent of the American forces in the initial attack would be engineers.[36]

The American DD tanks had their fair share of training mishaps. A major rehearsal exercise took place off the English south coast, dubbed Tiger, in late April 1944. This involved the 70th Tank Battalion. The DD tanks were successfully launched, but Staff Sergeant Gibson's tank began belching smoke and he and his crew had to abandon ship. 'In a few moments,' said Captain Harry Butcher, who was watching with Eisenhower, Tedder and Bradley, 'the tank crew was in the yellow dinghy and the tank had sunk.'[37]

Tiger was supposed to put the US 4th Infantry Division and 1st Engineer Special Brigade through its paces ready for the landings on Utah Beach. Where the tanks were concerned, the overall results of the exercise were not good. The engineers took too long clearing the beach obstacles, which left the armour exposed. 'If there had been enemy fire, the tanks, being quite close together, would have been easy targets,' observed Captain Butcher, 'as, indeed, would the landing craft. I came away from the exercise feeling depressed.'[38]

To add to the general air of despondency, on the night of 27/28 April, German motor torpedo boats, or E-boats, had got in amongst some of the vessels involved in the exercise, resulting in considerable loss of life. The majority of them were combat engineers who did not know how to properly use their life preservers. Rather than wearing them, they had strapped them round their waists.[39]

This attack was a highly embarrassing security breach, and to compound matters not all the dead were accounted for. This caused a panic because some of the American officers involved had knowledge of Operation Neptune, the naval aspect of D-Day. For a while, Eisenhower had to monitor Ultra (the secret decoding of German communication by Bletchley Park) to see if the Germans had been tipped off.[40]

Just before D-Day, the DD tanks of the 741st and 743rd Tank Battalions took part in Exercise Fabius. To give the crews a flavour of what to expect following a naval bombardment, they were launched 3,000 yards from the shore at Slapton Sands in order to hit the beach at H-Hour. However, afterwards they remained on the shore and were then sent back to Torcross.

9

A NICE LUNCH

Brigadier Arthur Walter was feeling rather pleased with himself. He had just come back from a very nice lunch at the In and Out Club in Cambridge House on Piccadilly in central London.[1] The brigadier was one of the unsung heroes of the war. As Director of Ports and Inland Water Transport, very few people had ever heard of him, and even fewer cared much about what he did. He would be the first to admit it was not one of the most glamourous jobs in the British Army. Nonetheless, he and his men had an important role to play in Overlord, now that they were involved in a top secret project known as codename Mulberry.

Once back in his office in Norfolk House in St James' Square, he decided to put his plans for D-Day back under lock and key.[2] 'Now,' he thought to himself, 'where did I put my brief case?' To his 'utter horror',[3] there was no sign of it. He mentally retraced his steps as he hurried past sandbagged doorways and taped-up windows, beneath the shadows of the barrage balloons tethered over central London. Walter was certain he had not but it down anywhere on the way. Come to think of it, he did not recall having it at all. He had committed mishaps in the past, but this he knew really 'took the biscuit'.

Brigadier Walter realised he had placed his case under the table during lunch and had foolishly forgotten to pick it up. His standard black civil service bag 'contained not merely the plans for Mulberry but also information as to where we were going to invade. At that moment, I wanted to die.'[4] Walter had accidently carried out the most appalling security breach. He could just imagine what his boss, Rear Admiral William Tennant, might say.[5]

Only a very small circle of people knew what Mulberry was: even the men building it did not know what it was for. Initially, it had been felt that in the first stage of an Allied invasion of France, they would need to capture a port in order to land supplies. Only this would be able to sustain an Allied build-up. However, the Dieppe raid had swiftly put paid to such notions. The supporting tanks had been unable to get off the beach and the whole operation had turned into a brave fiasco. However, Churchill had ordered the development of floating piers before Dieppe.

In putting his mind to the task of planning D-Day, Churchill was to show exceptional brilliance and foresight. He appreciated that the appliance of science and technical know-how could be used to ensure victory. Churchill had written a memo in May 1942 to Mountbatten, Chief of Combined Operations, advising they would need piers that 'must float up and down with the tide; the anchoring problem must be mastered. Let me have the best solution worked out.'[6]

Once the Allied planners had chosen the beaches of Normandy, they were presented with a tidal problem. The tide rises and falls by 25ft, which meant that supplies could only be landed across the beaches at selected times of the day either side of high tide. Furthermore, if the weather turned really bad in the Channel, nothing could be landed on the beaches at all. 'It was only then that bright boys – British boys,' recalled Brigadier Walter, 'thought up the idea of an artificial harbour which would be built in pieces in England, towed a hundred miles to the beaches and there put down, piece by piece by piece. And so came about the building of the Mulberry Harbours.'[7] A team under Vice Admiral John Hughes-Hallett produced the final design for an artificial port the size of Dover. Two were to be deployed: one at Arromanches off Gold Beach and the other at Omaha.

In a state of some panic, Walter phoned the In and Out Club. In the back of his mind, there was the nagging fear that someone official or otherwise had discovered his case. In a cold sweat, he imagined a visit by the military police, or a Nazi spy signalling his findings back to Berlin. Thankfully, the hall porter picked up the phone and, when questioned, cheerfully replied, 'Yes sir, a case was left here and I've got it in my cubby hole.'[8] The brigadier rushed back to the club to find that his case was still locked. No harm had been done.

Secrecy regarding the Mulberries was paramount. By late May 1944, Allied Supreme Commander General Eisenhower was content that Allied deception plans were working and that the Germans feared there would be two major landings, with the first a diversion. To maintain this delusion, Eisenhower instructed 'the use of devices for an artificial harbour should be kept secret and the Joint Intelligence Committee be instructed to place a ban on any public mention of Mulberries'.[9]

Walter was very lucky that his actions did not come to the attention of Hugh Astor, who was working for a counter-intelligence section within MI5.[10] Astor was acutely aware of how important Mulberry and PLUTO, the proposed underwater fuel pipeline, were to the success of the Normandy landings. Security on this matter was vital. Astor understood that they were 'the two top-secret elements in all [signals] traffic and we could say an awful lot but never, ever touch on these two things'.[11]

The worry at MI5 was that the Germans already had aerial reconnaissance photos of the Mulberries under construction. 'In fact they never did spot them,' said Astor, 'and we were spared any embarrassing questions.'[12] When the Directorate of Ports and Inland Waterways had requested a code word to use rather than employing the term 'artificial harbours', the head of security had simply selected the next available name in the code book, which happened to be Mulberry.

Shortly after his security mishap, Brigadier Walter attended a briefing conducted by Montgomery with around 400 officers in a cinema in Portsmouth. Walter's role became clear as Monty explained the overall plans for D-Day. He recalled, 'It was terribly inspiring, because I'd been planning my own little corner of the invasion, getting more and more puzzled, not knowing quite where it fitted in, and he suddenly put everything into perspective and I can only say that he raised my morale just like that.'[13]

While the artificial harbours were a sound concept, in some quarters it was felt that the enterprise had simply been left too late. The Royal Navy in particular were vocal in their concerns. 'Admiral Sir Andrew Cunningham has expressed anxiety lest the progress of construction of Mulberries and Gooseberries [the breakwaters for the harbours] ... should fail to meet operational requirements,'[14] wrote Eisenhower's naval aide Captain Harry Butcher.

Brigadier Walter and all those involved had almost been overwhelmed by the enormity of the task, especially when some of the contractors said what was required was impossible. 'Perhaps the greatest difficulty in getting the project underway after the plan was approved,' said Major-General Sir

Harold Wernher, who, as Co-ordinator of Ministry and Service Facilities, was given charge of the Mulberry project in August 1943, 'was the vast number of interested parties who had to be consulted or thought they ought to be consulted.'[15]

Creating the floating concrete caissons was a herculean task. According to Captain Alan Adcock from Walter's directorate:

> The design and construction of these was really a prodigious work; 147 of them were built and hadn't even been designed before the beginning of October 1943. And they were designed and built and floated round to the south coast ready for D-day between then and April 1944: seven months … it was a miracle that it was all done in the time.[16]

'One of the basic assumptions was that any port captured by the invasion forces would be mined,' recalled Colonel David Belchem, head of Monty's planning staff, 'its quays, cranes and handling equipment damaged or destroyed by the retreating German forces.'[17] As the need to design and build two artificial harbours had not been agreed until mid-1943, those involved only had 'some eight or nine months'.[18]

There could be no concealing the work from the public, or the Germans for that matter. 'In Southampton, I had watched the great concrete caissons … being built across the estuary, then towed to sea by their attendant tugs,' recalled Brian Selman, 'also the great drums of the PLUTO petrol lines, each with a gaggle of tugs on either side.'[19]

Their purpose, though, baffled everyone. 'My father was working at the time at Marchwood on the concrete Mulberry harbour,' said Bert Bragg, 'that's where a lot of it was made. They didn't know what they were building, they were just building concrete barges, but for what they had no idea.'[20] 'There was talk about PLUTO and then there were the Mulberry harbours,' remembered Patricia Cameron in Portsmouth, ' – we knew about them, but we didn't know what they were for.'[21]

Although the Mulberries were supposed to be top secret, the authorities were keen to have the construction process recorded for prosperity. Official war artist Muirhead Bone[22] was sent to the docks with his easel and watercolours to paint two of the enormous caissons being built. Although Bone delighted in painting industrial architecture, he was baffled by these enormous concrete barges, whose scaffold-shrouded superstructures were rising steadily skyward. Richard Eurich, who was also tasked with sketching the Mulberries, was equally perplexed. 'They wouldn't tell me what it was for,' he grumbled, ' … it was like a lot of factories standing out of the water.'[23]

Sitting on the quayside, Bone watched as the ant-like workforce scurried around the beached hulls while the tide was out and clambered up the towering scaffolding. He worked quickly and efficiently in sketching the stranded behemoths, but when he turned to his paints he faced a problem. The vista before him was grey, the sky was grey, the concrete was grey, as was the harbour floor. This hardly conveyed an impression of impending victory. To give his picture greater depth, and to make it three-dimensional, he opted for beige and brown. The result was that the picture had an almost golden hue.[24] It was as if he was harkening back to the days of the Spanish Armada and the gaudy galleons.

Ordinary Seaman Kenneth Bungard volunteered to help with trials involving a 200ft-long and 60ft-high concrete block off Dungeness early one morning. Next to it was a tug. When the vessel got underway, Bungard appreciated that the block was actually tethered to the tug and was floating. He and the other volunteers remained perched on top until, out in the bay, 'we promptly went down inside this concrete box, opened the sluices and sunk it on the sand and wondered what the hell we were doing – 'cos nobody tells you anything. We soon realised why they asked for volunteers, because these things had never been taken across an ocean. I mean, it was like trying to drag bricks across the Thames.'[25] Bungard and the others could only assume that the blocks were part of some elaborate air defence platform.

Movement of these caissons was painfully slow. Captain Butcher noted, 'In a test, two 1000-h.p. tugs towed one sample of Phoenix [codename for the concrete barges] in calm water at four knots.'[26] Unsurprisingly, the trials did not run smoothly. There was no hiding the Phoenixes sunk off Selsey Bill. 'I could see this from my bedroom window,' recalled Patricia Roach. 'Two or three blocks would appear each day and it grew to look like a village, which is what we eventually called it.'[27]

Captain J.B. Pollard, Deputy-Director of the Admiralty Salvage Service, was summoned to a meeting with his boss, Admiral Dewar. Apparently some sort of flap was on with the top brass, including Downing Street. He was instructed to get himself down to Selsey Bill to examine a sunken concrete caisson that had gone aground near Littlehampton. He was not informed of its function, but it was clearly misnamed as it could not be refloated in a hurry. The caisson had been constructed in haste and was defective, which greatly hampered pumping out the water.

When Pollard looked out to sea off Selsey, he saw more of these sunken caissons 'protruding from the sea like modern blocks of flats'.[28] He was at a loss as to what they were doing, but many were occupied by anti-aircraft guns and their crews located in a small flak tower. Between them were amphibious DUKW trucks carrying food and ammunition. When he asked around, the response was yes, these were to be refloated. He was told the War Office was in charge of the project, with the Army's engineers responsible for lifting the blocks off the sea bed.

Pollard was aghast, as many of the caissons were in the same faulty condition as the one off Littlehampton. The War Office was called, along with its responsible directorate, known as Transportation 5, under the command of Major Bruce White. He immediately despatched Major Steer, a former Port of London Authority engineer, to join Pollard and assess the situation. When Steer arrived, Pollard knew all about Mulberry and both returned to London to report that currently there was no way that eight caissons a day could be sent to Normandy.

In the meantime, Captain A. Dayton Clark, who was responsible for the American Mulberry, sent his salvage expert, Commodore Edward Ellsberg, to Selsey.[29] He had been overseeing the clearance of wreckage from Mediterranean and Red Sea ports. Ellsberg's prognosis was equally damning, 'Had the Royal Engineers deliberately started to find the worst pumps possible for the task in hand, they could not have chosen better.'[30] He reported to US naval headquarters in London that the British Army was not up to the job and that the task should be given to the US Navy.

On 11 May 1944, Admiral Dewar delivered the bad news to Major-General Donald McMullen, Director of Transportation in the War Office, that the Army's pumping equipment was unable to shift the Phoenixes. When Admiral Cunningham was informed, he drafted a memorandum for the Chiefs of Staff, urging responsibility be passed to the Admiralty. Churchill, who was a copy addressee, travelled to Selsey to see the situation first-hand for himself. Ten days later, Cunningham got his way and by the end of the month the pumping situation was in hand.

Hugh Spensley was a 20-year-old sub-lieutenant with the Royal Navy Volunteer Reserve serving on a landing ship tank. He had taken part in two previous D-Days, having been involved in the landings in Italy. His

vessel had been sent to India to conduct amphibious operations against
the Japanese, but by February 1944, he was back off the south coast of
England. 'It was decided that we should return to Britain for the invasion
of Europe,' said Spensley, 'wherever that might be.'[31] It was clear to everyone that preparations were underway for 'The Great Crusade'. Spensley
wrote:

> As the weeks rolled by, the ships and craft and Mulberry caissons
> increased in number all along the south coast and the day seemed to
> be not long off. Nowhere was this more apparent than in the great
> stretch of water protected by the Isle of Wight, the Solent, Spithead
> and Southampton Water.[32]

By 2 June 1944 Captain Pollard was able to report that everything was
ready for D-Day, though they had lost three caissons: one had been sunk
and two others had to be beached because they were leaking. All things
considered, it was not a too bad casualty rate.

10

BLINDING THE ENEMY

On Thorney Island, the RAF armourers drove their towing tractors out onto the hardstanding. Behind them were articulated trailers carrying a deadly cargo of finned rockets. Each had a large bulbous 60lb explosive warhead. It took two men to lift a rocket up into the launch rails; there were four under each wing. Once fitted, the rocket was slid back and connected to an electric firing cable. The waiting pilots, having checked their kit, climbed into the cockpits, powerful engines were started and the 'thumbs up' signal was given for 'chocks away'.

On 16 March 1944, Wing Commander Johnny Baldwin and twelve Typhoon fighter-bombers of 198 Squadron[1] from 84 Group conducted an attack on a German Wassermann radar[2] near Ostend using rockets. After approaching the target at 8,000ft, Baldwin dived down and hit the tower. This was some achievement as the rockets were unguided. He was followed by Warrant Officer Mason, Flight Lieutenant Niblett and Flight Lieutenant Plamondon. To their frustration, the tower remained intact.[3]

They returned in the afternoon and were met by increased flak that damaged several aircraft. Although they hit the radar tower again, it remained defiantly upright. The men of 198 Squadron were slightly baffled why they were not allowed to finish the job the following day. What they did not know was that they were being used as guinea pigs by Dr R.V. Jones, under the watchful eye of the Belgian Resistance.

Reginald Victor Jones had his hands full. He had started the war as a scientific officer serving on the staff of the Air Ministry, looking at air defence. Since then he had become one of the leading lights in the British scientific intelligence community. By 1944, he and his colleagues were grappling with numerous intelligence problems:

> At the same time as we were watching the flying bomb trials, dealing with the Baby Blitz, and wrestling with the German night defences, another problem was approaching its climax: this was the coming operation to land in force in Normandy. Ever since 1940 I had known what my part must be, whether or not it was formally assigned to me: to see that everything possible was done to knock out by jamming, deception, or direct action, the chain of coastal radar stations that the Germans would inevitably build up.[4]

Jones, his fellow boffins and the intelligence gatherers had catalogued 600 radar installations serving 200 stations,[5] extending from Bayonne in western France to Skagen in northern Denmark.[6] Such a vast sweep seemed wholly unnecessary, but Jones pointed out, 'Even though we knew that the attack was to be made in Normandy, we covered a very much wider coastline, so that if any leakage of information were to occur, the Germans would have no clue regarding the selected area.'[7]

Jones had made himself rather unpopular with the RAF as he advocated the best way to blind the German radar was by direct attack. In response, Fighter Command had rather feebly argued against such action as their fighters could not locate them. Jones then 'shamed' the RAF by suggesting if each fighter squadron was guided by a photo reconnaissance plane, then they might be able to find their way.

Johnny Baldwin was not privy to the full results of the attack on the Ostend radar. He knew he and his men had hit it, leaving it 'broken and badly battered'[8] but not completely destroyed. In the meantime, Belgian Resistance reported that the rotating mechanism was broken and that the station had been taken apart for repair.[9] This proved that the Typhoon and its rockets could take out the German radars. The Belgians also reported that there was another radar installation 23km up the coast ripe for such an attack. 'But once the technique had been established,' explained Jones, 'we then held off until the campaign for D-Day should start in earnest.'[10] In the meantime, Johnny Baldwin was awarded the Distinguished Flying Cross and took command of 198 Squadron.

Despite all his efforts, Jones was baffled as, '[E]ven as late as March 1944, I still had no formal request for information on German radar, nor was

I formally brought into the invasion planning.'[11] When he was finally approached by an RAF liaison officer, Jones was perturbed to discover the size of proposed operations would simply not be effective enough.

Jones resolved to take matters into his own hands. By good fortune, on 13 April 1944 he was asked to speak at the RAF Staff College. It so happened that Air Chief Marshal Sir Arthur Tedder, the Deputy Supreme Allied Commander, was speaking straight after Jones. He asked Air Vice Marshal Medhurst if he might get some one-on-one time with Tedder, so that he could discuss the inadequate countermeasures intended to silence the German coastal radars. Medhurst obliged and set up a meeting with Tedder, who was a veteran of the operations in North Africa and the Mediterranean, having served as CinC RAF Middle East Command.

Tedder was always receptive to new ideas and inter-service cooperation. In North Africa, the RAF had enjoyed what he called a 'happy marriage'[12] with the army. Close liaison and prioritising targets was always Tedder's goal.

Jones recalled with some relief, 'He was quickly convinced and asked me what to do – after all, the Invasion was less than two months away.' Jones' recommendation was that Victor Tait, Director General of Signals, should head a special unit within the headquarters of the Allied Expeditionary Air Force to conduct countermeasures. Sure enough, shortly afterwards Jones received a call from Tait asking for his help. Jones had conducted a Trojan horse exercise and was able to bring his own people on board.

Jones was disconcerted to discover during a visit to Supreme Allied Headquarters in Bushey Park that he was believed to be dead. A Canadian planning staff officer thought that he had accompanied the Dieppe Raid to help dismantle a radar. In light of Jones' expertise, orders had been given to shoot him should he be in danger of falling into enemy hands.[13]

Being very much alive, Jones set about coming up with the best way to destroy the enemy's radars. He appreciated that there were three options in dealing with them: they could be deceived, jammed or destroyed. A very low tech-solution had been found in 1942. Dr Robert Cockburn had devised 'Window', essentially foil strips designed to fool enemy radar during bombing raids. Jones reasoned that if they destroyed some of the stations, the remaining ones would not fully appreciate the significance of jamming and 'Window' when the time came.

This was wise, as the Germans were fully aware of the Allies' radar-jamming capabilities. Reichsmarschall Hermann Göring, CinC of the

Luftwaffe, grumbled, 'Whatever the equipment we have, the enemy can jam it without so much as a by-your-leave.'[14] Amazingly, the Germans had been incredibly slow, if not downright resistant to waging electronic warfare. Ironically, General Wolfgang Martini, the Luftwaffe's Chief of Air Signals, opposed a jamming campaign against the British on the grounds, 'There is a simple means whereby the enemy can jam our entire radar system, against which we have no antidote.'[15] As a result, no research was carried out for six months.

Their hand was forced once the British started employing 'Window'. In light of his lack of countermeasures against British radar, Göring had raged at Martini, 'What am I supposed to tell the Führer! He would think me a complete nincompoop if I repeated to him what you tell me.'[16] Infuriated by Martini's intransigence, and what he saw as incompetence, Göring took responsibility for electronic research and development from him.

The Germans eventually developed jamming transmitters to interfere with radar carried by Allied bombers. British intelligence erroneously concluded that the Germans had twenty-three jamming stations, but only five of these were confirmed and only four were in the invasion area. These could interfere with the invasion fleet's navigational aids. Jones' best countermeasure was bombs.

The British knew from experience in 1940, when the Germans had tried to wreck the country's radar network, that it was not easy to bring down the transmitter and receiver masts.[17] Unless struck by a direct hit, the British radar masts proved blast-proof.[18] German bombers could not see the masts from the air, and even dive-bomber attacks were not very effective.[19] The failure to silence Britain's radars convinced Göring that he was wasting his time and, fortuitously for Fighter Command, ordered that there be no further attacks.

Jones and his team already had their solution thanks to Johnny Baldwin and his rocket-armed Typhoon attack on Ostend. Even once the air attacks commenced on the German radar sites, it remained vital not to single out Normandy. Jones fully appreciated that partially blinding the enemy's radar would also serve operations to deceive Hitler about the actual location of the landings:

> As regards the tactics of the campaign, it would clearly be danger-
> ous to attack only the radar stations that could cover our intended
> landing area, and so we had a general rule that for every one attack

that we made in the area there should be two outside it, so that the Germans should not be able to deduce from the intensity of our pre-invasion attacks exactly where the landings were to be made.[20]

Jones, Tait and Cockburn were involved in another major effort to deceive Hitler's radars. To dupe German defences, it was decided to convince Hitler that D-Day would take place north of the Seine, somewhere between Le Havre and Calais. To achieve this required creating two spoof or fake fleets that would head for Fécamp and Boulogne. Crucially, this would serve to tie the bulk of the German infantry divisions north of the Seine.

Cockburn, who had devised 'Window', reasoned it could be used to create the impression of vast armadas. The first was to cover an area 16 miles long and 14 miles wide. Motor launches would also be deployed under the 'Window' to boost and extend the radar echoes. It was therefore important that the Fécamp radar station be left functioning.[21] Squadron Leader John Shannon of 617 Squadron, who was to be involved, recalled, 'The operation was called Operation Taxable and it was one of the biggest spoofs ever played on the Germans.'[22]

German air defence radars were also to be jammed by a large-scale operation. According to RAF radar and jamming expert Sergeant Jack Nissen, 'Two hundred ships were each equipped with two to three kilowatts of Mandrel jammers, which were used on that "one-night-only" basis. When Eisenhower said "Go", everybody on board their ships, wherever they were, threw this big master switch.'[23] The jammers would create 'hash' on German radar screens, which was consistent with a faulty valve. The hope was that the operators would wait until morning before calling the engineer, by which time it would be too late.

This was not all, as MI5 was also involved in highly elaborate counter-intelligence deception operations. Hugh Astor was privy to these at the highest level:

The cover plan created an imaginary army and gave the Germans the impression that we had available almost twice the number of troops that were in fact in existence … we were able, up to a point, to persuade them that the Normandy landings, when they started, were a diversionary attack and that the main force was still in East Anglia waiting to go across the Channel to Calais.[24]

There was a second landing deception plan designed to convince Hitler that the Allies were considering a diversionary attack on Norway.[25] Former Polish fighter pilot Roman Garby-Czerniawski, who was a double agent working for Astor, provided convincing but bogus intelligence to the Germans on military preparations in Scotland and the south-east of England.[26]

The Allies knew that their deception plans were working thanks to Bletchley Park's codebreakers. Captain Jerry Roberts and his colleagues were able to confirm 'that Hitler and his commanders expected an Allied invasion along the French coast at Calais, preceded by a feint at Normandy'.[27] They could do this because they had cracked the Lorenz cipher used by Hitler to communicate with his senior commanders. 'It was crucial,' said Roberts, 'for us to know whether the main bulk of the German Army was held in the Calais region (as Hitler wanted) or in the Normandy area (as his generals wanted).'[28]

Once Tait and Jones' team were up and running at Allied Expeditionary Air Force headquarters at Bentley Priory, they began briefing the squadrons assigned to attack the German radars. The man given the job was Squadron Leader Birtwistle, who had been working with Jones' unit. He was ideal: not only did he had a science degree, but he had also served as a Fighter Command intelligence officer during the Battle of Britain.

Birtwistle rose to the occasion admirably, making sure Group Captain Gillam's pilots at Thorney Island and Group Captain Davoud's at Hurn knew exactly what was expected of them. Assessing the results as the attacks progressed was equally important, so Group Captain Moncrieff's Canadian 39 Reconnaissance Wing at Odiham and Group Captain Donkin's 35 Wing at Gatwick were to conduct the photographic sorties. Also, British listening stations would monitor German transmissions to see how many were still functioning.

The anti-radar operations commenced on 10 May, and as they escalated it soon became apparent to the Germans what was happening.[29] In response, the air defences for these installations were strengthened, making the attacks ever more dangerous for the pilots. The Cherbourg area in particular was heavily defended by anti-aircraft guns, which meant the pilots could expect a very hot reception.

Squadron Leader Johnny Keep conducted a large attack on two sites near Cherbourg on 23 May. This involved nine Typhoons from his 181 Squadron, seven from 247 Squadron plus another fourteen from the Canadian squadrons of 143 Wing. Anti-flak Typhoons went in first to draw fire, and the others managed to target both radars. Keep's plane was hit and he nursed his aircraft 10 miles out into the Channel before ditching. In the process he broke a cheek and his jaw, but was luckily rescued by an RAF seaplane.

That same day, Squadron Leader Johnny Niblett and his men were briefed at Thorney Island that their target for tomorrow was at the northern end of the Cherbourg Peninsula. At Cap de la Hague was a radar aircraft reporting station, and they were to take it out of commission. For the operation, Niblett commanded eight Typhoons, half from 198 Squadron and the rest from 609 Squadron.

They were due to take off at 0650 hours on 24 May; however, fog ensured they were not in the air until 1007 hours. It was not a good start. Niblett and his men approached the target almost at ground level, and during the run-in the Germans opened up with everything they had. Valiantly, they pressed on to deliver forty rockets as well as cannon fire. One German soldier recorded his attacker's bravery:

> Three Typhoons came in from the valley flying very low. The second aircraft got a direct hit from 37mm flak which practically shot off its tail. The pilot, however, managed to keep some sort of control and continued straight at the target. He dived below the level of the target structure, fired rockets into it, and then tried at the last moment to clear. The third aircraft, in trying to avoid the damaged Typhoon, touched the latter's fuselage with a wing tip. Both aircraft locked together and crashed some 100yds beyond. The radar installation was never again serviceable.[30]

Niblett's success cost him the lives of Flying Officer Freeman and Flight Sergeant Vallely. Freeman almost crashed into the target.[31] By the end of the month, the RAF had conducted 619 missions against twenty-nine sites, of which twenty had been very badly damaged. Jones was delighted with the results, remarking, '[T]he attacks were going rather well, and Birtwistle – who had been briefing the pilots personally had clearly done it excellently.'[32] Birtwistle persuaded him and one of his team, Wing Commander Rupert Cecil, who was a bombing expert, that they ought to visit the fighter stations involved.

On 27 May, the three of them took off from Hendon, with Cecil at the controls, and headed for Thorney Island, Hurn and Odiham. To Jones' alarm, he soon discovered that Cecil was 'a spirited pilot'.[33] What Jones really meant was that Cecil was highly aggressive, recalling, '[A] Spitfire from Northholt thought that he would surprise us with a dummy attack from our starboard flank, heading straight for us. From his subsequent manoeuvre I imagined that he was as surprised as I was when Cecil, with all his old bomber pilot's reactions, banked us sharply into a turn heading directly at the fighter.'[34]

A head-on collision was avoided, but Cecil continued to throw poor Jones and Birtwistle about. He practically dropped the aircraft onto the Thorney Island and Odiham runways. On their return to Hendon, Cecil cut in front of a transport aircraft, forcing it to abort its landing, and narrowly missed a train. During their meetings, Jones found that the pilots, who had initially been less than enthused by the lack of 'bang' when they hit their targets, were beginning to realise the importance of their sorties. In addition, they wanted to have a go at Fécamp. Jones agreed that it would be unwise to leave the site untouched, and it was duly attacked on 5 June.[35]

In the meantime, the attacks continued, as did the losses. Flak claimed Johnny Niblett over Dieppe and Flight Lieutenant Johnny Saville over Guernsey. Group Captain Gillam noted, 'This was a very expensive time in that we lost about three wing commanders and about five squadron commanders in just over a month … But we did it very successfully and managed to do the job so they were all out of action with the exception of two that were deliberately left.'[36]

Just three weeks before D-Day, the Germans had forty-seven radar stations, but on the night of the invasion only about a dozen were functioning. Leigh-Mallory, the Allied Expeditionary Air Force commander, was fulsome in his praise, stating, 'The application of radio counter-measures immediately preceding the assault proved to be extraordinarily successful.'[37]

The Germans despaired that they were unable to stop the Allies from destroying their radars and France's bridges, railways and marshalling yards. By the end of May 1944, it was obvious the Allies were operating with impunity over France. Admiral Krancke, who was in charge of German coastal defences and the ports, lamented that Allied bombers and fighter-bombers 'had almost complete mastery of the air'.[38] The Germans, remarkably, seemed to have no real idea of what was going on. Just two days before D-Day, on 4 June, Krancke assessed that he doubted the Allies had gathered their full invasion fleet.

The following day, the Luftwaffe conducted just five reconnaissance sorties over the English Channel. By then the Allied fleet was on the move; however, the Luftwaffe signalled that there was 'nothing to report'. At the same time, R.V. Jones noted that the RAF 'had given Fécamp everything they could carry'.[39]

After a campaign to cut France's railways, RAF Bomber command, under Air Marshal Arthur Harris, turned their attention to the destruction of Hitler's Atlantic Wall. The problem faced by the bomber crews was that they could not concentrate on Normandy for fear of giving the game away. 'The only way of doing this,' said Harris, 'was by the wildly extravagant method of bombing at least two coastal batteries or defences elsewhere for every one that was attacked on the invasion coast of Normandy.'[40]

Such attacks largely consisted of carpet bombing the concrete gun casemates and hoping for the best. In late May, an attack on the St Martin-de-Varreville battery scored 'several direct hits',[41] causing the casemate to collapse. According to Harris, on the night of D-Day, ten German batteries in the assault area received over 5,000 tons of bombs. This amounted to the largest weight of bombs dropped by Bomber Command in a single attack to date. Some 14,000 tons of bombs were dropped on the Atlantic Wall. The results were to prove very unsatisfactory.

11

THE WEATHERMAN

The weather has always been a very British preoccupation, and Churchill was no exception. On 30 May 1944, he wrote to Admiral Andrew Cunningham, the First Sea Lord, seeking guidance, 'Pray let me have the weather forecast. How does this hot spell fit in with our dates? Does it tend to bring about a violent reaction or is it all clear ahead? Let me have the best your meteorologist can do, but do not fill it up with technical terms.'[1] It is notable that Churchill wanted the prognosis in layman's language and did not want to be bamboozled by the science. Two days later, unhelpfully, the fine weather broke.

Also on 30 May, an unhappy Air Chief Marshal Leigh-Mallory, CinC of the Allied Expeditionary Air Force, went to see Eisenhower. 'Ike had a tough one today,'[2] noted Captain Butcher, who was present at yet another difficult meeting. Leigh-Mallory explained that he was still extremely concerned about the prospect of two American airborne divisions jumping onto 'Rommel's Asparagus'. The British airborne division's route and drop zone was much less perilous, whereas the Americans were facing 'futile slaughter', warned Leigh-Mallory. Flying in from the west, they would be completely exposed by the full moon and have to run the gauntlet of German searchlights and flak.

Leigh-Mallory estimated that the Americans would suffer heavy losses, including the bulk of their gliders, and recommended that the western drop be cancelled.[3] Playing for time, Eisenhower asked that he put his concerns in writing. The problem Ike face was that if he heeded Leigh-Mallory's warning, then he would have to cancel the attack on Utah Beach, which would impact on Omaha. Afterwards, Eisenhower sought the advice of his airborne commanders. 'I was encouraged to persist in the belief that Leigh-Mallory was wrong!' he concluded.[4]

By early June, all the preparations for Operation Overlord were complete and everyone from Eisenhower down were keyed up and increasingly tense. Getting to this stage had required unending problem-solving and decision-making. At the pinnacle of this process was Eisenhower. It understandably took a toll on him. 'Ike looks worn and tired,' observed Butcher. 'The strain is telling on him.'[5]

The men and ships were ready: camps and ports up and down the UK were crammed with every accoutrement of war. Weather-wise, it was now or never. Eisenhower was reliant on his weathermen, headed by 'a dour but canny Scot, Group Captain J.M. Stagg'.[6] The senior commanders were meeting twice daily, at 0400 and 0930 hours, at Southwick House. Timing for the landings was everything, and although 5 June was selected, with a decision to be made the previous day, some units in the north had to depart on the 3rd in order to be in place in time. However, by Saturday 3 June, the weather was deteriorating, much to the dismay of Eisenhower, Tedder, Ramsay, Leigh-Mallory and Montgomery.

That morning, Montgomery wanted to be away, saying, 'My own view is that if the sea is calm enough for the Navy to take us there, then we must go.'[7] After the 0930 hours meeting that day, he scribbled in his diary:

> The weather forecast does not look good, and tomorrow, 4 June, will be an interesting day; at 0800 hours tomorrow the final decision must be taken, and once taken must be stuck to; everything will be at sea, and if it is to be turned back, it must be turned back then.[8]

Then, as an afterthought, he added, 'Strong and resolute characters will be very necessary.'[9] Although he was no doubt referring to his fellow commanders, he was especially thinking of Eisenhower, who was shouldering the ultimate burden.

When Eisenhower and his senior commanders gathered on the morning of 4 June, Group Captain James Stagg had the worst possible news: they could expect strong winds and low cloud – which was not good for sailing or flying. 'The meteorologists said that air support would be impossible,' noted Eisenhower, 'naval gunfire would be insufficient, and even the handling of small boats would be rendered difficult.'[10] Admiral Ramsay adopted a neutral stance, and while Montgomery was all for going, Tedder, disagreed: they needed their bombers and fighter-bombers to pave the way. Eisenhower had little choice. 'We will postpone it for twenty-four hours,'[11] he said.

The Royal Navy officer charged with alerting everyone was Captain Richard Courage in the operations room of Southwick House. This proved to be a rather nerve-wracking task:

> In the early hours of 4 June I got a signal to send out in cipher giving a twenty-four hour postponement of the Operation. I sent that off, but we didn't know whether it had got through to everyone. They couldn't answer back because of radio silence and we could not guarantee that they had received the signal.[12]

Just to be on the safe side, seaplanes were sent to check on progress. Steadily, everyone was rounded up and they headed back to the nearest port in the face of a growing storm. It was not confirmed to Admiral Ramsay until 0900 on Sunday that all wayward vessels were heading for shelter, and the Admiralty issued a gale warning for the Channel.

Alarmingly, one convoy of almost 140 ships ferrying men of Major-General Raymond Barton's US 4th Infantry Division could not be located. By 0900 hours, it was wallowing in rough seas 25 miles to the south of the Isle of Wight. A sense of panic prevailed in the Southwick ops room at the prospect of the convoy pressing on and arriving unsupported off the invasion beaches. It took all day for an aircraft to locate them, by which time the cloud was down to 100ft. The first message canister fell into the sea, and although the second one found its mark, the captain seemed to take no notice. Then, to the relief of the pilot, the convoy put about and headed north.[13]

When they reconvened early on 5 June, Eisenhower was relieved to learn he had made the right decision. The prevailing weather for the day would have caused 'a major disaster' if the invasion had gone ahead. Eisenhower was then astonished to learn that 'the following morning a period of relatively good weather, heretofore completely unexpected, would ensue, lasting probably thirty-six hours'.[14] However, the long-term forecast was not favourable. Essentially, there was a small window of opportunity created by a gap in the bad weather.

Group Captain Stagg arrived, clutching his briefing materials, and said, 'The fair interval that has now reached here and will extend through all southern England during the night will probably last into the later forenoon or afternoon of Tuesday.'[15] There was much nodding of heads around the conference table. He added that the winds were tolerable and that visibility would be good. For the rest of the week, his prediction was that the weather would be variable, with a mixture of fair and overcast periods. 'The relief that statement brought into the room,' recalled Stagg, 'was a joy to behold.'[16] He then left, leaving Ike and his commanders to their deliberations.

Looking at Montgomery, Ramsay and Tedder, Eisenhower considered the implications of what he was being told. His immediate concern was that they might get several assault waves ashore, only to have the beachhead cut off by the weather and then destroyed by a German counterattack. If they did not go now, they would have to wait another two weeks for the tides to be right, and even then who knew what the weather would have in store. He appreciated that it was now or never, or at least until later in the year. Such a delay would not go down well with Stalin, who was planning his own version of D-Day. Montgomery and Ramsay thought the risk was worth taking, but Tedder and Leigh-Mallory were reluctant.

'This is a decision which I must take alone,' said Eisenhower. 'After all, that is what I am here for.'[17] He paced the room for a tense 45 seconds, then stood looking at his expectant subordinates' faces. 'I quickly announced the decision to go ahead with the attack on June 6,' Ike said. 'The time was then 4.15 a.m., June 5.'[18] He looked around the table and there were no objections. If anything he felt a lightening of the mood as if a great weight had been lifted from everyone. He then uttered the immortal words, 'OK, let's go.'[19]

'We were all glad,' recalled Montgomery. 'This conference did not last more than 15 minutes. Eisenhower was in good form and made his decision quickly.'[20] Afterwards, Stagg found himself the centre of attention, with senior commanders coming over to congratulate him on his work. 'I think you've treated this whole business in a most masterly way, Stagg,' said Air Chief Marshal Tedder. 'The Supreme Commander and all of us have appreciated it.'[21] Stagg was grateful that his efforts, and those of his American counterpart, were trusted, but there remained a nagging doubt that the weather could still change when they least expected it. He was unaware that his rivals in Paris, Professor Stoebe and Major Lettau, had completely missed the looming gap in the weather.

Across southern England there was no missing that D-Day was now very imminent. Dr R.V. Jones, busy overseeing the destruction of Hitler's radars, recalled that day, 'Before returning to Stanmore, we flew on to Hurn, and it was clear that the Invasion was "on" because the large armada of ships which had been in Spithead two days before was no longer there. I was silently wishing them Good Luck when we had a head-on encounter with a whole wing of American Thunderbolts.'[22]

At his chateau near Paris, Field Marshal von Rundstedt read the Luftwaffe's latest reports, 'The enemy command is still trying by all means to prevent us from observing his activities. The continued air attack on Dunkirk and the coast as far as Dieppe leads us to suppose that the enemy will attack in that sector.'[23] Such raids were now routine and seemed little cause for immediate alarm.

At the back of his mind, Rundstedt must have wondered when the waiting game would finally come to an end. His eyes, skimming to the end of the reports, saw that the Luftwaffe assessed 'it is unlikely that the invasion is imminent'.[24] He could relax for another day at least. Later, he set off for the Côq Hardi, his normal restaurant, to enjoy a leisurely lunch. He would have choked on his food had German intelligence known that a great invasion armada was about to be steaming across the Channel heading for Normandy.

'Within half-an-hour of sunset on the night of 5 June, while the leading ships of the seaborne assault moved into the buoyed channels to steer for France,' wrote war correspondent Captain R.W. Thompson, 'the Pathfinders of the United States and the British Air Forces took off from their English fields to light their beacons in the fields of Normandy.'[25] They would also soon be causing alarm and confusion behind enemy lines.

Back in France, Rundstedt's headquarters at St Germain-en Laye was warned of an imminent invasion and alerted Dollmann and Salmuth's Seventh and Fifteenth armies. 'Soon after 2100 hours on 5 June we intercepted messages from England to the French Resistance Movement,' said General Blumentritt, Rundstedt's Chief of Staff, 'from which it was deduced that the invaders were coming.' The two armies' headquarters responded differently. 'Our Fifteenth Army east of the Seine at once issued the "Alarm", though for some reason the Seventh Army in Normandy delayed doing so until 0400 hours.'[26] Blumentritt was clearly vexed about this, adding, 'That was unfortunate. Soon after midnight news came that Allied parachute troops had begun dropping.'[27]

This warning posed a threat to Overlord because it gave Rundstedt time to move the armoured reserve, I SS Panzer Corps located north-west of Paris, under the cover of darkness toward Normandy. There was only one snag: it could not be released without Hitler's personal permission. 'As early at 0400 hours I telephoned,' recorded Blumentritt, 'and asked for the release of the Corps – to strengthen Rommel's punch.'[28] Hitler's staff refused to wake him, suspecting that it was just a feint. The Führer slumbered on, oblivious to what was happening.

Had Rommel been at his headquarters, things might have gone very differently. 'Rommel,' noted Blumentritt, 'often spoke to Hitler himself on the telephone, which Rundstedt never did.'[29] Hitler had forbidden his commanders to travel by air because of the Allies' air superiority, so Rommel had set off very early by car on his way to confer with the Führer. General Speidel, Rommel's Chief of Staff, was unable to get hold of him at Herrlingen until 0600 hours on 6 June. Rommel promptly turned around, but would not be back until the end of the day. He could have got the I SS Panzer Corps released much sooner, and indeed deployed the panzer division nearest the beaches; yet neither happened.

The Invasion Coast

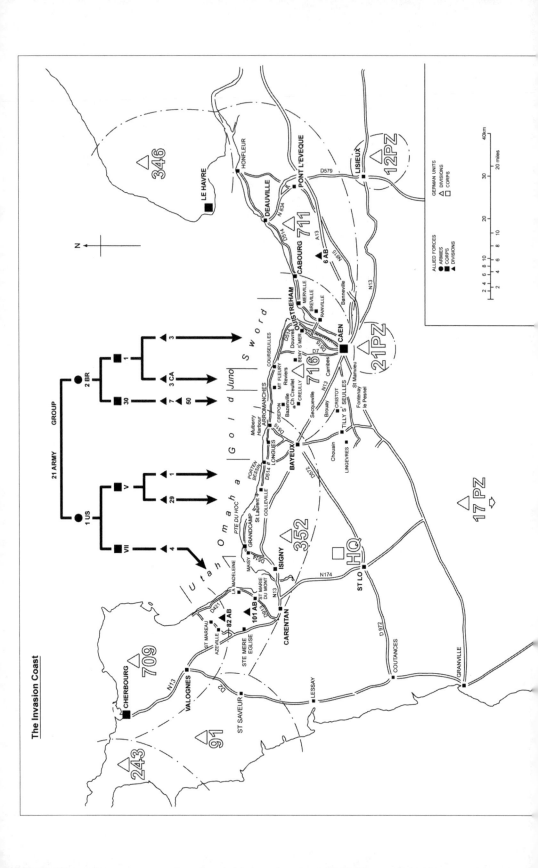

12

BROKEN CRICKET

Late on 5 June, an anxious Eisenhower visited the US 101st Airborne Division in the Newbury area. He was encouraged to find the men 'in fine fettle'.[1] They were packed and ready to go. Captain Butcher recalled Ike wanted to watch them 'load for the great flight – one which Leigh-Mallory said would cost so heavily in lives and planes'.[2] Jokingly, the men told the Supreme Commander not to worry. Their overriding confidence was a testimony to their high level of training. This was to prove a vital asset in the coming hours.

Looking round at all the young faces, Eisenhower must have secretly fretted: after all their meticulous planning and problem-solving, had they got it right? If they had not, then tens of thousands would die, slaughtered on the beaches and fields of Normandy. Even after making the decision to go, the burden of command still weighed heavily on Ike's shoulders. He probably went to see the paratroopers just to drive home exactly what it was he was doing.

'In the preparation of an immense military enterprise, the staggering multiplicity of decisions and details can tend to dwarf other things in life,' noted Eisenhower philosophically. 'But like all men in the services, I had personal concerns and worries, prides and fears, and a good thing too – they helped save us from degenerating into one-track machines.'[3]

Leigh-Mallory's concerns also weighed heavily with Eisenhower, who observed that the paratroopers' 'participation had been so severely questioned by the air commander'.[4] Ike had been warned that the airborne assault could suffer over 80 per cent casualties. Turning to some of the officers, he said, 'I've done all I can, now it is up to you.'[5]

Kay Summersby, Ike's driver, recalled:

General Taylor was about the last person to get aboard his ship. E. [Eisenhower] walked with him to the door of the C-47. By this time it was getting quite dark. We returned to 101st headquarters ... then proceeded to climb on the roof of the building to watch the aircraft circling over the field getting into formation. It was one of the most impressive sights anyone could wish to see.[6]

'I stayed with them until the last of them were in the air,' said Eisenhower, 'somewhere about midnight.'[7] 'At Control Tower level,' recalled BBC reporter Robert Barr, who was one of four correspondents shadowing Ike, 'we could no longer see the riding lights of the gliders. We could see the tow-planes circling but hear nothing.'[8]

Kay Summersby and reporter Merrill 'Red' Mueller saw that Eisenhower's eyes filled with tears as he watched the last of the planes take off.[9] Earlier, Meuller had watched Ike 'bowed down with worry'.[10] It was then a 2-hour journey back to his headquarters to start the waiting game.

Amongst those taking off was Lieutenant Dick Winters with E Company, 506th Parachute Infantry Regiment, 101st Airborne. Their transport aircraft lifted off from Upottery airfield in Devon in the south-west of England. While waiting to get on their planes, Winters reflected, 'It's here that a good jumpmaster can do the most for his men. Getting all that equipment on, tied down, make it comfortable and safe.'[11] Little, though, could be done to lessen the burden of each man, who carried up to 150lb of gear. Some were so overloaded that they could not put on their reserve chute. Once in the air, Winters pondered, 'Every man, I think, had it in his mind, "How will I react under fire?".'[12]

That night, Captain Courage at Southwick House recalled, 'I remember the tension was greatest when we felt that the time was approaching when any German E-boat patrols from Cherbourg might have met the invasion fleet in mid-Channel. But, contrary to expectations, they didn't appear.'[13] At Bletchley Park, codebreaker Harry Hinsley had the task of informing the top brass in London the moment that the German Navy reported the presence of the Allied invasion fleet. Understandably, there was great concern about the havoc E-boats and U-boats could cause if they got in amongst the invasion forces. This was well-founded after the losses incurred during Exercise Tiger off Slapton Sands.

Just before 0300 hours, the first signal was decrypted by Bletchley and the contents transmitted to the Admiralty.[14] Not long after, the phone rang and a woman said she was calling from Downing Street and had the Prime Minister on the line. Although he was very tired, Hinsley composed himself. 'Has the enemy heard were are coming yet?'[15] demanded Churchill's very distinctive voice. Hinsley replied that the first message was on the teleprinter. The line abruptly went dead.

Ninety minutes later, Churchill called again. 'Is anything adverse happening yet?'[16] This time Hinsley was able to inform the Prime Minister that a 'Torpedo Boat Flotilla were ordered to attack landing boats off Port-en-Bessin and Grandchamp'.[17] Again, Churchill hung up without a word of thanks. Hinsley did not leave his office until about midday, by which time he had been at his desk for 24 hours.

Once in the air, Major-General Matthew Ridgway's 82nd Airborne Division and Major-General Maxwell Taylor's 101st Airborne Division headed west of the Cotentin Peninsula and then looped south-east past the Channel Islands. It was a tense time for the pilots of Troop Carrier Command. Few had flown combat missions at night in bad weather or experienced flak.[18] The plan was for Ridgway's men to come down west of Ste-Mère-Église and the Merderet River, while Taylor's would land further east just behind the flooded areas that backed onto Utah Beach. Much of the Merderet and the River Douve had also been flooded by Rommel's engineers.

Taylor's men needed to neutralise the enemy's batteries and then take control of four of the causeways between Saint-Martin-de-Varreville and Poupeville. Meanwhile, Ridgway would take and hold the crossings over the Douve and Merderet as well as capturing Ste Mère-Église. In addition, they had to clear the glider landing sites for the first wave at 0400 hours. A lot depended on how quickly the Germans responded to what was happening.

The German garrison on the Channel Islands was alerted to the great airborne armada flying to their east and opened fire in the darkness. 'Below us we could see glints of yellow flame from the German anti-aircraft guns on the Channel Islands,' observed General Ridgway. 'We watched them curiously and without fear, as a high-flying duck may watch a hunter, knowing that we were too high and far away for their fire to reach us.'[19]

Graf von Schmettow, the garrison commander, was not there as he had been summoned to Rennes, along with all of Rundstedt's divisional and corps commanders, for a wargame exercise. While Schmettow departed Guernsey on 4 June for St. Malo, many of his colleagues had left it to the last minute. The timing of this gathering could not have been worse and was to sow confusion amongst the German chain of command. In a preliminary meeting with General Marcks, Schmettow had been reassured that an Allied attack on the west coast of the Contentin seemed unlikely as the Allies would not want to first assault his heavily fortified Channel Islands.

In the meantime, when the American transport aircraft crossed the French coastline, the troublesome weather once more intervened. A bank of cloud caused the pilots to scatter for fear of colliding with one another. When they emerged they were greeted by German searchlights and flak. 'It seemed almost impossible to fly through that wall of fire without getting shot down,' recalled Pilot Sidney Ulan of the 99th Troop Carrier Squadron, 'but I had no choice.'[20]

Dropping to 600ft, the pilots were supposed to slow down ready for the paratroopers to jump. Instead, they opened their throttles in a bid to escape the incoming fire and some began to climb while others dived. The result was that when many men jumped, there were aircraft not only above them but also below. Others were simply too low. Private Donald Burgett, with the 101st, witnessed the horrific results of this:

Seventeen men hit the ground before their chutes had time to open. They made a sound like large ripe pumkins being thrown down to burst against the ground.

'That dirty son of a bitch of a pilot,' I swore to myself, 'he's hedge-hopping and killing a bunch of troopers just to save his own ass. I hope he gets shot down in the Channel and drowns real slow.'

Burgett himself only just survived having leapt from his aircraft at less than 300ft. Looking up at the flak illuminating the night sky, he recalled, 'I couldn't help wondering … if I got the opening shock first or hit the ground first; they were mighty close together.'[21]

As the troopers queued to exit their aircraft, they could see the tracer rounds arcing up towards them. Burdened by all their equipment, many of them kept falling over before they reached the door. Once in the air, the paratroopers ended up scattered everywhere, miles from their allotted drop zones. Men of the 82nd and 101st became mixed up. It was not a good start.

In the case of the 506th Parachute Infantry Regiment, they were to land 10km to the south-west of Ste-Mère-Église, which lay directly behind Utah Beach. Unfortunately, some men dropped straight into the town and were promptly shot by the German garrison as they descended. In anticipation of such an airborne attack, some of the landing zones were defended by machine-gun teams and mortars, which opened up on the helpless paratroopers. The flooded areas also proved death traps for the overburdened paratroops.

A very low-tech solution was employed to help the paratroops find each other in the dark without having to call out. 'Every man in the division had been issued a little cricket snapper to use in place of a password,' explained Private John Houston of the 101st. 'One click is the challenge and two clicks is the answer.'[22] This device led to some close shaves.

Lieutenant Jack Tallerday, having gathered a group of men from both the 82nd and 101st, moved down a hedgerow. Spotting another group coming toward them, he used his cricket and got a reply. To his alarm, Tallerday saw 'it was quite evident by the configuration of their helmets that they were Germans'.[23] Each group passed each other without taking any action, until at last they were swallowed up by the night. Inevitably, the Germans captured some of these crickets, soon cottoned on to how they were being used and were able to ambush some paratroops.[24]

Simple as the crickets were, they could be broken, as Private Woodrow Robbins of the 101st discovered almost to his cost. Creeping through the night trying to find his unit, he heard a friendly sounding click-clack and stepped forward with his hands raised. 'You dumb shit, what the hell's wrong with you?' admonished Private Pat Christenson from the darkness, angry that his comrade had not used his cricket in response. Seeing that Christenson was pointing a revolver at him and poised to fire, Robbins apologised, saying, 'I lost the clicker part of my cricket.'[25]

On another occasion, a group of three men, failing to use their crickets or to respond correctly to the challenge 'Flash' with the reply 'Thunder', had a grenade thrown into their midst. Luckily, they managed to jump clear before it exploded and their assailant disappeared, thereby avoiding a lynch mob.[26]

While Rommel's anti-aircraft batteries responded well to the airborne assault, on the ground the reaction was much slower and confused. This was not helped by the absence of Lieutenant-General Karl von Schlieben, who was also in Rennes for the exercise, and Major-General Wilhelm Falley, who was en route there. Before leaving Chateau Haut,

Falley had remarked to his chief of operations, 'Nothing's going to happen in this lousy weather.'[27] The generals' departure left the 709th and 91st Divisions defending the region rudderless and with little idea of what was going on.

'Wherever they landed, they began to cut every communication line they could find,' said General Ridgway, 'and soon the German commanders had no more contact with their units than we had with ours.'[28] The paratroops and the French Resistance set about systematically severing all the telephone cables. Thanks to good local intelligence, the Americans located a concrete communications casemate that acted as the hub between the Cotentin and Carentan. This was swiftly blown up. South of the town, at the headquarters of Colonel Frederick von der Heydte's 6th Parachute Regiment, they received word of the airborne landings. 'I tried to reach General Marcks,' said Heydte, 'but the whole telephone network was down.'[29]

One of Heydte's officers was 'astounded' that the Americans severed their 'communication so quickly'.[30] Heydte's unit post was way to the south-west of Carentan at Périers, and even if he had wanted to prepare a counterattack, his regiment lacked lorries to transport them north.[31] While Heydte was a highly decorated veteran, most of his re-formed command comprised inexperienced teenagers. Later, he drove up to Carentan and saw prisoners from the 101st Airborne.

He tried to call Schlieben's headquarters near Valognes but could not get through, so he called Marcks again. 'This is the invasion,'[32] he told Major Viebig, Marcks' chief of operations. In the meantime, Schlieben, who was eventually contacted in his hotel in Rennes, did not get back to his command post until around midday.

At Etreham, Major Pluskat and his German Shepherd, Harras, were woken by the sound of bombers hitting their coastal defences. In just his underwear, he peered from his chateau's windows and listened for some 20 minutes, waiting for someone to tell him what was going on. From what he could make out, his artillery batteries were okay. Taking matters into his own hands, he called his regimental commander, Lieutenant-Colonel Ocker. He did not know anything either, but promised to call back.

In the distance, Pluskat could still hear the droning of aircraft engines and he instinctively knew something was seriously wrong. Pluskat next tried contacting divisional headquarters and managed to get hold of Major Block, the 352nd's intelligence officer. Block dismissed it as 'just another bombing raid'. Then Pluskat's telephone rang. 'Paratroopers are reported on the peninsula,' said Lieutenant Colonel Ocker. 'This could be the invasion.'[33] Pluskat felt vindicated.

The American glider troops did not have much of an easier time than the paratroops. They approached from the east after being towed across the Channel. The 101st's reinforcements were destined for Hiesville, some 4 miles from Ste-Mère-Église, where they had to brave trees, hedgerows and 'Rommel's Asparagus'. Once committed to landing, the pilots had few options when it came to avoiding these deadly obstacles. Nor did they get any help from their co-pilots, who were all untrained troopers. Upon hitting the ground, many of the flimsy gliders came apart, scattering men and equipment in all directions.

The first senior officer to be lost on either side was Brigadier-General Don Pratt, assistant divisional commander of the 101st. He was killed by the impact of hitting a hedgerow and his pilot, Colonel Mike Murphy, was thrown from the cockpit and broke both legs. Incredibly, apart from this the 101st's losses at Hiesville were relatively light, and most of the gliders found the landing zone and successfully unloaded their cargos. These included jeeps, anti-tank guns and even a bulldozer.

North-west of Ste-Mère-Église, half of the 82nd's gliders missed the landing zone, smashing into woods, buildings and stone walls or the flooded areas. Sergeant James Elmo Jones, an 82nd pathfinder, was horrified by the carnage, saying, 'There's never been a greater slaughter than what took place that night.'[34] Gliders crashed all over the place, with the loss of eighteen pilots with the opening wave. Altogether they suffered a 16 per cent casualty rate, and some of the jeeps and anti-tank guns were damaged. Even on the landing zone, the medics were confronted by horrific injuries. Sergeant Zane Schlemmer of the 508th Parachute Regiment witnessed one glider hit a tree. 'I could just visualize the poor pilot,' he said, 'with that baby bulldozer smashing into him.'[35]

Despite these setbacks, the paratroopers were trained to be incredibly adaptable. Lieutenant-Colonel Edward Krause with the 82nd's 505th Regiment soon seized Ste-Mère-Église after it became apparent the German garrison had left. Once this was secured they could prevent the Germans from counterattacking toward Utah Beach. Major-General Falley, desperate to get back to Picauville, was caught in an ambush on the road by Lieutenant Malcolm Brannen of the 82nd Airborne. Falley, his aide Major Bartuzat and their driver were all gunned down.

Ridgway and Taylor found it very difficult to control their scattered forces. Communication was all but impossible because the bulk of their radios were lost or damaged during the drop. Although Ridgway set up a command post outside Ste-Mère-Église, he lacked even maps. Nonetheless, the airborne forces showed initiative and formed ad hoc battle groups and got on with their missions. The most crucial of these was securing the exits across the flooded fields from Utah. Ridgway was lucky enough to be one of those who was not lost. 'My own little command group of eleven officers and men set up division headquarters in an apple orchard, on almost the exact spot we had planned to be before we left England,' he said with some pride.[36]

By 0600 hours, General Taylor, Brigadier-General Anthony McAuliffe and Colonel Julian Ewell had gathered about sixty men in the vicinity of Ste-Marie-du-Mont.[37] He now had to decide whether to move to take exits 1 and 2 off Utah or go south to the Douve and prepare for German counterattacks. The exits seemed more important, so they headed for Poupville and promptly ran into a small garrison of similar strength from Falley's division. The fire fight lasted almost 3 hours before the German soldiers surrendered. Taylor now had control of exit 1 and sent Lieutenant Eugene Brierre with a patrol down the causeway to link up with Barton's US 4th Infantry Division. This was achieved at 1110 hours.

To the north, Lieutenant Colonel Robert Cole, commanding the 3rd Battalion, 502nd Parachute Infantry Regiment, gathered what men he could and made his way toward exit 3 near Audouville-la-Hubert and exit 4 near St-Martin-de-Varreville. They bumped into a German patrol, and, after an exchange of fire, captured most of them. One group arrived at exit 4 at 0930 hours and ambushed German soldiers retiring across the causeway from the beach. By midday both exits had been captured. Cole was unaware that the focus of the 4th Division's assault had inadvertently slipped south opposite exit 2.

An added bonus of the American airborne landings was the spooking of German guns crews. Alarmed by the distant clatter of small-arms fire, most of the gunners grabbed their rifles and took to their trenches. As a result, the batteries at Brécourt Manor and Holdy to the north and south of Ste-Marie-du-Mont did not immediately bombard Utah. Likewise, the battery near St-Martin-de-Varreville was found abandoned and bomb-damaged.

The Brécourt battery was linked by telephone to a well-placed observer in a pillbox just off Utah Beach. The camouflaged guns had just gone into action when the Americans pounced. Lieutenant Dick Winters, with just a dozen men from E Company, 506th Parachute Infantry Regiment, successfully overcame five times that number of Heydte's paratroops defending a network of trenches and emplacements. This again showed the excellence of their training. For the loss of four dead and two wounded, Winter's men killed fifteen Germans and captured a dozen prisoners, as well as successfully destroying four 105mm field guns.[38] The battery at Holdy was also stormed and destroyed by members of the 506th.[39]

Colonel Heydte, who had moved a battalion to Ste-Marie-du-Mont, was also driven back. However, he managed to hold on to St-Côme-du-Mont to the south-west. The flanking battalion that was supposed to be supporting his left became distracted by the American presence at Ste-Mère-Église. Heydte found himself conducting defensive actions rather than his anticipated counterattack

Leigh-Mallory was highly relieved as the news filtered in that the 82nd and 101st, despite all their difficulties, were still achieving their objectives. He was straight on the phone to Eisenhower. Ike was pleased, recalling, '[H]e was the first to call me to voice his delight and to express his regret that he found it necessary to add to my personal burdens during the final tense days before D-Day.'[40] Eisenhower fully appreciated that Leigh-Mallory had just been doing his job.

Across England, both American and British bombers also took to the skies to pound the Atlantic Wall. In addition, 218 and 617 Squadrons headed for Boulogne and Cap d'Antifer to conduct their radar deception mission to dupe the enemy into believing there was another invasion fleet. The pilots had to drop their 'Window' from the right altitude and in a way that suggested approaching ships. This was done by flying over-lapping circles, with each one getting closer to the coast. 'To do this so accurately that the enemy did not suspect that aircraft and not ships were producing the reactions was,' said Air Marshal Harris with pride, 'a remarkable feat of navigation.'[41]

Other groups of bombers were to limit the range of Rundstedt's early warning radar, but not to the extent that they missed the 'Window'-dropping Lancasters, jam the communications of German night-fighters and drop dummy parachutists. Harris adds they also dropped 'machines which made noises like rifle fire and other sounds of battle'.[42]

On the morning of D-Day, R. V. Jones was at Stanmore and under-standably wanted to know how things were going. In response to his questioning, an RAF Group Captain remarked, 'I haven't heard, but it must be going well – there is a marked increase in saluting, this morning!'[43] He was also delighted to learn that the remaining enemy radars had been fooled, '[T]hese were so shaken that their operators fell easily for Cockburn's spoof, and German guns and searchlights were brought into action against the bogus Fécamp convoy.'[44]

After all the months of intensive preparations in camps around England, it soon became obvious that the Americans had gone. Harry Patch, who was working as a maintenance worker in the American camps in Devon, left his job on the evening of 5 June without realising quite what was occurring. 'Came back in the morning, and not a soldier was to be seen,' he said, 'they were gone. It was quite eerie.' He wandered round the camp in rather a daze. 'There were urns of cocoa, coffee, tea, all hot. Cheese, butter, bacon, it was all there in the dining room, half-consumed meals on the table.'[45] Secrecy was such, said Harry, that, 'It came as a complete surprise to me to hear that D-Day had happened.'[46] This was testimony to the success of Overlord's operational security.

13

ORNE BOUND

Major John Howard of the British 6th Airborne Division suffered more than his fair share of frustrations thanks to the delay in D-Day. Despite extensive training since mid-April, he had not been permitted to share his objectives with any of the members of his company, not even his second-in-command, Captain Brian Priday, until the end of May. That was only once they were confined to a transit camp at Tarrant Rushton near Bournemouth, such was the requirement for complete secrecy. No one was allowed to leave, except for Howard, and that was only to visit divisional headquarters. When he finally informed his officers and men where they were going, they were amazed by the amount of detailed intelligence that was available.

The British 6th Airborne Division had the tough job of securing and holding the British left flank. To accomplish this, they were to be dropped by parachute and Horsa glider to the north-east of Caen. Their target was the wooded ridge in the Bois de Bavent area, the German battery at Merville and several local bridges. The River Orne and Caen Canal run parallel from the city to the coast. Between the villages of Bénouville and Ranville, the coastal road was carried over the waterways by two bridges. Elements of two German infantry divisions were responsible for defending 6th Airborne's drop zone.

Possession of the bridges was crucial because it would permit Montgomery to break out eastward and prevent Rommel from bringing up reinforcements. After much scratching of heads, the planners decided the best way to take the bridges was by a glider-borne *coup de main* ahead of the main parachute drop. To the men of Major John Howard's D Company,

2nd Battalion, Oxfordshire and Buckinghamshire Light Infantry, fell the honour of being the very first British troops of the invasion force to set foot in Nazi-occupied France.[1]

'My company was lucky to be selected for what turned out to be a wonderful operation,' recalled Major Howard. 'It would be a night landing and they chose gliders to do the job as distinct from parachutists in order to get complete surprise … gliders will land thirty men on the spot.'[2]

At Tarrant Rushton, Howard had set about preparing his men. In this he was greatly aided by an enormous 12ft model of the bridges' location that had been produced as a result of RAF reconnaissance flights. These were flown on a daily basis to ensure that the model was regularly updated.[3] He was also furnished with intelligence on the local population, including Georges Gondrée who ran the little café close to the bridge on the west bank of the Caen Canal. Howard was interested to learn that Gondrée spoke perfect English, which he had kept from the Germans.

D Company met the crews of the Glider Pilot Regiment, volunteers and veterans of the Sicily campaign. They also had been extensively training to the point that they boasted they could land on a sixpence.[4] Howard was suitably impressed, remarking, 'I knew that we had the very best glider pilots.'[5]

Amongst them was Captain Alexander Morrison.[6] 'The Horsa … glider … had a wing span wider than the bombers that towed it,' he explained. 'Made completely of wood, it could carry a load of up to three-and-a-half tons and was designed to deliver 28 fully-equipped men, or a jeep with gun, right to the forefront of the battle.'[7]

British intelligence assessed that the bridges were held by a company of about fifty German soldiers, most of whom were billeted at Bénouville. Both bridges were rigged for demolition, and the Caen Canal bridge was thought to be the most heavily defended. The latter was protected by a pillbox on the eastern side of the bridge, which was thought to house the detonator for the demolition charges. In addition, the Germans could call on several other companies in the area should they be needed.

East of the Orne was home to the 711th Infantry Division belonging to General Salmuth's Fifteenth Army, forming the boundary with Dollmann's Seventh Army. This was one of the weakest divisions in Normandy, with just over 7,000 men.[8] They were supported by two battalions of artillery equipped with captured French and Russian guns. Most of this division was billeted east of the river Dives and south of Cabourg.

The main cause of concern for 6th Airborne was the presence of elements of the 716th Division, in particular its 736th Infantry Regiment, which was equipped with machine guns and mortars. Luckily for the airborne troops, the 716th was stretched very thinly, with much of its other infantry regiment deployed way to the west at Grandcamp and Bayeux.[9] Although these units had some anti-tank weapons, they lacked any means to move them.[10] Mobility was also a problem for the infantry, with some companies relying on bicycles to get about.

Howard's reinforced company numbered 150 men plus thirty engineers, whose job was to deal with the explosives on the bridges. They were to be airlifted by six Horsas towed by Halifax bombers. Two drop zones were selected between the waterways, one to the south of the Caen Canal crossing and one to the north of the Orne crossing. Major-General 'Windy' Gale, Howard's divisional commander, warned him that the best he could hope for was half his force landing in the right place.

From the start, Howard knew that he would have to be flexible and adaptable with his planning. He simply could not guarantee how many gliders would reach their target or in what order. This meant that each of his six platoons would have to be capable of doing everything. The very first platoon on the ground by the Caen Canal bridge was to grab the pillbox and get over the bridge. Once he had both bridges, Howard would conduct fighting patrols into Bénouville in anticipation of any German counterattacks.

Just before they were about to go, aerial reconnaissance indicated that the Germans had been warned of Howard's operation. The latest photographs showed that on his selected landing zones, the Germans were erecting long poles to deter any airborne assault. After all their intensive training, it seemed as if the whole thing was now off. Howard summoned his leading glider pilot, Staff Sergeant Wallwork, and showed him this unwelcome development.

'That's just what we needed,' said Wallwork after examining the photos closely. Howard's heart sank. 'You remember that embankment where we end up by the road,' continued Wallwork. 'Well, we've always been worried about piling into that if we overshot the landing zone.' Howard nodded, not sure where the conversation was going. 'A heavy landing and one grenade going off by accident.' Howard nodded again. 'Now these stakes are just right. They're spaced so as to take a foot or two off each wing and pull us up just right.'[11]

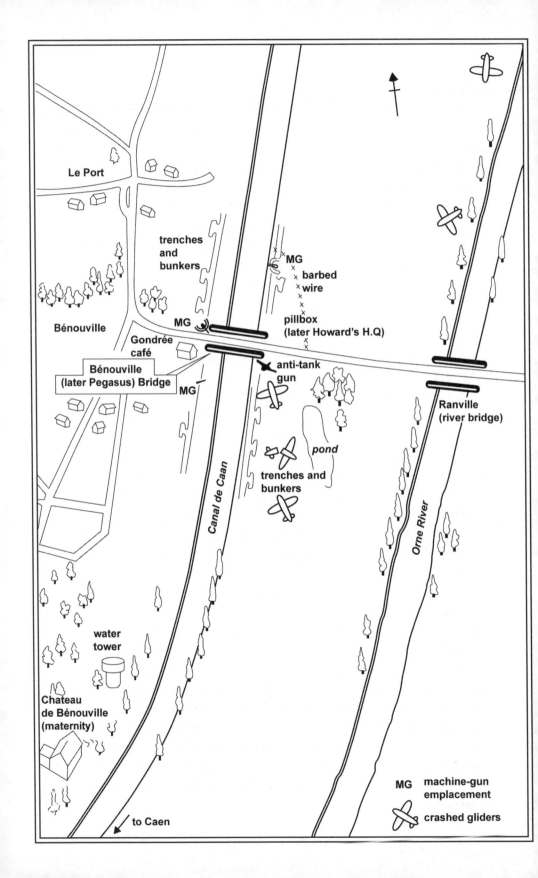

The plan was for the airborne bridgehead to be reinforced by the commandos landing on Sword Beach. Unfortunately there was a clash of personality, with the commando commander taking an instant dislike to his airborne superior. Lord Lovat of No. 4 Commando commented that General Gale 'struck me as vain and egotistical'.[12] Gale understandably had a lot to oversee, but Lovat grumbled that 6th Airborne 'seemed preoccupied with their own affairs'. Relations were not helped when Pat Porteous' orderly knocked out a Canadian paratrooper during a friendly boxing match. Lovat suspected that Gale 'was jealous of the green berets', but added that the airborne 'were fine people'.[13]

A despatch rider arrived at Tarrant Rushton at 0900 hours on Friday 4 June with the move order. Everyone's adrenaline began to flow – D-Day was on. Then the weather deteriorated and the order was cancelled. The following morning there was no cancellation. At 2200 hours on 5 June, Howard and his men drove out to the airfield. As they loaded their equipment and clambered into their gliders, he said goodbye to all of them. The first Halifax rumbled along the runway with its glider behind it at 2256 hours. Aircraft then followed in one-minute intervals, rising into the sky to form part of the Allies' huge aerial armada heading for Normandy.

At the same time, six aircraft took off from Harwell carrying the pathfinders of the 22nd Independent Parachute Company. They were to mark three drop zones north-east of Ranville, between Varaville and the Dives River and north-east of Giberville. 'The first member of the Allied forces to land in Normandy … was Lieutenant Bobby de la Tour,' recalled glider tug pilot Flight Lieutenant Oliver Kingdon, who flew him to his target. 'He commanded a small detachment of ten Pathfinders whose job was to lay out patterns of lights in a small field to guide the following waves of parachutists and gliders.'[14]

Gale watched his division's departure. 'That night the moon shone. The sky was clear as one by one the great aircraft boosting up their engines, roared down the runways,' he observed. 'Next to go were the two parachute brigades and the engineers accompanying them. Then our turn came.'[15] Shortly after, three gliders took to the air with an assault party to make a pinpoint landing near the Merville battery. The massed airlift involved moving 7,000 men with all their equipment and supporting weapons.[16]

'Suddenly we became airborne,' said Private Harry Clarke with the Ox & Bucks. 'We could barely see, it was quite dark, there were a few cigarettes going and there was obviously a tenseness and nervousness because there wasn't the usual idle chatter.'[17] They flew in from the east, near Cabourg, through a known gap in the German anti-aircraft defences. Although there was heavy flak on either side, they got through unharmed.

The bombers cast off the gliders at 5,000ft, which turned toward their landing zones. The glider pilots descended to about 1,000ft ready for the run-in. In Howard's glider, platoon commander Lieutenant Den Brotheridge opened the door and saw the lines of the canal and river below them. There was a rush of air, the glider skids hit the ground and the aircraft bounced into the air again. The second time it came down it stayed there, crashing along until finally lurching to a halt. It was 0020 hours and they had landed just 47ft from the German pillbox. For a few seconds the shaken men gathered their wits.

Howard bumped his head and for a moment could not see. At first, in a panic, he feared that the impact had blinded him, then realised to his embarrassment that his helmet had simply slipped over his eyes. 'Den Brotheridge ... said "Gun out", which was me,' said Private William Gray. 'Out I jumped, stumbled on the grass because of the weight I had on me, and set the Bren [gun] up facing the bridge and the rest of the lads jumped out.'[18]

By a stroke of good luck, the glider's nose had gone through the German barbed wire. Back in England, Howard had cheekily asked the pilot if he could do this so they would not have to use explosives to make a breach. Howard was delighted, recalling, '[W]e really caught old Jerry with his pants down.'[19] Men ran forward and tossed grenades through the pillbox slits, and then sprinted over the bridge. 'I saw a German on the right-hand side and let rip at him and down he went,' observed Private Gray. 'I still kept firing going over the bridge and on the other side was another German and he went down too.' The crossing was not without casualties. Lieutenant 'Sandy' Smith, who had broken an arm on landing, 'arrived at the other end to find Brotheridge dying'.[20] Howard's other two gliders also landed right on target.

The men under Lieutenant Dennis Fox assigned to take the Orne bridge captured it without firing a shot. This was fortunate, as two other platoons, including Captain Priday, went astray. Once informed, Howard instructed his radio man to signal the code words for success, which were the suitably British 'Ham and jam'. At 0050 hours, the 7th Parachute Battalion (7 Para) were dropped to relieve Howard's men, and the rest of the division, comprising 3rd and 5th Parachute Brigades, were also dropped on the other objectives.

D–Day was only an hour old when Brigadier Nigel Poett's 5th Brigade jumped over Normandy either side of Howard's bridges. Once on the ground, they were able to assemble quickly. While his 12th and 13th Battalions moved to cover the high ground and roads, after taking Le Bas de Ranville and Ranville the 7th Battalion raced towards Howard's force. However, 7 Para would not get to them until 0245 hours. The battalion's drop did not go smoothly, as Captain Richard Todd recalled, 'The men had been so scattered … we only had about 150 men out of 600.'[21]

At the same time the 9th Battalion and the 1st Canadian Parachute Battalion of Brigadier James Hill's 3rd Brigade jumped further east near Varaville. His 8th Battalion landed to the south-west with the task of taking the Bures and Troarn bridges and securing the woods of Bois de Bavent.

Howard had been warned to expect a German counterattack within an hour of landing. At 0130 hours, Howard 'heard the ominous sound we most dreaded … two tanks were slowly coming down the road'. They were heading along the Ouistreham road toward the junction just to the east of the Gondrée café. The only anti-tank weapon his men had was the largely unreliable PIAT, which had a range of just 50 yards and often fired duds. Nonetheless, they engaged the lead tank, 'then there was a sharp explosion as Sergeant Thornton … had fired at it at point blank range', said Lieutenant Smith.[22]

Thornton, positioned 30 yards from the junction, had first watched in amazement as the tank commanders climbed out for a chat before getting back in. Despite his violently shaking hands, he knew that his comrades were relying on him. 'The first tank, a Mark IV, had begun moving slowly down the road,' said Thornton. 'I pulled the trigger. It was a direct hit. Machine-gun clips inside the tank set off grenades, which set of shells.'[23]

In the darkness, the tank was a cascade of 'green and orange and yellow' flames. Private Clarke was rattled by it 'cooking off', noting, 'This, coupled with the cries and screams of the trapped tank commander did little good for our nerves.'[24] The second vehicle quickly disappeared.[25] So far, 6th Airborne's luck had held.

It was at this point that Captain Todd and men of 7 Para were trotting over the Orne bridge to get to the canal. Looking ahead, Todd saw the explosion, 'I thought oh God, a real battle has started.'[26] Their job was to hold the perimeter west of the canal ready for the arrival of Lord Lovat's commandos.

In the meantime, the café was liberated and Georges Gondrée dug up almost 100 bottles of champagne, which he had hidden from the Germans in 1940. Sergeant Thornton lamented, '[U]nfortunately I missed out on the celebration!'[27] The café was used as a first-aid station and Major Howard observed, 'The sick and the wounded were having quite a good time, there was a lot of cork-popping going on.'[28]

Two British pathfinders gave Major-General Josef Reichert, commander of the 711th Division, the fright of his life. Disturbed by the sound of planes, he abandoned his card game with his officers and went outside just in time to witness the men landing on his lawn. They were disarmed and brought before him. 'Awfully sorry, old man,' said one of them nonchalantly, 'but we simply landed here by accident.'[29] Reichert called his corps headquarters to inform them that the British had conducted a raid on his headquarters. This was then eventually relayed to General Salmuth's staff, who unhelpfully recorded, 'No details given.'[30]

Brigadier James Hill's 3rd Parachute Brigade had two key tasks. The first was to screen Howard east of the Orne. This they accomplished by destroying five bridges over the River Dives and occupying a ridge. The second was assigned to Lieutenant Colonel Terence Otway's 9th Battalion, who were to take the Merville battery about a mile inland from Sword Beach.

The Merville battery, reportedly armed with four 150mm guns, posed a major threat to the Allied invasion fleet. It was believed that the emplacements were built using concrete that was up to 2m thick, making them bomb-proof.[31] They were protected by dense barbed wire and a minefield enclosing an area over half a mile by a third of a mile dotted with machine-gun posts. On the seaward side there was a 14ft-wide anti-tank ditch.

Otway and his men were well prepared for their mission. They had trained on a full-scale mock-up of the Merville battery built in England at some considerable expense. This was based on valuable intelligence provided by the French spy network headed by the unassuming looking Eugène Meslin. As the government engineer for the Caen area, he had regular contact with the Todt Organisation and, through his spies, was able to monitor building of the Atlantic Wall.[32]

The plan was that 100 RAF Lancaster bombers would pound the battery at 0030 hours. Otway would gather his men and march on the battery; once there, five gliders full of heavy equipment would arrive to support the assault. However, things did not go smoothly.

Hill's 3rd Brigade was spread out over a wide area and many men ended up in the marshlands created by the Germans. The brigadier was among them. 'To my horror I found myself dropping in to the flooded valley of the Dives,' recounted Hill. 'I was two or three miles from where I ought to have been.' For many, weighed down by 60lb kit bags, there was no escape. He was lucky to eventually wade through the water as 'a lot of chaps were drowned that night'.[33] Earlier, pathfinder Lieutenant de la Tour almost suffered such a fate in a muddy duck pond, but was rescued by his vigilant sergeant.[34]

Otway who found himself chest deep in water managed to gather only 150 men; he should have had 750. Getting out of the marshes proved a real struggle. 'The suction was unbelievable,' recalled Otway. 'I lost a lot of men in there. They just went in and were drowned.'[35] Although he rounded up double that number on the way, he soon discovered that the RAF had accidently bombed his approach route. This meant clambering in and out of 9ft-deep craters in the dark, though this did enable him to avoid detection by a German patrol.

Tragedy struck his glider force. Only three gliders took off from base, and one of these broke its tow rope before reaching the Channel. Of those that reached Normandy, one crash-landed half a mile from Merville and the other came down 200 yards from the Merville wire only to burst in flames. The survivors leapt out to hold off the Germans while Otway stormed the battery.

The German commander, Lieutenant Raimund Steiner, and his senior NCO, Sergeant Johannes Buskotte, were initially taken by surprise. Steiner was at a forward observation bunker overlooking the coast when the attack started. He responded by calling a battery near Cabourg and directing them to fire on Otway's men who were picking their way through the wire.

Despite this, by 0500 hours Otway had overcome most of the defenders. Frustratingly, he subsequently had to withdraw because of a scheduled Allied naval bombardment. 'I went in with 150,' said Otway, 'and came out with 65 only on their feet including myself.'[36] Nearly all of Steiner's garrison, numbering about 130 men, were casualties.[37]

While the Merville operation had the desired result of preventing the guns from firing on D-Day, they were not completely neutralised and the Germans reoccupied the site. Despite their best efforts, 9th Para ran out of time and failed to completely destroy the guns because they had lost their demolition charges during the drop.[38] Although it was 'a tremendously brave thing to do', said Lieutenant Hubert Pond, who fought with the battalion, 'it didn't really have the outcome on the battle that we thought it would'.[39]

Nonetheless, as Colonel Belchem noted, '6th Airborne had accomplished its primary objectives' and there was cause for optimism.[40] 'Sitting back at headquarters at Portsmouth on the morning of June 6th, I felt considerably excited,' said Freddie de Guingand, Monty's Chief of Staff. 'The airborne operations had been outstandingly successful.'[41]

By 1330 hours, Lovat's 1st Special Service Brigade pushed inland to link up with the exhausted airborne troops, who had beaten off repeated counterattacks by German panzergrenadiers. When the commandos crossed the canal bridge they came under fire. 'Sorry about the mortaring from that ruddy chateau,' yelled Howard. 'The bastards have got the range, but it happens to be a maternity hospital and I have strict orders not to disturb the inmates!'[42 43]

Despite the professional rivalry between the airborne forces and the commandos, both sides were very relieved to see each other. 'John Howard's nocturnal coup de main,' said Lovat, 'was a notable achievement.'[44] Fortunately for 6th Airborne most of the German armour had been diverted north of Caen in a futile and belated attempt to stem the Allied landings.

14

ASHORE WITH THE 'FUNNIES'

On the morning of 6 June, the big question facing Major-General Hobart, Brigadier Duncan and the other officers of the 79th Armoured Division was how the 'Funnies' would perform. Despite their rigorous training, there was no way of truly knowing what was going to happen when they hit the beaches. From their sea exercises, the biggest worry with the DD tanks was that they would sink before ever reaching the beaches. If that happened, the Crab flail tanks and the Churchill AVREs would initially be unsupported. The Crabs inevitably would miss some of the mines and fall victim to them. For the sappers of the Royal Engineers, they could only conclude that their AVREs would draw the bulk of the enemy fire simply because the Churchill presented such a large target. Everyone knew what had happened to the Churchills at Dieppe, and that was not an encouraging thought.

In the early hours, the mighty Allied invasion fleet gathered off the Normandy coast. As the preliminary bombardment commenced, the lead assault elements of the 79th began to embark into their LCTs and DD tanks. Their task was not an easy one. They had to swiftly destroy the steel and concrete beach obstacles and silence the German gun emplacements, all of which threatened to stall the invasion on the shoreline.

The men in 8th Armoured Brigade's DD tanks can have had no time to consider the fate of their American cousins, who had also trained to use the swimming tanks. On Juno Beach, the Canadians were to be supported by the 'Funnies', but on Utah and Omaha, the two American DD battalions were on their own.

Both British and Canadian forces utilised elements of the 79th, with each landing allocated a 'menu' of different types of specialised vehicles. The first British invasion beach on the right, codenamed Gold, centred on Le Hamel and was the responsibility of the British XXX Corps, with the British 50th Infantry Division heading the assault. Supporting units from the 79th were the 81st and 82nd Squadrons Armoured Royal Engineers (with AVREs), B and C Squadrons of the Westminster Dragoons (Crabs), the Sherwood Rangers Yeomanry and the 4th/7th Dragoon Guards (DDs).

Sword Beach on the far left, centred on Lion-sur-Mer, under the British I Corps, was to be assaulted by the British 3rd Infantry Division. It was supported by the 77th and 79th Squadrons Armoured Royal Engineers (AVREs), A Squadron of the 22nd Dragoons (Crabs) and the 13th/18th Hussars (DD). Juno in the middle, centred on Bernieres, also I Corps' responsibility, was to be assaulted by the Canadian 3rd Infantry Division. Its support came from the 26th and 80th Squadrons ARE (AVREs), B Squadron of the 22nd Dragoons (Crabs), plus the 6th and 10th Canadian Armoured Regiments (DDs).

Gold

Royal Engineer R.J. Mellen, with the 82nd Assault Squadron bound for Gold Beach, remembered, 'Our tank, a Churchill AVRE, with two others, an armoured bulldozer and a flail tank, loaded onto a LCT, left Southampton at 2000 hours on Sunday, 4 June ... A group of us stood at the side of what was no more than a flat-bottomed barge. We were very quiet, thinking would we ever see England again?'[1]

Gold Beach was semi-circular, bisected by regions of soft clay, which required the Churchill 'Bobbins' to pave a way. The beach area was divided into three by the heavily fortified villages of Arromanches to the west, Le Hamel in the centre and La Rivière to the east. Unfortunately, the aerial and naval bombardment did not take out many of the German guns. This meant they would have to be silenced by the Churchills' Petards.

For the initial assault on Gold, the Sherwood Rangers comprised three Sabre Squadrons, one equipped with regular Shermans, the other two with DDs. The latter were to land at H-Hour minus five minutes and consisted of B Squadron supporting the 1st Hampshires and C Squadron assisting the 1st Dorsets.

Approaching Gold Beach, it was clear that the DD tanks of 8th Armoured Brigade were going to have their work cut out at H-Hour, timed for 0725. The choppy waters were not going to make the operation easy and the swell was exactly what the tankers had learned to fear during their training exercises. The men of the 4th/7th Royal Dragoon Guards and Sherwood Rangers in the four DD squadrons braced themselves for the worst and began to double-check their escape equipment and dinghies.

They were relieved when common sense prevailed. 'The sea was so rough that it was not possible to launch the DD tanks,' said Brigadier Duncan, 'and the 4th/7th Dragoon Guards and Sherwood Rangers were brought ashore in their landing craft.' This inevitably meant a delay in getting tank support onto the beach. 'The assault teams had to assist in overcoming hostile fire,' noted Duncan, 'to open the gaps to help the infantry forward as best they could, improvising local tactics to meet entirely unexpected circumstances.'[2] This flexibility and adaptability was exactly what they had trained so hard to perfect.

Ironically, although the DD tanks were all beached from their LCTs, this did not stop some of them drowning as they still had to wade ashore. In the western sector of the beach, the Sherwood Rangers came in from 700 yards and lost eight tanks in the process. Trooper Kenneth Ewing, driving one of the tanks, quickly spotted the reason:

One of the troubles was that there were gullies. On most beaches when the tide goes out you'll see lines of water, gullies. Well, some of these were quite deep and unfortunately that was what caused the problem. Some of them, they touched down, they lowered their screens and they went forward and went down into a gully and of course that was it.[3]

As the Allied bombers withdrew, and with naval gunfire still whizzing over their heads, the first flotillas bearing the Sherman Crabs and AVREs of the Westminster Dragoons and 81st/82nd Assault Squadrons hit the beach. Their flat-bottom LCTs ground onto the shore at Le Hamel and La Rivière. As soon as the ramps dropped, a hail of German machine-gun, mortar and artillery fire greeted them.

Frogman Sergeant Peter Jones and his team 'swam into a maze of steel pylons, gates and hedgehogs and concrete cones'.[4] There they tried to clear a way for the 'Funnies'. It was difficult work and it was not long before the DD tanks and first assault troops were amongst them. It was impossible to remove all the obstacles, with predictable results. Sergeant Jones, joined by the Royal Engineers, watched in horror as a landing craft was lifted by the swell right onto a series of mined obstructions. The occupants 'shot up into the air ... and parts of bodies spread like drops of water'.[5]

On Gold, Brigadier Duncan's Crabs and the 79th Armoured Division's other specialised armoured fighting vehicles were inevitably in the firing line from the start thanks to this delay. One Crab, having successfully disembarked from its landing craft, began to flail up the shore, but then veered to the right, struck a mine and was disabled.

Elements of the Sherwood Rangers did not arrive until 90 minutes later, which meant it largely fell to the Crabs of Duncan's Westminster Dragoons to provide fire support taking out gun emplacements and machine-gun nests.

Lieutenant Commander Irwin, commanding a bomb-firing landing craft, witnessed the fate of a Crab coming ashore east of La Rivière. After firing off his spigot bombs, he recalled the lull before the storm:

Hard aport and the LCT beached. The first tank moved out. Amazing, unbelievable, not a shot fired! All was quiet for a minute or two – nobody on the beach but one tank. An explosion as the water-proofing was disposed of. Her flails started. Then black smoke came from the tank as she was hit and it caught fire. This was H–1 minute.[6]

One of the LCTs grounded in 6ft of water and its AVRE drowned on the ramp. The craft then struck several obstacles and mines that ripped its hull wide open. The crippled LCT blocked the path of the second approaching vessel, but its crew managed to land one AVRE and its sapper section. The third LCT negotiated the jam and landed its AVREs safely.

'I could see two AVRE Churchills brewing up on the beach,' said Lieutenant Hills of his run-in to Gold. 'The tanks had been completely destroyed, and their crews killed, by 88mm shells which had ignited the explosives they had been carrying to clear beach obstacles – I wondered if this would soon be our fate too.'[7]

On the eastern half of Gold, the 4th/7th Dragoon Guards faired a little better. It was decided to run them in as close as possible so all they had to do was negotiate the breakers. To be on the safe side, the crews still erected their screens and some of them promptly ran into soft patches of sand. Their tanks became stuck and were drowned by the incoming tide.

On Item and Jig sectors, the left-hand section of Gold, three Crabs roared up the beach tearing gaps through the minefields and barbed wire. German anti-tank guns knocked out two, but the third from 231st Brigade made it off the beach. A further three assault teams serving the left flank fared better. The Crabs successfully beat their way across the shoreline and reached the coast road half a mile inland.

Onshore winds had resulted in a higher tide than expected, rising some 30 minutes ahead of time. Lieutenant Hills, with C Squadron, Sherwood Rangers, preparing to launch his DD tanks 700 yards from the shore, was alarmed to see two knocked-out flail tanks. 'Without more ado I gave my driver the order to go,' said Hills, 'and down the ramp we went. The screen was very flimsy in the rough sea and the water poured in everywhere.'[8]

He and his crew then had a narrow escape as their tank refused to float in the choppy water and sank like a stone. 'The Sherman DD tank was about to become the Sherman submarine,' joked Hills. 'I gave the order to bale out or abandon ship.' Two other tanks from his LCT did not make it either. 'Even during those hectic and exacting moments,' he recalled, 'I could not help wondering what old Father Neptune would think about the sudden appearance of a tank on the bottom of the sea.'[9]

Engineer Mellen, with his Churchill AVRE bridge-layer, arrived on Jig beach near Le Hamel. Driving into 6ft of water, he recalled:

Suddenly my periscope began to clear and I could see a sandy beach dotted with gun emplacements and tank traps. The roar of the engines and the sound of exploding shells seemed insignificant now we were on dry land. There was a babble of shouts from my crew, my seasickness disappeared. We had arrived.[10]

Meanwhile, Lieutenant Hills and his crew were rescued by a landing craft, from which he watched the DD and AVRE tanks in action:

A company of infantry appeared to be pinned down behind a sea wall by enemy fire coming from the large building they seemed to be attacking. A LCT with 25-pounder guns opened up on the building from close range, as did a Churchill and two Shermans. Fire from the building ceased.[11]

At Le Hamel, the 1st Hampshire Regiment leapt from their landing craft 30 yards from the beach. Although supported by Sexton self-propelled guns, they soon found themselves exposed to the withering German fire raking the shore. To make matters worse, German artillery knocked out most of the supporting Royal Marine Centaur tanks as they came ashore. Nonetheless, the left flank companies of the Hampshires advanced east; seizing Les Roquettes, they then swung to the right, taking Asnelles-sur-Mer.

The Le Hamel sanatorium, which had been converted into a German strongpoint, was also assaulted. Initially every attack was beaten off, so several AVREs were called up. They drove to within point-blank range and crumpled the building. Major Peter Selerie, also of the Sherwood Rangers, with five DD Shermans and an AVRE, was involved in this attack. He found the main resistance was coming from a multi-storey building. 'The petard fired and something like a small flying dustbin hit the house just above the front door,' recalled Selerie. 'It collapsed like a pack of cards, spilling defenders with their machine guns, anti-tank weapons and an avalanche of bricks into the courtyard.'[12]

Colonel Belchem was impressed by the performance of the 'Funnies' on Gold:

> The German defences facing the eastern half of the 50 Division landing beach had not escaped the preparatory bombing, and most of la Rivière village was in ruins. But one heavily protected stronghold remained, and the troops racing ashore to find cover were subjected to sustained machine-gun fire, and an 88mm gun brewed up two engineer beach clearance tanks. But a flail tank, taking advantage of the enemy's limited power of traverse, moved in from the flank and fired a belt of 'Besa' [machine-gun bullets] through the embrasure at point-blank range.[13]

He was equally impressed by the actions of the AVREs to the west of La Rivière:

A party of three of these tanks moved against a pillbox and its adjoining wall, from which the enemy were firing automatic weapons and hurling grenades. The pillbox was shattered by petard (blockbuster explosive) and the tanks broached the wall – and unsuspectedly dropped four feet on to a roadway behind.[14]

To the left, on the King sector, the Green Howards, acting as the vanguard for 69th Brigade, managed to cut their way inland. By 1100, two lanes had been cleared off Gold Beach. The DD tanks were by then thrusting inland, supporting 151st and 56th Brigades. By nightfall, the 50th Division was 6 miles inland.

Juno

Tank driver Corporal William Dunn, with the 26th Assault Squadron, found crossing the English Channel to Juno beach nerve-wracking, not least because all the transport vessels were ordered not to stop under any circumstances to help others in distress. He listened in alarm to the announcement, 'If anybody falls overboard you don't stop to pick them up.'[15] This order was enforced by motor torpedo boats acting as escort. If anyone dropped out of line, they were swiftly and sternly shepherded back into position.

Dunn watched as some of the smaller craft overturned and the skipper of his vessel slowed to take on survivors. Immediately, an escort came alongside and, Dunn recalled, instructed 'leave them, other MTBs would come along and pick these lads up, to make sure the timing would be exact'.[16]

Spearheading the landing for the Canadian 3rd Infantry Division were the Canadian DD tanks of the 1st Hussars and Fort Garry Horse. It was now time to put all their training with the 79th Armoured Division to the test. The landing beach was divided into two sectors – Mike and Nan – which were to be assaulted at 0735 and 0745 hours respectively

Preceding the landing craft at H-1 came the demolition frogmen. Amongst them was Royal Marine Sergeant Keith Briggs with his ten-man team who were to clear a 600-yard gap for 'the 'Funnies'. He recalled, 'We were told exactly where we were going … we were given the exact landing points, we were given photographs of the exact landing points.'[17]

However, things did not go according to plan. 'By the time we put to sea, there was a gale blowing ... the sea was so rough,' said Briggs.[18] Their landing craft were dropped by their parent vessels about 7 miles out, each filled with several tons of explosives.

Nearing the beach, Briggs' craft snagged on one of the obstacles which he had been trained to clear. Although miraculously it did not have a mine attached to it, the steel tore right through the vessel's hull and it promptly sank in about 3ft of water. If there had been a mine, the craft, packed with demolition charges, would have been blown sky-high along with all it occupants.

Briggs and his men abandoned ship and headed for the shore, where they sheltered beneath the sea wall. It seemed only a matter of time before they were spotted by the Germans and mown down. Instead, another miracle happened. Briggs recalled, 'We could see German soldiers getting on transport ... we assumed they were going out for the day.'[19] Nevertheless, for the time being they were stuck. 'We couldn't put our explosives on the obstacles because the sea was too rough,' said Briggs. 'And we couldn't get at our explosive because it was in the sunken craft.'[20]

From Juno, the 3rd Canadian Infantry was to drive for Carpiquet airfield west of Caen. The DD tanks were to act as the vanguard for the Canadian 7th and 8th Brigades. A Squadron of the 6th Canadian Armoured Regiment launched ten DD tanks 1,500 yards from the shore. Three floundered, but the rest safely reached the shoreline.

As only a third of the DD tank showed above the water, the Germans thought they were small craft and did not bother firing on them. Although small-arms fire was capable of penetrating the screen, a bilge pump could compensate for this. The main danger was from artillery fire and high waves. B Squadron launched their tanks a lot further out, at 4,000 yards. Of the nineteen launched, five were lost. Due to the roughness of the water, all the 10th Canadian Armoured Regiment's tanks were then landed in their LCTs, along with six from A Squadron of the 6th Canadian Armoured Regiment. When the 22nd Dragoons and 26th Assault Squadron landed on the right, they found the DD tanks had done most of the work.

The high tide brought the assaulting craft over the rocks and reefs, but they still had to negotiate the submerged obstacles. On the left, the first three approaching landing craft were instantly destroyed. The Landing Craft Assault of the Queen's Own Regiment and the North Shore

Regiment, the vanguard of 8th Brigade, managed to negotiate the rough seas and beach obstacles in order to reach the shore. Unfortunately, they lacked armoured support and their advance faltered.

Lieutenant D.S. Hawkley, commanding LCT 513 and in charge of the 20th LCT Flotilla, found the cross beach tide and the partially submerged obstacles made the approach treacherous. He attempted to negotiate a gap between two obstacles as quickly as possible before his vessel was carried sideways:

> I was lucky enough to get to the beach, unload, and get off again but unfortunately many of the other LCTs hit the obstacles and were badly damaged as a consequence. All the time we were on the beach the only opposition we encountered were what seemed like mortar shells landing around us.[21]

'We waited for the engineers to come in with their DD tanks,' said Sergeant Briggs,' … and then we prepared, with them, to clear the obstacles manually.'[22] With the help of armoured bulldozers driven by Royal Engineers and Canadian engineers, they helped clear gaps and rendered safe over 100 enemy explosive charges on the beach. Under constant sniper fire and occasional mortar rounds, they achieved this by attaching 'wires, ropes and hawsers' to the obstacles and the bulldozers.[23] Briggs was extremely annoyed that the second frogman team, which he spent time looking for, had returned to the Isle of Wight because of bad weather. He was of the view that their officer in charge should have been court-martialled.

On Juno, the AVREs of the 26th Assault Squadron soon went to work. 'The atmosphere in the tank as we hit the beach was a little tense,' recalled driver Corporal Dunn, 'because we were battened down and I was the only man that could see.'[24] His main concern was not to run over the men who were lying on the shore. However, he and his crewmates' war was to be short-lived.

Dunn's tank was ordered to deliver their wooden fascine into a culvert. Unable to find the ditch, he shifted the tank into first gear and dropped it into some flooded ground. This was so deep that water began to pour into the turret and everyone frantically clambered out, except for Dunn. He began to drown, but luckily his co-driver managed to pull him out in the nick of time. They had just taken shelter in the dunes when a mortar bombed dropped into their midst, killing three of his mates and mortally wounding a fourth. Dunn fell into a minefield and, despite having one of his legs broken in five places, managed to make a run for it and was rescued by some Canadians.

Ian Hammerton came ashore on Juno with the Crabs of the 22nd Dragoons. Moving up the beach, he watched a Spitfire get accidently hit by a flight of rockets. His tank and another Crab headed for the sea wall, planning to rendezvous with an AVRE assault bridge. The latter, he discovered, had been hit and had dropped its bridge prematurely. His only alternative was to use a nearby stone ramp, but another supporting AVRE trying to clear the obstruction at the top was disabled by a mine. In the process of clearing the blockage, Hammerton's tank was drowned.

Luckily, an AVRE clanked across the beach and blasted a hole in the 12ft-high sea wall. By 0930 hours, Crabs east of the River Seulles had managed to open up the exits. As more equipment landed, including AVREs, the Canadians forced their way inland, capturing Bernieres and Courseulles.

On the right, 7th Brigade, headed by the Royal Winnipeg Rifles and the Regina Rifles, fared slightly better. Supported by about ten DD tanks of the 1st Canadian Hussars, with the 80th Assault Squadron behind, they were soon punching inland. At the end of the day, the 'Funnies' had cleared twelve exits off Juno. The 7th Brigade thrust on to reach the main Bayeux-Caen road at Bretteville, and the 9th, supported by the 8th, straddled the Courseulles-Caen road.

The Centaurs supporting the Canadians not only helped spearhead their landing but also the fight inland. Amongst the Royal Marine crews assaulting Juno was Pat Churchill. Such was their reception that his tank was the only one to get off the beach unscathed. He and his crew mates managed to push 5 miles inland.[25] At around 1730 hours, 'Six Centaurs with their 95mm guns had arrived at Reviers,' said Captain J.G. Baird with the Regina Rifles, 'and were able to assist the forward companies.'[26]

Sword

Even at the peak of the naval bombardment of the invasion beaches, there were moments of humour. Sub Lieutenant John Pelly was serving on the destroyer HMS *Eglington*, supporting the landings on Sword. 'At 0630 hours we opened up and so did the cruisers astern and the battleships behind them,'[27] he recalled. His vessel was to hit any weapon positions along a 2-mile stretch of sea front. 'The Captain chose his own targets and we were so close we couldn't miss,' said Pelly. 'In fact we all had the time of our lives – pointing out targets that took our fancy – like the greenhouse the captain thought to be an eyesore.'[28]

On the approach to Sword Beach, the 13th/18th Hussars prepared to put their DD tanks into the water. All the crews were wearing their escape kit, praying that they would not need it. Generally, the drill was that only the driver remained inside to keep the engines running, the rest of the men riding on top. Their job was to make sure the screen struts stayed up and to bail out the water when it slopped over the sides. Trooper Mawson was amazed. 'The run-in over the last few miles was wonderful,' he said, 'nothing happened at all.'[29]

At 0730 hours, the 13th/18th Hussars were launched 5,000 yards from Sword. Of the forty DD tanks launched, six failed to leave their LCTs, while, of the remaining thirty-four, three were lost before reaching the shore. Off Sword Beach, two DDs were rammed and sank, the breakers swamped five before clearing the shoreline, enemy gunfire accounted for another four on the beach and five were brought in by their LCTs.

The conditions were far from ideal. 'The sea was very rough,' said Corporal Patrick Hennessy, commanding one of tanks, 'and the landing craft was heaving around.'[30] The ramp was lowered and his troop sergeant successfully disembarked into the sea. It was then Hennessy's turn, and with the wind behind him, his tank was soon climbing up and down the waves.

Glancing back, Hennessy saw disaster strike as a DD tank came off another LCT. Just as it reached the exit, the vessel was struck by a wave. The tank caught the steel sides, gashing open its screen. The crew were helpless as there was nothing they could do. They were blocking the ramp and could only go forward. Hennessey watched in horror as the tank continued forward and sank like a stone. He then heaved a sigh of relief as he watched the crew bobbing around in their escape dingy.

Trooper A.V. Tribble was with the nineteen tanks of C Squadron, 13th/18th Hussars, which were to be delivered by LCTs. He remembered that morning that most of the crews had skipped their breakfast of 'porridge, fried tinned sausages and tea'[31] because of seasickness. Tribble watched as, 'Our friends in "A" and "B" Squadrons, who were in duplex drive Sherman tanks, had been launched into the rough sea a considerable distance from the coast, and were going round in a circle before lining up for their final assault on the enemy-held beaches.'[32] 'At the rear, yellow flashes could be seen from the big guns of the Navy ranged on inland targets,' witnessed Tribble, 'but these later subsided before the final assault of all the various types of landing craft.'[33]

Corporal Bob Barnes, also with the Hussars, knew that this was the most dangerous time. He said, 'Getting there from the LCT, that part – two and a half miles at four knots – is the thing most on your mind and you're praying a shell doesn't land on you.' All about them were exploding German mortar bombs, shells and machine-gun rounds. Suddenly the ordeal was all over and Barnes' tank reached its destination. He recalled, '[As] soon as the tracks hit the beach, the driver pulls the lever and the tracks take over and once you're out of the water the skirts drop and your firing at everything you can see.'[34]

R.M.S Neave, with a DD tank, was one of the first to arrive:

The tide was absolutely rock bottom low. Arranged in rows along the beach were various anti-tank obstacles. We had landed amongst a variety of flimsy poles, on top of which were balanced a series of large 7.5 shells, each with an instantaneous fuse sticking out like a pimple on their noses. We edged the tank between the posts, being delighted to discover that there was about two inches to spare each side of the tank.[35]

The enormous volume of craft meant that nothing could stop. 'Anything that faltered just had to be run down,' observed Mawson. 'Due to slow speed, one of our tanks was overtaken in the rough water and the occupant [driver] only survived because a rope was flung to him accurately from a passing ship when he was at his last gasp.'[36] Mawson and his fellow crewmates had almost got to the beach when they themselves were inundated:

We touched land, dropped our front screen and, I believe, let off a round or two but the breakers from the fast incoming tide immediately swamped us. The water came up and reached the turret at just about the same time as we did. We threw out the inflatable dinghy.[37]

They found themselves surrounded by exploding enemy mortar shells and underwater obstacles fitted with mines. Luckily for them, the rising tide helped neutralise some of the shrapnel and carried them over the obstacles to the beach. Others were not so lucky. Looking back, Mawson saw, 'Around the obstacles were poor devils drowning as they tried to neutralise the booby-traps in the rough sea.'[38]

Nineteen-year-old Trooper R. Cadogan and his crew had a similar experience. He remembered their 'tank behaving magnificently in a sea that would have daunted many a larger craft'. They got to within 200 yards of the beach when the tank in front of them ran into a mine. Its canvas screen was ripped open, allowing in the sea, and the crew calmly clambered onto another tank. Cadogan's driver bumped into an anti-tank obstacle and attempted to reverse. As they had already lowered their canvas screen, the sea flooded their engine. 'So there was nothing else for it but to abandon our tank,' said Cadogan.[39]

Major Tim Wheway, with the 22nd Dragoons and the flail tanks, observed:

We land at 0725 hours and the impact nearly shoots the tanks through the doors [of the landing craft]. The flails stream out in three feet of water, followed by the AVREs. We are met by terrific shell, mortar and 88 and 75[mm] AP [armoured piercing] and small arms fire at 300 yards range … Mines are sighted on top of wooden beach obstacles.[40]

Eight assault teams of the 22nd Dragoons beat their way over the beach. German resistance was fierce; the first Crab reaching the dunes drove into a minefield and promptly lost its tracks, while a German 88mm anti-tank gun immediately knocked out a second. Even so, the armour pushed on. After this hot reception, it was discovered that only eleven out of twenty-six flails were fit to leave the beach.

Corporal George Agnew was with the Crabs of the 22nd Dragoons. After getting ashore on Sword, he and his crew nearly had a short-lived D-Day. 'I ran slap-bang into an 88mm gun emplacement,' he said, 'which didn't take long to neutralise my tank.'[41] He was hit by two rounds, one of which caught his turret and the other his engine. Agnew's tank burst into flames, but he had the presence of mind to turn the turret to the side so his driver and co-driver could get out their hatches. He and his men took cover in the dunes. Agnew then found another Crab whose commander had been killed, so he took charge of that.

Things did not run smoothly in Major Wheway's sector. 'The AVREs follow the flails and the Bridging AVREs dropped their bridges,' he noted, 'but the crews jump out to make them fast and in doing so are killed or wounded and the tanks receive direct hits and are brewed up.'[42] German infantry then counterattacked from some nearby houses. On the beach, all the clearance engineers had been killed, leaving the task solely to the flails.

In the meantime, Corporal Hennessy and his crew were swamped. They had expected the Royal Engineers to clear mines and mark clear paths, but they had been delayed. They landed at low tide but the tide was now coming in fast. All around them infantry landing crafts sped by, and Hennessy kept firing in support. His driver began to complain that the tank was rapidly filling with water, and then the engine died. Unable to start it, Hennessy and his men had little choice but to abandon ship and climb into their dingy. This was sunk by German machine-gun fire and the driver wounded, but the five men managed to reach the shelter of the dunes.

Trooper Tribble, with C Squadron, successfully dry-landed:

Along the shore were several other landing craft disgorging their tanks ... and soon all the vessels were withdrawing from the beach, except the one next to us which had yellow flames and black smoke coming from the far side. No doubt it had hit an undersea Teller mine which had not been cleared earlier in the day by the frogmen.[43]

Alongside French troops, No. 4 Commando landed at 0820 hours hot on the heels of 8th Brigade, with the task of capturing Ouistreham at the mouth of the Orne. After some tough fighting, with the support of four Royal Marine Centaur tanks they took the Riva Bella battery.[44] The Centaurs assaulting Sword included *Vidette*, which landed between Hermanville-La Brèche and Lion-sur-Mer.

Unfortunately, neither the La Brèche strongpoint nor Quistreham had been silenced when the five landing craft carrying Lieutenant-Colonel Peter Young's No. 3 Commando came in at about 0900 hours. 'A shell landed in the water 100 yards away and to the port we could see a tank landing craft blazing,' said Young. 'The crew were going over the side as the ammunition exploded.'[45]

The South Lancashire Regiment, acting as vanguard for 8th Brigade, landed on the right side of the beach. Supported by DD tanks, they soon followed the 'Funnies' off the beach and inland. The East Yorkshire Regiment was held up by German machine-gun and mortar fire, but the 22nd Dragoons and the 77th/79th Assault Squadrons cleared seven out of the eight lanes off Sword Beach.

'The clearance of the foreshore presented no great problems,' noted Colonel Belchem, 'but along the sand dunes behind lay a maze of fortifications, obstacles and mines. Thanks to the timely arrival of the tanks and engineers, by 0930 the assault brigade had captured Hermanville-sur-Mer, about a mile and a half inland.'[46]

The 'Funnies' were directed to help the infantry seize Lion-sur-Mer and Quistreham. By 1100 hours, the South Lancashires and 185th Brigade were at Hermanville. Fighting against elements of the 21st Panzer Division, the 185th had, by 1600 hours, reached Bieville about 3½ miles from Caen. At nightfall the British had stalled at Lebisey, a mere 2 miles from their goal. The units of the 79th had fought well.

Major Wheway appreciated just how crucial the Crabs had been, saying, 'General Rennie, 3rd British Division Commander, congratulated the flails on the magnificent show they had put up and stated that if it had not been for them he doubted if the landing would have succeeded on this strongly held front.'[47] 'Many of the swimming tanks of "A" and "B" Squadrons were sunk in the heavy sea,' recalled Tribble sadly, 'and some of the crews drowned.'[48]

'The AVREs had distinguished themselves and with eleven tanks of 79th Squadron succeeded in getting the Bridge at Ousitreham,' recalled Major Wheway. '77th Squadron also successfully battling forward with only four tanks left. Their casualties were extremely heavy, somewhere in the region of 70 per cent tanks and 60 per cent personnel; they were extremely brave men.'[49]

Brigadier Duncan was delighted with the achievements of the 79th Armoured Division on Gold, Juno and Sword, commenting, 'For the first time a sea-borne assault had been preceded by armour in such strength that it was able to win the firefight on the beaches and open a way for the infantry to reach their objectives at relatively low cost.'[50] By the end of the day, the 79th Armoured Division had suffered 179 killed, wounded and missing. 'An incredibly low figured,' said Duncan, 'for a difficult and hazardous operation.'[51] From the assault engineers' 120 AVREs committed to the landings, twenty-two were destroyed, while from a force of fifty Crabs, Duncan's 30th Brigade lost twelve.[52]

Major-General Feuchtinger, commander of the 21st Panzer Division, designated one of Rommel's reserve units, had been reduced to ninety tanks and did not start moving northwards until 1600 hours on D-Day. His weak counterattack towards Bieville failed and his troops were driven eastwards. By the end of the day, Feuchtinger's armour numbered just seventy serviceable panzers. In the meantime, by 1400 hours, the German mobile reserve, the 12th SS Panzer Division and the Panzer Lehr Division, had been released for action. The 12th SS headed for Caen, but was subjected to continual Allied air strikes. Crucially, it was not until 7 and 9 June that the two divisions were brought into action.

15

TOUCH & GO

To the west of the British and Canadian landings, the Americans were to be confronted by very different conditions. The tidal movement in the English Channel meant that the tide rises first from the west, so H-Hour was set at 0630 hours. Three men who were particularly anxious that the American landings should run smoothly were Colonels Frank Holmes, Allan G. Pixton and Paul W. Thompson. They had invested a great deal of time and effort ensuring that American troops were well prepared thanks to their efforts at Depot 0-617 and the assault training centre.

Omaha

Thompson, now in command of 6th Engineer Special Brigade, was personally due to set foot on Omaha at H+140, to join his men in support of the 29th Infantry Division.[1] Pixton, serving with 5th Engineer Special Brigade, was also destined for Omaha with the 1st Infantry Division. While they were anxious about inevitable losses, they knew that speed was of the essence in getting off the beaches and clear of the German killing zones. Armoured close-fire support was going to be a problem. At Omaha Beach, the Calvados Reef ensured that the waves were shorter and steeper, making the water wholly unsuitable for the Americans' swimming tanks.

Up until his departure from England, General Bradley had been led to believe that his troops at Omaha would be attacking the overstretched static 716th coastal defence division. Just before he left, this intelligence was updated, warning that an extra division had moved into the area. This was the 352nd Infantry Division, but it was too late for him to do anything about it.

The opening attack consisted of two regimental combat teams, totalling 1,500 men from the 1st and 29th Infantry Divisions, who were to land at H+1 minute. They were to provide covering fire for the special engineer task force teams. Unfortunately for them, the bomber and naval bombardment designed to destroy the German defences missed their targets. The unharmed garrison, as soon as the bombing and shelling ceased, hurried to man their machine-gun and mortar positions. They waited until the first wave was only about 400 yards from the beach before unleashing a torrent of hot metal along the 4 miles of Omaha Beach,[2] where many of the landing craft carrying the American troops were British-crewed.

The naval bombardment of the American beaches did not commence until 0550 hours, 20 minutes later than that on the British ones. The German fortifications on the British and Canadian beaches endured 2 hours of bombardment before H-Hour, compared to just 40 minutes in the American zone. Later, Admiral Kirk, the commander of the Western Task Force, was to admit, 'The period of bombardment was extremely heavy but was of too short a duration to silence or neutralize all the defences, particularly in the Omaha area.'[3] In light of the firepower laid down on the Germans, something clearly went wrong.[4]

Lieutenant Wesley Ross and his engineers were deafened by the bombardment as they made their run in to Omaha. '[W]e passed near the bow of the battleship *Texas* just as she fired a broadside from her big guns,' observed Ross. 'The blast would have blown my helmet away if the strap had not been fastened.'[5] They also witnessed the rockets fired from the 'Grasshoppers', which, Ross said, 'cut loose with three or four salvoes of several hundred rockets each. We could see the flashes as they hit the hill behind the beach.'[6]

Major Pluskat, along with Captain Wilkening and Lieutenant Theen, of the 352nd Division, were trapped by the heavy shelling in their forward observation bunker near Ste Honorine. Having already spoken to his divisional headquarters about the arrival of the enemy fleet, he hurriedly phoned his battery commanders. He was surprised to discover that none of them had been hit, nor had any of the crews been killed or wounded. Pluskat could only conclude that the Allies were targeting the observation bunkers along the coast in the mistaken belief that they were gun emplacements.[7] 'Remember, no gun must fire until the enemy reaches the water's edge,' Pluskat instructed his officers.[8]

'When the ramps of the leading assault craft went down, the enemy machine guns tore through living flesh,' wrote war correspondent Captain R.W. Thompson, 'so that the front cavities of the vessels became in seconds raw wounds, thick with blood.'[9] Machine gunner Private Franz Gockel opened up with his weapon almost immediately. All the dust and sand thrown up by the naval bombardment soon fouled it. 'I tore the belt from the feed tray, shook it clean, and slapped it back into the tray,' he said.[10] A sudden blast and the weapon was taken from his hands, so he took up his rifle.

This hail of fire immediately pinned down the Americans on the exposed shore. Roy Holmes, with the 146th Engineer Combat Battalion, was horrified by what he found, saying, 'The infantry troops ahead of us were seeking shelter from the murderous fire from the beach and were hiding behind the steel hedgehog obstacles that our men were to blow up, so delays were caused until we got them out the way.'[11] Private Gockel watched as 'the first wave of assault troops collapsed making only a few meters headway'.[12]

Half the engineer teams were 10 minutes late landing, with just five coming ashore in their assigned sector. In the opening minutes, of the planned sixteen paths, they succeeded in clearing only five and a half.[13] The engineers simply did not have the time to carry out their allotted tasks, and found themselves fighting a losing battle. The Germans seemed to deliberately target the engineers, either by sniping at the mines on the obstacles or waiting until the engineers were almost ready to detonate and then dropping mortars onto them, with devastating effect.

The engineers also found themselves in danger of being run down by the successive assault waves. Sergeant Barton A. Davis of the 299th Engineer Combat Battalion, looking up, saw a boat full of 1st Division men heading his way. In the seconds it took for him to consider his options, the boat hit a mine. Davis was aghast at the mess, 'I saw black dots of men trying to swim through the gasoline that had spread on the water and as we wondered what to do a headless torso flew a good fifty feet through the air and landed with a sickening thud near us.'[14] Just two badly burned men survived the blast.

In the sector ironically designated Easy, twenty-nine swimming tanks of the 741st Tank Battalion were launched around 5,000 yards from the shore. The crews cannot have been happy driving their vehicles out into such inhospitable waters, and disaster quickly struck. The tide and winds first blew them off course, and then one by one inundated each tank. The waves crashed against their canvas screens, ripping them open or snapping the support struts. Engines flooded and spluttered into silence.

Despite their training, the crews can only have felt a sense of panic as they jumped from their stricken tanks, struggling to inflate their lifebelts. Last out, if they were lucky, were the drivers, who paddled toward the nearest dinghy. Some were not quick enough and went down in their steel coffins. In all, thirty-three crewmen were drowned.[15]

Just two tanks survived to reach the beach, and were eventually joined by three more that were landed from their LCTs. As elements of the 1st Infantry Division came in, they passed numerous orange dinghies, full of what they thought were shot-down aircrew. They were actually all that remained of the 741st. This tragic loss of almost all of 1st Division's supporting tanks would cost hundreds of casualties at the beginning of the landings. It meant that of the ninety-six tanks intended to support the first wave, a third had been lost already.

Private Gockel watched as the 75mm gun protecting his position opened fire on an American tank moving up the beach. In the confusion, it seems the gunners missed because the Sherman crew zeroed in on the concrete casemate opening and returned fire. Remarkably, such was the gunner's accuracy that his round went into the bunker, destroying the gun and its crew.[16]

Many of the amphibious DUKWs of 6th Engineer Special Brigade shared a similar fate to the DD tanks. Launched over 10 miles out, they suffered with the heavy seas. Some were overloaded and sank, while others lost power and also foundered.[17] Back on the beach, the surviving engineers discovered that the loss of much of their equipment and the incoming tide meant they struggled to complete their missions.

Captain R.W. Thompson reported:

Disaster had also met the attempts to ferry the supporting artillery ashore in the DUKWs … The 11th Field Artillery Battalion lost all its 105mm howitzers save one. The 16th Infantry Cannon Company shared the same fate, and the 7th Field Artillery was very little better.[18]

Riding low in the water, the men in the struggling DUKWs could do nothing as the waves washed into the hulls from aft and starboard. At least eleven of these vessels suddenly dropped like stones, taking the guns and their gunners with them.[19]

In Dog sector to the west, the crews of the three companies of the 743rd Tank Battalion supported the 29th Infantry Division. They were spared the ordeal of having to swim their tanks in, it being decided that their LCTs would carry them up to the shoreline. Only the timely arrival of these tanks alleviated some of the pressure on the engineers and infantry trapped on the beach.

To the west, C Company managed to arrive before the Vierville exit but was shelled on the run-in. All the senior officers were lost in swift succession: first the company commander's LCT was sunk with him on board, then four other officers were killed or wounded. Nonetheless, half of the sixteen tanks were soon engaging enemy positions. The DD tanks acted in support of the naval beach battalion, which attacked up the shingle bank to destroy a number of pillboxes.

Even an hour after the landings had commenced on Omaha, the engineers were still losing vehicles in the sea. Many of the landing craft dropped their ramps onto the edge of runnels and many trucks were driven into 6ft of water. From a force of thirty-five trucks landed to support 5th Engineer Support Brigade, just thirteen reached the shore.[20] Six were lost in one go in the same runnel.[21] Many of 1st and 29th Divisions' landing craft became mixed up in all the confusion, resulting in men coming ashore in the wrong places. Dead and wounded soldiers were strewn all over the beach.

Lieutenant-Colonel Thompson came ashore around 0830 hours and discovered a team of his men struggling to get through the wire along the beach road. 'Some of the engineer personnel were trying to blow it up with Bangalore torpedoes,' observed Thompson, '... and it seemed to me they were going about it kind of clumsy.'[22] Moving forward to show them what to do, a rifle round smashed through his jaw, with a second one going through his right shoulder. Because he had been shouting orders, the round hitting him in the head passed through his open mouth and out through his jawbone. Amongst the casualties evacuated that morning was Thompson, who was found severely injured beneath a German bunker.

Lieutenant Ross of the 146th Engineer Combat Battalion was also wounded. His legs and feet were peppered by shingle and shrapnel thrown up by a mortar round. Recovering sufficiently to hop away, he narrowly avoided three more which impacted at the same point. 'I dug a small foxhole in the sand with my hands,' recalled Ross, 'cutting them on buried

barbed wire in the process – to gain some protection.'[23] He was not rescued until the afternoon.

'Apart from lightly armoured bulldozers the Americans had no mecha-
nised equipment,' said war correspondent Chester Wilmot, 'for dealing
with the obstructions and fortifications.'[24] Instead, the men were expected
to use pole-charges and man-pack flamethrowers whilst braving German
machine-gun and mortar fire. 'That they often failed is not surprising,'
added Wilmot.[25] The armoured superstructure on the bulldozers only
protected the driver from rifle and machine-gun fire, while the exposed
tracks were easily disabled by mines.

Colonel Goth of the German 352nd Division, from his bunker on
Pointe et Raz de la Percée, reported the mayhem he was witnessing to
Lieutenant-Colonel Ziegelmann, the divisional chief of staff. Goth stated:

> At the water's edge the enemy is in search of cover behind the
> coastal zone obstacles … many … vehicles … burning on the
> beach. The obstacle demolition squads have given up their activities.
> Disembarkation from the landing-boats has ceased … The fire of our
> battle positions and artillery is well placed and has inflicted consider-
> able casualties on the enemy.[26]

For the first few hours of the Omaha landings, the Americans suffered one
casualty for every 6ft of the 4-mile-long beach – this equated to almost
2,000 men.[27]

Ziegelmann concluded that they were facing 'inferior enemy forces',[28]
and he briefed his commanding officer, General Kraiss, to that effect.
By 1100 hours, subsequent optimistic reports convinced Kraiss that the
American landings had been thwarted and he decided to deploy the
352nd's reserves to strengthen his right flank facing the British sector.
These reports greatly helped the Allies.

Now would have been a good time for Marcks and Kraiss to authorise
a counterattack at Omaha, which if they had got reinforcements there
in time could have tilted the balance. Kraiss' 915th Infantry Regiment,
acting as LXXXIV Corps reserve to the south-east of Bayeux, could
have counterattacked the British heading for the city or the Americans
at Omaha. Indeed, they had practiced attacking toward the coast on
numerous occasions. Instead, they had been sent west of the Vire to help
fight the American airborne landings in the Carentan area. Although

Kraiss countermanded the order and the regiment turned about, it was too late.

Such was General Dollmann's misplaced optimism that when General Salmuth phoned to offer to redeploy an infantry division from the Le Havre area, he was curtly informed, 'We don't need them.'[29] At 0820 hours, Colonel Goth tried telephoning General Kraiss to update him on the situation. 'Naval guns are smashing our strongpoints,' he said. 'We are running short of ammunition. We urgently need supplies.'[30] Before he could finish his report, the line went dead. It had either been cut by the bombardment or by American paratroopers.

Colonel Benjamin Talley, US V Corps deputy chief of staff, was sent in a DUKW to try to assess the situation at Omaha. At 0930 hours, he signalled his corps commander, General Gerow, 'The assault craft are milling about off the coast like a stampeding herd of cattle and dare not venture on land. Such vehicles and armour as have reached the beach cannot advance any further while the German guns remain intact.'[31] What Talley did not know was that an hour earlier, the beachmaster had suspended the landings because of the mess.

'Throughout the morning tanks, guns and vehicles were immobilised at the water's edge,' wrote Chester Wilmot, 'because the engineers could not clear gaps in the shingle banks, a comparatively minor obstacle.'[32]

By noon, General Bradley, aboard the cruiser *Augusta*, was considering abandoning the assault at Omaha. Rather than continue the bloodletting, it seemed prudent to send the remaining assault forces to Utah and the British and Canadian beaches. For some men on the beach, the horror was simply too much. Sergeant William McClintock, one of the survivors of the 741st Tank Battalion, saw a man sitting under machine-gun fire at the edge of the sea 'throwing stones into the water and softly crying as if his heart would break'.[33]

Major Stanley Bach, the liaison officer for 1st and 29th Infantry, also recorded the horror that was Omaha, stating, '12:15: Heavy mortar and 88 fire started from E end to W end – series of five shells in spots. Direct hit on Sherman tank, men out like rats – those alive …12:30: LCT hit two mines, came on in – hit third, disintegrated and rear end sank.'[34]

The deadlock at Omaha was broken partly by the brave action of two large landing craft which had distracted the defenders' fire.[35] Despite the obstacles, mortaring and shelling, their skippers ran their vessels aground on the beach off Colleville. Even after beaching, their crews continued firing at the enemy defences. Two destroyers also closed to within 1,000 yards of the beach and targeted German positions at Les Moulins. This enabled the assault troops to rally just as the engineers' bulldozers cleared two paths through the St Laurent dunes.

On Dog sector, Brigadier-General Norman Cota rallied the troops to blow the anti-tank wall blocking the Vierville exit. In the centre, the opening up of Exit E-1 cleared a route toward St Laurent. By late afternoon, the engineers had managed to clear five large and six small gaps between the designated exit routes. After almost 7 punishing hours, the Omaha assault was finally making progress.

Later that day, a traumatised Major Bach wrote, 'I've seen movies, assault training demonstrations and actual battle but nothing can approach the scenes on the beach from 11:30 to 14:00 hours – men being killed like flies from unseen gun positions. Navy can't hit em, air cover can't see em – so infantry had to dig them out.'[36]

To the west of Omaha, three companies of US Rangers conducted a daring assault against a battery at Pointe du Hoc. They clambered up the cliffs using ropes and ladders, under covering fire from two destroyers, and stormed the position, only to find that the guns had been removed.

A dazed and dust-covered Major Pluskat managed to escape his bunker, with the aim of reaching his headquarters at Etreham. He discovered that his Volkswagen staff car had been destroyed by naval gunfire or prowling enemy fighter-bombers. He had little choice but to cover the 4 miles on foot, and when he finally arrived at 1300 hours he demanded a brandy. His next thought was ammunition for his guns. Not long after, the phone rang. It was his regimental commander, Lieutenant-Colonel Ocker, who said, 'I've got bad news. I've just learned that the ammunition convoy has been wiped out. It will be nightfall before anything gets to you.'[37]

The paucity of Pluskatt's ammunition was highlighted by delays in his barrages, which were hitting the eastern end of the beach every 15 or 20 minutes. Two of Goth's guns on the Pointe et Raz de la Percée also continued to be little more than a nuisance. Pluskat knew his batteries would be out of ammunition by nightfall, when it would be a question of who got to them first, the Americans or the ammunition. Lacking orders to withdraw, he issued instructions for the gunners to be ready for close-quarter fighting.

Pluskat's fears were well-founded. Back at divisional headquarters, Lieutenant-Colonel Ziegelmann knew only too well that they 'lacked the ammunition needed to smash strong enemy attacks'.[38] Within three days, when Ziegelmann did an inventory check, he found the division only had fourteen operational guns.[39]

Utah

The assault was completely different on Utah to the west. Sheltered by the expanse of the Cherbourg Peninsula, the sea conditions were not quite so bad. The plan was for the 8th Infantry Regiment from the 4th Infantry Division to open the landings. Elements of 1st Engineer Special Brigade would support the first wave, followed by the DD tanks.

Just after 0630 hours, Major Herschel Linn of the 237th Engineer Combat Battalion landed with the task of creating eight 50-yard gaps in the beach obstacles. Such was the smoke screen caused by the aerial and naval bombardment that the assault infantry got slightly lost and landed 2,000 yards from their objectives. By good fortune, they encountered very little opposition. This meant that within 8 minutes of the engineers landing they had created the first gaps, and within 3 hours had removed all the obstacles.[40]

As more and more men came in, what they did not know, according to war correspondent Captain R.W. Thompson, was that 'they were more than a mile south of their target, that the southeasterly set of the tide, and the loss of their control craft, had brought them astride Exit 2, instead of the more heavily defended Exit 3'.[41]

About thirty swimming tanks of the 70th Tank Battalion were launched at 3,000 yards, and luckily only one foundered.[42] However, an LCT manoeuvring to disembark four tanks hit a submerged sea mine with its ramp. Sergeant Orris Johnson on another craft saw the explosion and was transfixed as a tank 'soared more than a hundred feet into the air, tumbled slowly end over end, plunged back into the water and disappeared'.[43] Johnson subsequently discovered that his friend Don Neill was amongst the crew killed. The LCT sank with all its tanks. As a result of the shift south, the tanks were not greatly pressed once ashore. War correspondent Tom Treanor observed, 'The general lack of fortifications at this point was astonishing.'[44]

Sub Lieutenant Herbert Male, who was with a LCT crew, recalled:

We were attached to the American Assault Engineers. We were loaded with tanks and we went into Utah about twenty minutes after

H-Hour ... There were lots of mines on the beaches and obstructions that had to be got through but we had a team of underwater
divers who'd disposed of most of those anyway. We weren't bothered
at all. We had a free run into the beach.[45]

It was around this point that the 237th Engineer Combat Battalion's demolition unit, along with Navy divers, landed to clear underwater obstacles. Their
losses proved light.[46] At 0730 hours, the 531st Engineer Shore Regiment also
arrived to help clear beach obstacles and exits inland.

While the DD tanks had worked perfectly on Utah, other preparations
proved less satisfactory. The shore regiment reported, 'Although all vehicles had been waterproofed for seven feet of water, many of them were
drowned coming in. Every effort was made to tow these vehicles out of
the water ... however, vehicles discharged in [the] incoming tide were
often covered before they could be towed out.'[47]

By the time the third wave arrived, the engineers had blown a 50-yard
gap in the defences and breached the sea wall made of reinforced concrete some 50ft above the high-water mark. The key exit off the beach
lay behind this. While many men found the landing an anti-climax after
all their training, the assault was not spared the horror of war. Second
Lieutenant Herbert Taylor, serving with 1st Engineer Special Brigade, was
shocked when he witnessed a soldier 'decapitated by an artillery burst just
twenty feet away'.[48]

Colonel Eugene Caffey of 1st Engineer Special Brigade knew that the
commanders of the 4th Infantry Division now had a difficult decision to
make. He was with Brigadier-General Theodore Roosevelt as the latter
agonised over whether to let the follow-on troops land in the wrong place
with a single exit causeway, or divert them to the original landing zone
with two causeways. The success of the first option hung on the men
taking and holding Exit 2; if they did not, the beachhead would become
bottled up. Roosevelt gathered his battalion commanders, and after a brief
discussion decided not to waste time and to press on. 'I am going on ahead
with the troops. You get word to the Navy to bring them in. We're going
to start the war from here,'[49] he instructed Colonel Caffey.

Not long after, Roosevelt stood with his divisional commander,
Major-General Raymond O. Barton, directing traffic at the entrance to
the secured causeway. As Major Gerden Johnson of the 12th Infantry
Regiment marched by, Roosevelt greeted him, 'Hi, Johnny! Keep right

on this road, you're doing fine! It's a great day for hunting, isn't it?'[50] Remarkably, the two lead regiments only lost twelve killed.[51] Both the generals fretted that a German counterattack could bring the whole show to a stop. Luckily for them, at about 1100 hours they received word that just a mile away, Exit 3 had been opened.[52]

Back in England at his headquarters at Southwick House, Eisenhower was very pleased with Barton's remarkable success on Utah:

> Our good luck was largely represented in the degree of surprise that we achieved by landing on Utah Beach, which the Germans considered unsuited to major amphibious operations, and by the effective action of the two airborne divisions, the 82nd and 101st, which had landed almost in the centre of the peninsula.[53]

Subsequently, British officers were critical of the American assault at Omaha. Key amongst these criticisms was the tactical decision to attack the main German fortifications head-on. British experience had shown that it was wise to land between enemy strongpoints, which enabled the assault force to turn the enemy's flank and attack them from the rear.

Likewise, much debate had raged ever since over Bradley's decision not to employ Hobart's 'Funnies' except for the DD tanks. Colonel Belchem, amongst others, was critical of this in his account of the landings:

> The decision not to use flail (mine-clearing) tanks and specialist armoured engineers' tanks, deprived the troops of any specialist equipment with which to deal with pill-boxes, clear wire entanglements, place explosives on concrete barriers, or lift mines. Even as late as the afternoon, troops were crossing the shingle bank in single file because the clearance of mines by hand was taking so long.[54]

16

SMASHING THE MULBERRIES

In part thanks to the 'Funnies', the Allies successfully landed 155,000 troops, 6,000 vehicles – including 900 tanks – 600 guns and about 4,000 tons of supplies on 6 June. It was simply a quite remarkable achievement. Shipping elements of the Mulberry harbours over to Normandy also commenced on D-Day. Getting the artificial harbours across the English Channel was an enormous technical challenge from start to finish.

According to Colonel Belchem:

> In all, some two million tons of preformed steel and concrete had to be towed or carried by sea to form two Mulberries, including more than 200 Caissons, some of them the size of five-storey buildings, and 70 block-ships. All available tugs in Britain, and even some from America, were requisitioned for the massive towing operation.[1]

With a sense of anticipation, Brigadier Walter and the team responsible for Mulberry B had boarded the cruiser HMS *Despatch* two days earlier. Now all their hard work would come to fruition. The task facing them was immense: not only did the caissons or Phoenixes have to be assembled, but ships also had to be found to create a much wider breakwater to protect vessels using the Mulberries and anchored off the beaches. These were dubbed Gooseberries. Likewise, pier heads and floating roadways had to be built.

Chief Petty Officer G.C. Brown, who had been assigned to an LST off Gosport, recalled, 'After several postponements waiting for the better weather conditions, we finally set sail in the early hours of 6th June with a contingent of REME, together with their various vehicles and equipment, and towing part of the Rhino ferry for the Mulberry Harbour.'[2] Commodore Rupert Curtis, who was in charge of a landing craft flotilla, ordered his vessels to anchor off Gold Beach. 'Already parts of the prefabricated Mulberry harbours were under tow from England to be placed off Arromanches and St. Laurent,' he observed.[3]

Dick Cowlan, with the British Mulberry construction team, noted, 'We landed at 1800hrs on D-Day at Arromanches and spent the first week clearing up the debris, getting ready for the Mulberry. Parts arrived over the next ten days and we sank the blockships and all was fine … until D plus 13 when the storm blew up.'[4]

Towing the Phoenix concrete caissons across the Channel started the day after D-Day. While the tug crews had a tough time, the men on the caissons did not have it any better. Each carried an anti-aircraft gun with four crew, plus two sailors whose job was to communicate with the tug.

Chief Petty Officer Albert Barnes was the quartermaster of a Royal Navy tug that struggled to tow a caisson across in a Force 9 gale. The crew had a harrowing time with what Barnes describe as 'one of the worst tows that we ever had'. After a tense journey, when it was not clear if they were towing the caisson or it was towing them, Barnes recalled:

When we got over there, we shortened the tow and went to this long row of ships that had been sunk as a marker for us. Small tugs tied up alongside and guided her in and then they opened the seacocks and sunk them and that was more or less the start of the Mulberry Harbour.[5]

According to Admiral Tennant, a total of 150 tugs were selected as suitable for the Channel crossing. These were marked with an M for Mulberry on their funnels; 'all took great pride in their M'.[6]

To prevent German snooping in the English Channel, Eisenhower even took the extraordinary step of banning fishing for a period of a week three days after D-Day commenced. In light of these waters being clogged with thousands of naval vessels of all shapes and sizes and the skies full of Allied aircraft, it is hard to imagine any fishermen wanting to venture out for fear of mishap. While Eisenhower may have been concerned about public safety, it is also likely that he did not want any word of the Phoenixes being towed to Normandy reaching German intelligence.

The BBC European Service issued an urgent warning on behalf of Eisenhower to the fishermen of Belgium, Denmark, France, the Netherlands and Norway, instructing:

All fishing should cease in these waters for a period of seven days beginning at 9pm on Thursday, June 8, and extending until 9pm on Thursday, June 15. Fishermen now in port must remain there. Those at sea must return to port immediately. Failure to do so may be fatal to yourself and hinder the operations of the Allied Forces.[7]

This ensured that there were no 'innocent' civilian craft bobbing around the Channel getting in the way, or worse, spying for the enemy.

During the assault phase, four Phoenixes were lost along with many of the crew. One hit a mine, another was torpedoed and two were lost in rough weather.[8] Persistent German artillery fire delayed things at Omaha, where the first two caissons for Mulberry A were not sunk until 10 June. However, within four days, thirty-two of fifty-one Phoenixes had been manoeuvred into place. 'Lost another Phoenix last night by torpedo,' noted Captain Butcher, Eisenhower's naval aide, on 12 June, 'but the Mulberries and Gooseberries are all in and working as expected.'[9]

Doctor Patterson, No. 4 Commando's medical officer, witnessed the results of German efforts to stop the Mulberries. He was heading for Portsmouth with casualties, when the vessel he was on picked up twelve Americans from an M-tug that had been torpedoed by a U-boat. The Phoenix survived the encounter, but the tug had gone to the bottom. 'Nine out of the twelve men had fractured thighs,' noted Patterson, 'due to the deck coming up under them when the torpedo hit.' They were very lucky to have survived. 'The sub had biffed the harbour section with two torpedoes,' added Patterson, 'but it remained afloat.'[10]

The breakwater known as Gooseberry 2, consisting of sunken block-ships, was in place by 10 June to provide shelter for the Mulberry being constructed off Omaha. Royal Navy officers warned that two gaps left to allow craft to reach the beach had divided the breakwater into three. These would allow water through in rough weather, which would endanger the Mulberry. Gooseberry 1 was completed three days later off Utah. The third one was placed to protect the Mulberry off Arromanches.

Incredibly, within five days, 326,547 troops, 54,186 vehicles and 104,428 tons of supplies had been delivered at the five invasion beaches.

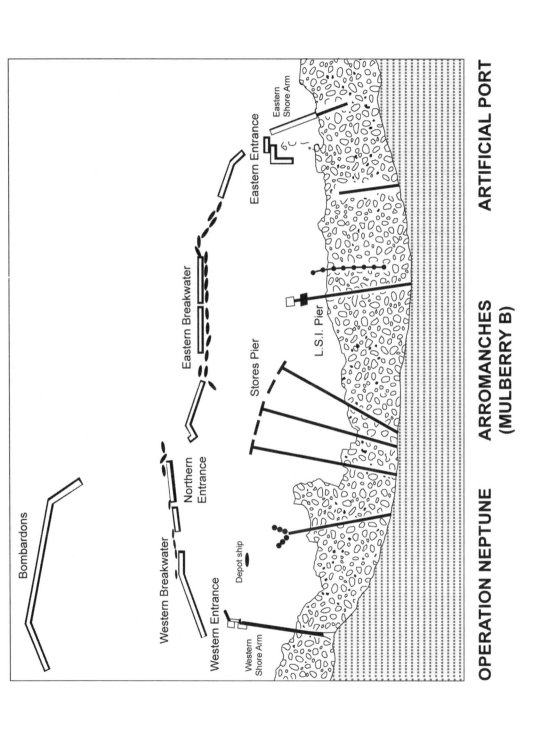

Bombardons

Western Breakwater

Northern Entrance

Depot ship

Western Entrance

Western Shore Arm

Eastern Breakwater

Eastern Entrance

Eastern Shore Arm

Stores Pier

L.S.I. Pier

OPERATION NEPTUNE **ARROMANCHES** **ARTIFICIAL PORT**
(MULBERRY B)

The Allied build-up continued at a pace. By the afternoon of 17 June, 589,653 men, 89,828 vehicles and almost 200,000 tons of supplies had been landed.[11] Naval losses were small, including four LCTs and a Landing Ship (Infantry).[12]

There could be no denying that the Mulberries were proving to be a great success. The main concern was that the Germans would realise just how important they were and make an all-out effort to destroy them. 'Their existence may not be mentioned in press stories, as there is strict censorship,' wrote Captain Butcher, 'although the Germans, with their recce planes and frequent bombing attacks, must know of their existence. We may fool them as to capacity, however.'[13]

It was not until mid-June that the Luftwaffe began to appreciate quite what the Allies were up to off the shores of Normandy. However, Allied air superiority, dense flak and barrage balloons made attacks hazardous. Despite this, they began to drop pressure mines.

Reg Plumb, with the 84th Light Anti-Aircraft Regiment, saw the results of this activity:

> Because of the constant mining by the Luftwaffe, in and around the harbour, we had plenty of night firing. One night a hospital ship struck a mine some way north of Port Mulberry and many casualties were caused, the remains drifting in to the north wall where we had the gruesome task of recovering them and locating their identity discs etc; many of the dead were nurses.[14]

While D-Day was all about overcoming enormous scientific and technical challenges, on 14 June an unwanted political problem arrived in the shape of Free French leader General Charles de Gaulle. The Allied planners had chosen to ignore this inevitable aspect of Overlord. He crossed the Channel in the French destroyer *La Combattante*, bringing with him a delegation. This included François Coulet, whom he had appointed as his commissioner for Normandy, and Colonel de Chevigné, his military representative.[15] Coulet arrived with a trunk containing twenty-five million francs with which to bankroll the Gaullist organisation.[16]

De Gaulle was invited to eat with Monty. 'We have not come to France,' responded de Gaulle haughtily, 'to have luncheon with Montgomery.'[17] Nonetheless, he arrived at Montgomery's caravan, which was used as his tactical headquarters, at around 1430 hours. Motioning to a photo of

Rommel, Monty said, 'I missed him in Africa, but I hope to get him this time.'[18] After an exchange of pleasantries and a military briefing, de Gaulle got to the point of his visit, 'I have brought with me Commandant Coulet, who will be concerned with the administration at Bayeux.'[19] Monty took no notice of this Trojan horse, nor its political ramifications.[20]

After quickly touring the British and American sectors, de Gaulle returned to England that very night. At the end of the month, General Pierre Koenig, whom de Gaulle had designated as head of the French Forces of the Interior, was formally accepted by the Allies. President Roosevelt feared that de Gaulle's presence in France could spark open conflict between Marshal Philippe Pétain's collaborationist Vichy government, the Communist Resistance, the Gaullist resistance and a myriad of other competing French factions. He felt that Eisenhower and his commanders had their hands full fighting Rundstedt and Rommel, without having to worry about being caught in the middle if the French set about each other.

A way to avoid this was to limit the number of regular Gaullist units deployed to Normandy. Apart from a few warships on D-Day, the French role had consisted of a company of commandos who accompanied the British at Ouistreham, plus commandos dropped into Brittany to assist the resistance. Some might argue that it was a cynical ploy to assign most of the Gaullist and other regular French divisions to the liberation of the Riviera later that summer in order to keep them out the way.

French politics were a distraction compared to the weather, which soon began to cause the Allied air forces problems. 'For a whole fortnight after D-Day the weather was most unfavourable for bombing,' wrote Air Marshal Harris, 'with continuous low cloud, more often than not completely unbroken.'[21] American bombers used to flying during the day either had their missions cancelled or had to abort after failing to locate their target. In contrast, Bomber Command, consigned to conducting night operations, managed to carry on for a week after D-Day largely unhindered.

Admiral Ramsey remained alarmed at the prospect of a major attack by the Germans' large fleet of E-boats operating from Le Havre and Boulogne. In response, Bomber Command was called on to do something about them. Harris decided to conduct both day and night attacks on the German Navy, with the raids scheduled for 14–15 June. 'They were attacked just before sunset,' said Harris, 'when we could be certain that the vessels would be out of their concrete shelters and collected together in the harbours, getting ready to operate during the night.'[22] Heavy-duty bombs were also dropped on the concrete E-boat shelters at Le Havre. According to Harris, the attacks proved highly successful.[23]

Eisenhower and Group Captain Stagg's luck now began to run out. Since D-Day, the wind and the waves had started to pick up. The wind, although variable, had only reached at the most Force 4, and likewise the height of the waves had been a steady 2ft. The latter began to double and the sea was too rough to continue towing operations. Brigadier Walter at Arromanches and Captain Clark at Omaha prepared themselves for the worst. Walter and his colleagues ordered precautions be taken, and all vessels not currently unloading were ordered to stop.

Just twelve days after D-Day, the weather in the English Channel deteriorated very rapidly. Eisenhower, Tedder, Ramsay, Leigh-Mallory, Montgomery and Bradley must have thanked their lucky stars that they had made the most of the weather on the 6th. The wind began to gather, and by 19 June had turned into a 30-knot gale that whipped the waves as high as 8ft. For the next three days, all shipping in the Channel was brought to a halt, as were ship-to-shore operations in Normandy.

The storm created mayhem, as an eyewitness recalled:

Ships were now dragging their anchors and parting their cables ... As night fell a big coaster grappled by two tugs bore down on us. Next came a signal: 'If the ship on your port bow is No.269 she contains 3,000 tons of ammunition,' but the tugs held her like terriers all night and she was saved.[24]

All eyes turned to the Mulberries which were still under construction. The waves smashed against them and the painstakingly assembled jetties and piers. It was now that the outer Gooseberry breakwaters seemed a good investment. At Arromanches, Walter's Mulberry was almost complete and the breakwater held successfully, sheltering 500 vessels. Some unloading was even achieved during the storm.[25] In contrast, the one in the American sector off St Laurent was not ready. The breakwater held for three days and then gave up the struggle.

By 20 June, the Mulberries were being lashed by waves that crashed over everything. The American and British tug crews fought valiantly to rescue drifting craft to prevent them smashing into the piers. The Phoenixes became completely flooded to the brim because the valves were designed to let water in, not out. The internal pressure was such that when the tide went out, five caissons split. Remarkably, the British blockships, apart from two that had their backs broken, stayed in position. The British towing launches survived, but all the American ones were lost.

'During the storm my cabin was flooded and I lost most of my kit in seawater covered with fuel oil,' said Royal Navy officer Fenton Rutter. 'For a while after that I wore an American Army uniform with Royal Navy epaulettes and cap and slept on netting on top of the ammunition boxes.'[26]

In Paris, the atrocious weather was a mixed blessing for the Luftwaffe's meteorologists, Major Lettau and Professor Walther Stoebe. Whilst it grounded the air force's planes, it did mean that the Army and Waffen-SS were able to move reinforcements to Normandy without fear of attack by the Allies' fighter-bombers. The Luftwaffe had a major presence in and around the city, with about a dozen airbases. Constant Allied attacks on its airfields had greatly eroded the Luftwaffe's strength, along with Hitler's ever-changing priorities. What pilots and aircrew were there, had to hang around while the rain lashed their hangers at Brétigny, Villaroche and Villacoublay.[27]

In the British and Canadian sectors, the arrival of three much-needed divisions was delayed by a week. Similarly, in the American sector, the delivery of men and vehicles was cut by two-thirds. The Allied build-up in Normandy ground to a halt, and their air forces' operations were greatly hampered. Rommel was given a much-needed breathing space in which to deploy his units largely unhindered to contain the enemy bridgehead. Given four precious days, he was able to position three divisions ready for contact with the Americans.[28]

At Omaha, Captain Clark did all he could, but his Mulberry received the full force of the storm. He tried to save the piers and pierheads, but drifting craft kept hitting them. Having endured regular fire from German batteries, he was soon exhausted and forced to return to England. His place was taken by Commander Ard, who faced the same thankless task.

One American naval engineer was dismayed at the level of damage as he looked upon 'wrecked landing craft in every direction and on such destruction as I could not have imagined possible from any cause – either from the fury of man at his worst or from nature at her most violent'.[29] The piers were wrecked, while twenty of the thirty-two caissons were destroyed. Most of them burst open due to the water pressure. Seven of the American blockships also broke their backs. The decision was taken to abandon Mulberry A as it was beyond repair.

'The destruction of the American Mulberry off St Laurent produced many arguments about the value of these artificial harbours,' said Colonel Belchem. 'What is quite certain is that the Gooseberry breakwaters were of inestimable value.'[30] 'At the height of the storm, Admiral Sir Philip Vian, commanding the Eastern Task Force, signalled, "The Gooseberries have saved the day",' recorded Captain Harold Hickling RN, the senior naval officer at Arromanches. 'Even at Mulberry B, it was possible to land 800 tons of much needed ammunition.'[31]

'Nine of the eleven Whales being towed were sunk by the high seas yesterday,' Captain Butcher recorded on 20 June, 'the worst loss we have suffered in the artificial-harbour devices.'[32] Two days later, he noted the growing concern about the weather:

The north-east wind continues to raise hell with our shipping, has stopped convoys, and is lashing our Mulberries and Gooseberries ... The weather man says that a great high, lying north of the UK and west of Iceland, is forcing bad weather from the Nordic countries across Germany and the French coast, giving poor visibility for air operations. He says that the weather records for forty years do not show similar conditions. Apparently, we are in an unlucky streak.[33]

Eisenhower slightly exaggerated when he called the storm a 'hurricane', but the effects were not dissimilar. For four whole days, all landing activity was stopped and communication between England and France by air and sea was cut, while the English Channel was whipped into a fury. Eisenhower was kept closely informed of what was happening in the Normandy beach-head and wanted to see the extent of the damage for himself. He wrote, 'On the day of the storm's ending I flew from one end of our beach line to the other and counted more than 300 wrecked vessels above small-boat size; some so badly damaged they could not be salvaged.'[34]

One unit that was stuck at sea was Major-General Robert Macon's 83rd Infantry Division, which was ironically nicknamed 'Thunderbolt'. With unloading halted, the men were unable to disembark at Omaha and had to ride out the appalling weather. 'I visited the men of that division the day they finally got ashore and found a number of them still seasick and temporarily exhausted,' noted Ike.[35]

The build-up was virtually bought to a halt, delaying 20,000 vehicles and 140,000 tons of stores. In the overall scheme of things, however, this terrible storm was only an inconvenient glitch: despite the weather, 850,000 men, 570,000 tons of supplies and 149,000 vehicles had arrived in Normandy by the end of June. Rommel could only marvel at such resources.

Once the Arromanches Mulberry was functioning it became a hive of activity, as Dick Cowlan recalled, '[I]t was on the go 24 hours a day, unloading military vehicles, lorries, tanks, food supply trucks, everything for the troops advancing.'[36] The loss of so many craft was a setback but not a disaster. By mid-July, of some 800 damaged vessels, three-quarters had been repaired and refloated.[37]

'The Germans have disclosed by a broadcast that for the first time their reconnaissance has detected our Gooseberries and Mulberries,' reported Harry Butcher in mid-July. However, added Butcher with some pleasure, 'they conclude that these shelters were a measure forced upon us by the "nor'easter" of June 19–20 and by our belated realization that their demolitions in Cherbourg would deny us the use of that port for a long time.'[38]

In the meantime, the storm forced Montgomery to postpone Operation Epsom, his assault to the west of Caen, until 25 June. Bradley, in order to conserve artillery ammunition for his attack toward Cherbourg, suspended all southward operations.

17

CHERBOURG CAPTURED

To the far west of the Allied bridgehead, Bradley's men faced a tough task. They had to guard their southern flank against counterattack by Rommel whilst fighting northward towards Cherbourg. When he had been briefed on the defences in the Cotentin Peninsula, General Graf von Schmettow, the Channel Islands commandant, was of the view that they were not as good as his own.[1] He managed to get back to Guernsey early on 7 June, and prepared for a long and miserable siege.

In the wake of D-Day there was no ignoring the Allied threat to Cherbourg's garrison. The Berlin correspondent for the Swedish daily newspaper *Aftonbladet* reported that the 'mass landings have sharpened the danger to Cherbourg, and the cutting off of the Cherbourg peninsula is now feared'.[2] His German hosts were far from ignorant about this danger.

Rommel knew all about the difficulties of defending Cherbourg, having swiftly captured the port with his 7th Panzer Division in June 1940. '[W]e succeeded in carrying out the Führer's special order to take Cherbourg as fast as possible,'[3] he later wrote, with evident pride. Speed had been the key. Despite the French having up to thirty-five forts operational and superior numbers, Rommel's men had carried the day. He used two columns to fight his way north. He had then employed artillery and dive-bombers to pound the naval dockyard and the forts. Fort Central, facing the sea, had been shelled into silence.

After Cherbourg surrendered, Rommel toured Fort du Roule to the south and Fort Querqueville to the west. At the latter he recalled, 'I was surprised to see how little damage our shell-fire had caused in the fort.'[4] He also noticed, 'The shell pits in the masonry … were some 12–16 inches deep and the garrison had apparently come to no serious harm.' The thoroughly demoralised French garrison claimed they had been forced to surrender due to insufficient ammunition. The truth was that they had been outfought.

Now Rommel's men were in a reverse position, as it was they who would have to defend the port. In early June 1944, Rommel's more immediate concern was the British and Canadian threat to Caen. This was the anchor for his much more important right flank. Nevertheless, he became distracted by the defence of the Cotentin. Instead of concentrating on massing his forces for an immediate counterattack against the Allied bridgehead, he ordered his reserves to the Cotentin. This was because captured Allied documents showed that the Americans were intent on taking St Lô and Cherbourg. Instead of remaining focused on an overall strategy, Rommel was increasingly reduced to tactical firefighting.

The western part of the Contentin was held by General Heinz Hellmich's 243rd Infantry Division. Two of his infantry regiments were deployed in the Barneville and Pieux areas.[5] The division's artillery consisted of second-hand Russian weapons and limited numbers of anti-tank weapons. However, its tank-hunter battalion comprised twenty-four assault guns and tank destroyers, which were more than capable of taking on the American Sherman tank.[6] To the east lay Schlieben's 709th Infantry and Falley's 91st Airlanding Divisions. Limited elements of the 77th Infantry, based near St Malo under the command of General Rudolf Stegmann, were sent as reinforcements and reached Valognes on 10 June.[7] His units were deployed both sides of the Merderet.

Like many German generals, Hellmich's headquarters was in a large chateau, that was located at Malassis. The Allies had bombed it and his nearby artillery regiment on 5 June, killing a guard and a civilian. According to Blanche Leroy, one of the daughters of the chateau's owner, Hellmich had told her mother, 'Gather your children and hide.' This they did and, she recalled, 'When we came back, the Germans had all gone.'[8]

The German view was that holding Cherbourg hinged on a successful defence of Montebourg. To that end, on 12 June Major Friedrich Wilhelm Küppers found himself in charge of an artillery group charged with the defence of a line Quineville-Montebourg-Gorse Hill.[9] The firepower of his five batteries was supplemented by a regiment of mortars and a flak group. Combined, they were giving supporting fire to the 919th Grenadier Regiment, from the 709th Infantry, and the battle groups Hoffmann and Müller from the 243rd Infantry. Küppers' guns, which were well camouflaged in their field positions, maintained a concentrated harassing fire night and day in order to make it difficult for the Americans to locate them.

The surrounding landscape greatly aided German defensive efforts. The Norman countryside was very ill-disposed for the conduct of armoured warfare thanks to the confining nature of the towering hedgerows known as bocage. Hindering visibility, this greatly hampered the use of artillery and tanks. Likewise, great swathes of marshland extending from the Douve to the Merderet also impeded Bradley's progress. West of the Merderet River and north at Montebourg, it took almost a week to secure objectives that ideally should have been taken on D-Day.

Four days after D-Day, the US 8th Infantry Regiment, from Barton's 4th Infantry, and the 82nd Airborne's 505th Paracute Infantry Regiment continued their attack northwards towards Montebourg. The unfortunate town, firmly held by the Germans, was devastated by Allied naval firepower, including its beautiful medieval church. The US 90th Infantry Division resumed its attack on 11 June, clearing Amfreville. After coming ashore, Barton's 4th Infantry struggled to capture the German batteries at Azeville and Crisbecq, though these were eventually secured, the first by force and the second after the Germans abandoned it. Welcome American reinforcements arrived at Utah on 10 June when the US 9th Infantry Division landed under the command of Major-General Manton S. Eddy.

The assault north fell to General Lawton Collins' US VII Corps. He was highly experienced in close-quarter combat, having fought in the swamps and jungles of Guadalcanal and New Georgia in the Pacific. Collins, known as 'Lightning Joe', learned that it was vital for his infantry to show initiative and fight with what they carried, rather than constantly relying on supporting firepower. First, though, on 14 June, with the 82nd Airborne on his right and 9th Infantry Division on his left, Collins struck west toward Sauveur le Vicomte on the far bank of the Douve. He did this employing four regimental columns, each with a thousand-yard frontage, either side of the two main roads.[10] Most of the town's buildings were destroyed and its imposing medieval castle dominating the Dove Valley was badly damaged.

Bradley and Collins knew that it was vital to cut off Cherbourg from external help as soon as possible. Rommel, misreading the situation, assumed that Collins would punch south-west with the aim of driving further into Normandy and possibly toward Brittany, and deployed what reserves he had to hand to counter such a move. Collins, by early on 16 June, had two bridgeheads across the Douve, and two days later the 9th Division rolled into Barneville on the coast. Bradley and Collins now had four divisions astride the Cotentin peninsula, consisting, east to west, of the 4th, 79th, 90th and 9th Infantry.

Major Küppers spoke to Colonel Reiter, his regimental commander, on 17 June and received the bad news. 'The Americans have broken out to the west from their bridgehead,'[11] warned Reiter. Disastrously for them, an American corridor had been cut to the Cotentin's western coast. The LXXXIV Corps now found itself in the uncomfortable position of fighting on northern and southern fronts. The only good news was that 1,200 men of Stegmann's 77th Division had been directed south and had narrowly avoided being cut off. This left Rommel with the remnants of four exhausted divisions trapped in the Cotentin. These were reorganised into two battlegroups, dubbed Hellmich and Schlieben. To make matters worse, General Stegmann, commander of the 77th Infantry, was killed by an American fighter-bomber on 17 June. General Hellmich was also killed in an air attack that day.

Colonel Bacherer took charge of the 77th Division. Captain Dr Schreihage, the divisional intelligence officer, witnessed their escape, 'The few Volkswagens and radio-vans that were still intact sneaked through enemy lines in dread secrecy. In the grey light the marching columns were passing through enemy-occupied villages. The American sentries got quite a fright when they saw the silent processions, and were quickly disarmed.'[12] Heading for Villot, they were rescued by some self-propelled guns from the 243rd Division. They then forced a crossing over the Ollande, capturing a bridge and driving the US 47th Infantry Regiment out of the way. In the process they ended up with 250 prisoners, but this was small recompense for the American breakthrough.

Rundstedt and Rommel, under Operation Heinrich, wanted their trapped forces to withdraw to prepared positions just outside Cherbourg and sit tight for as long as possible. Once Collins' troops were on a line Les Pieux–Brix–Valognes it would only be a matter of time before they reached the port. When such a move was suggested to Hitler, he flew into a rage at the very idea of giving ground to the enemy. Instead, he did his usual trick of trying to micro-manage the battle rather than rely on his commanders on the ground. He took a red pencil and scrawled a line westward on his map from just below Vauville across the peninsula to St Vaast. This would be their new defensive line and they would have to conduct a fighting withdrawal to it. In other words, they could only move when forced to.

This was madness because Hitler's proposed 30-mile long front line did not capitalise on Cherbourg's existing perimeter defences. These could exact a heavy toll on the Americans whilst the port facilities were blown up. Instead, by the time the battered German units reached them, they would not be in a fit state to resist. To Rommel it looked like Tunis all over again, the needless defence of a city that offered one prospect: the loss of the entire garrison. He called Rundstedt to protest, warning, 'If the Führer's order is interpreted literally, and all the forces in the Peninsula remain in their positions, then the enemy will drive right on to Cherbourg along undefended roads behind our own troops.'[13]

Bradley and Collins, keen not to give the trapped Germans time to solidify their defences, renewed the attack on 19 June with the 4th, 9th and 79th Divisions. To the east, the German defences at Montebourg were swiftly cracked, placing Collins firmly on the road to Valognes. Just prior to the American assault on the German positions at Montebourg, the town was heavily bombed. In order to give local civilians the chance to escape, it was decided to shower the town in leaflets. However, when NBC correspondent William W. Chaplain tried to report this positive step, he experienced the heavy hand of the official censor. The leaflets were scattered by high winds and 'the people of Montebourg had died in the ruins'.[14] On the 20th, the Germans withdrew from around the Montebourg sector with Barton's 4th Infantry hot on their heels.[15] The town was bypassed by both the 4th and 79th Infantry, with the latter heading for Valognes.

Küppers' batteries and the other units in the immediate Montebourg area were 'hanging in the air'[16] as their flanks were now unprotected. Lieutenant Staake, 5th Battery commander, arrived to warn Küpper that enemy tanks were busy bypassing the town centre. 'We've got to get out of here, Herr Major; we're in a trap,'[17] cried the bedraggled lieutenant with urgency. Instead, Küppers calmly sought to drive the Americans back using his artillery and mortars. He then managed to phone Major Förster, the 709th's intelligence officer. Förster was aghast, replying, 'You're still there? We thought you'd moved back during the night.'[18] At that point the line went dead. Küppers and Staake realised they were on their own.

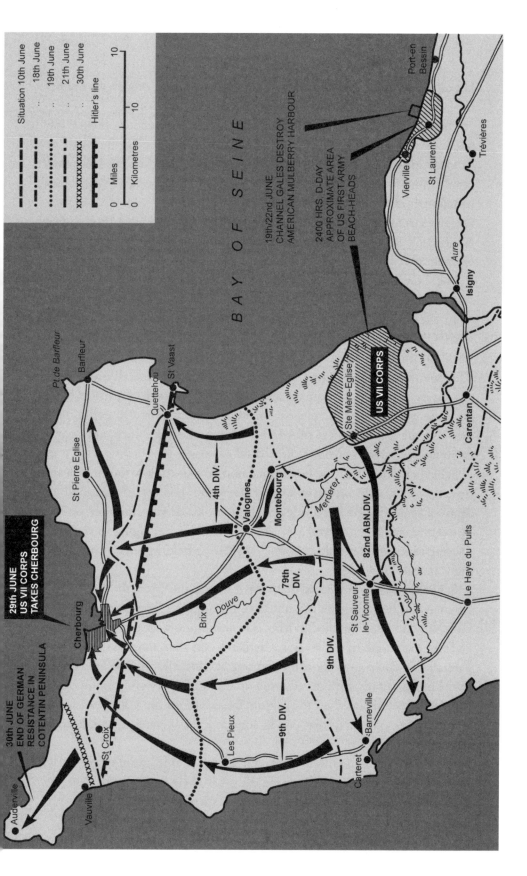

Situation 10th June
" " 18th June
" " 19th June
" " 21th June
" " 30th June
Hitler's line

0 Miles 10
0 Kilometres 10

BAY OF SEINE

19th/22nd JUNE
CHANNEL GALES DESTROY
AMERICAN MULBERRY HARBOUR

2400 HRS D-DAY
APPROXIMATE AREA
OF US FIRST ARMY
BEACH-HEADS

US VII CORPS

29th JUNE
US VII CORPS
TAKES CHERBOURG

30th JUNE
END OF GERMAN
RESISTANCE IN
COTENTIN PENINSULA

Port-en-Bessin
St Laurent
Vierville
Trévières

Isigny
Aure
Carentan
Port-en-Bessin

Ste Mère-Eglise

Pt de Barfleur
Barfleur
St Vaast
Quettehou
St Pierre Eglise

4th DIV.

Valognes
Montebourg
Merderet
82nd ABN.DIV.
St Sauveur
le-Vicomte

79th
DIV.

Brix
Douve

9th DIV.

Cherbourg

Les Pieux
9th DIV.

Barneville

Le Haye du Puits

Carteret

Vauville
St Croix
Auderville

Just as the weather turned bad, Küppers instructed his officers to fire off the last of their ammunition and retreat as quickly as possible.

There is little doubt that the failed defence of Montebourg proved the breaking point for the Germans in the Cotentin. 'During the battle at Montebourg the men were completely worn out by the incessant naval bombardments and by air attacks,' said Major Hoffman, one of Schlieben's battalion commanders. 'The withdrawal to Cherbourg, which took place under extreme enemy pressure, drained the last ounce of their inner fortitude.'[19] Had they been authorised to move sooner, they might have escaped unscathed; instead they were forced to fight running battles.

Local German forces were reorganised into a battle group using the survivors of the 709th Division and the 922nd Grenadier Regiment from the 243rd Division, which were removed from the control of LXXXIV Corps. General Schlieben became the garrison commander with 'an entirely battered division, with horse-drawn transport ... The enemy moreover, had an air force which prevented all movement during daytime.'[20] Cherbourg's landward defences were controlled from an underground command post located beneath Fort Octeville. This was also the headquarters of Admiral Hennecke, the Normandy naval commander, who controlled the coastal batteries.

Schlieben knew that the best they could do was to slow the Americans down, but the end result would be the same. His forces included an array of rear echelon personnel, such as cooks, drivers, military police, nurses and signallers, as well as frightened workers belonging to the Todt Organisation. He signalled Rommel requesting help, but there was nothing Rommel could do.

Schlieben fully appreciated that even if he had the forces for an effective defence at Cherbourg, he did not have the supplies. The garrison in the Cotentin had been doubled in May, but ammunition, food and fuel stocks had not increased. In addition, his artillery and mortar ammunition had been drawn down to support the fighting at Montebourg. Nothing could move on the roads without inviting attack, and Luftwaffe supply drops had been scattered all over the region, including on the Channel Islands. Ironically, the one thing that was in abundance was alcohol, with brandy, champagne and wine.[21]

Within three days, Hitler's so-called defensive line counted for nothing and Collins' troops were preparing for their final assault. On the night of 21 June, he called on Schlieben to surrender. He was given until

0900 hours the following day to ponder his decision. Schlieben had no choice in the matter. Hitler signalled, ordering him to hold until the last:

> Even if the worst comes to the worst, it is your duty to defend the last bunker and leave to the enemy not a harbour but a field of ruins. The German people and the whole world are watching your fight; on it depend the conduct and result of operations to smash the beachheads, and the honour of the German Army and of your own name.[22]

When Schlieben did not respond to Collins, ultimatum, at 1240 hours on 22 June American and British bombers pounded his defences across a 20 square mile area. The bombs fell like confetti, smashing everything they hit. This attack, however, did not go uncontested, with German flak accounting for twenty-four aircraft. 'Hand-to-hand fighting is proceeding at some of our artillery positions and command posts,' reported Schlieben on the afternoon of the 23rd. 'Positions which have not been destroyed are still holding out. Navy considers harbour has been destroyed for good.'[23] After two weeks of fighting, Rommel sensed that things were going against him. 'The enemy air force is dealing extremely heavily with our supplies and at the moment is completely strangling them,' he wrote. 'Even Cherbourg will not be able to hold out for long in these circumstances.'[24]

The town's defences comprised a ring of outlying forts on three ridges, as well as concrete emplacements built in the port area. The three largest batteries were armed with massive 280mm guns, so Bradley called on Allied warships to silence them. He deployed three battleships, four cruisers and eleven destroyers as a powerful bombardment force. These vessels tried to keep out of range of the 150mm guns at Fort Homat, but some German batteries opened up, sparking a one-sided duel. The Allied shelling lasted for 3 hours, while in the city Collins' infantry, using phosphorous grenades and pole charges, slowly destroyed Schlieben's remaining bunkers and pillboxes.

It was a truly miserable existence for the garrison, with absolutely no hope of rescue. They were mercilessly shelled by sea and by land, and bombed from the air. Those cowering in the bunkers, their will to resist ebbing away, listened to the noisy rattle of the ventilation generators and watched the swirling clouds of dust shaken loose by the heavy bombardment. In the poor electrical light, their faces were filthy and many were caked in blood. Other than some of the officers and NCOs, few had much stomach for the fight any more.

Every now and then they could also feel the shock waves caused by the German naval personnel and engineers finishing off Cherbourg's dock-yard facilities. Some 35 tons of dynamite were used to smash the piers and the dock railway. Even the old landmark tower was toppled into the harbour. In the depths of the Octeville command centre, the ventilator packed up and the network of corridors and galleries began to fill with noxious fumes. In the hospital gallery, many of the 300 wounded began to choke to death, but there was nothing the medical staff could do.

In desperation, Rommel did consider shipping a division from Brittany as reinforcements, but the presence of the Allied navies and air forces made such a move simply irresponsible. During 23 and 24 June, the attackers struggled forward, driving the defenders from their positions, remaining at the mercy of snipers hidden in the rubble. Around the port, resist-ance proved fierce particularly at La Glacerie and Fort du Roule. 'The American attacks on all strongpoints, however small, invariably followed the same pattern,' observed Lieutenant-Colonel Keil, commander of the 919th Grenadiers. 'First, bombing by fifty aircraft. Second, pasting by mortar fire. Then the charge by assault troops.'[25]

On the 24th, Collins' troops gained a foothold in the suburbs of Octeville and Tourlaville, as well as Fort du Roule. This meant that Schlieben and Hennecke's command bunker was now in the midst of the fighting. Major Harry Herman, with the US 39th Infantry, was involved in the attack on Octeville. He watched as their own artillery fell short, hit-ting a platoon and forcing the supporting tanks to back off:

Everything seems wrong … With my Sergeant Maachi in tow, we crawl under heavy but high machine-gun fire up to the fort that looms up like Grand Central Station. I don't quite remember what happens from here on, but piecing it together, we got two bazookas up to about sixty yards from the fort when we hit the outpost.[26]

He was then struck in the right hip by machine-gun fire and his right arm was caught in a grenade blast. Once the Fort du Roule battery was in American hands, they were able to shoot down into the heart of Cherbourg. Over the next few days, the Americans took 2,150 prisoners as the German defence began to rapidly collapse.[27]

Eisenhower sailed over to France in a destroyer on 24 June and met with Bradley. 'Among other things, he wanted to make certain that after the capture of Cherbourg,' recalled Captain Butcher, 'Bradley would turn the American First Army to the south and smash into the Germans to prevent the peninsula from being sealed.'[28] Eisenhower was worrying needlessly, as Rommel did not have the resources for such a move.

On the morning of 25 June, General Schlieben sent his depressing situation report to Rommel, stating, 'Enemy superiority in material and enemy domination of the air overwhelming. Most of our own batteries out of ammunition or smashed. Troops badly exhausted, confined to narrowest space, their backs against the sea.'[29] Furthermore, he highlighted that he had 2,000 wounded in Cherbourg whom he could not move. Rommel's reply simply said that in accordance with Hitler's orders, they must fight on until they ran out of ammunition. That night, Lieutenant Kruspe, Schlieben's orderly officer, signalled, 'Last phase of fighting begun. General fighting side by side with his men.'[30] If nothing else, it sounded good for Nazi propaganda.

Organised resistance finally came to an end late on 26 June. Schlieben and Hennecke knew they had run out of time, and surrendered their Octeville stronghold. Its demoralised inhabitants, some 800 strong, filed out onto the hillside and sucked in the welcome fresh air. The remaining wounded were a terrible sight. The pair were taken to General Eddy, who drove them to Collins' headquarters. There was some talk of them dining with Bradley, but he would have none of it because they had refused to surrender sooner, costing him even more American lives.

Although part of the garrison under General Sattler, holding the Arsenal strongpoint, lay down their arms the following day, some soldiers in the harbour forts needlessly resisted for another three days.[31] By this time the Germans had comprehensively wrecked the entire port; the basins and docks were filled with sunken vessels, and everywhere were different types of mines designed to avoid detection and defusing. Sattler insisted that his strongpoint be given a perfunctory shelling before he and his 400 men, who had already packed their bags, marched out.

One of the forts still holding out was Osteck to the east. This was held by Major Küppers and his men who had escaped from Montebourg. It covered a sizeable area, comprising bunkers, embrasures and observation posts protected by artillery, anti-tank guns and mortars, and was surrounded by an anti-tank ditch. There was also a minefield beyond the ditch, but luckily for the Americans many of the mines lacked detonators.

On 27 June, a combat team from the 4th US Infantry Division, supported by tanks, spent all day assaulting Osteck. The tanks were quickly
through the 'dummy' minefield, and it was not long before the American
infantry were in front and on top of the German bunkers. Küppers bravely
led a counterattack, but time was running out. His gunners were down to
just twenty smoke shells.[32]

The following morning, Major-General Barton arrived to call on the
garrison to surrender. Küppers took him to his command post, where
Barton produced a map clearly marked with the Americans' next ground
assault. One of the great advantages the Americans enjoyed at Cherbourg
was the quality of their intelligence regarding the fortifications. Küppers'
jaw dropped, as the map showed far greater detail of his defences than anything he had. Barton warned that if the Germans did not lay down their
arms, the map illustrated what would happen. He added for good measure
that the map did not show what would hit them from the air and sea.

Barton then adopted a more conciliatory approach, saying he had been
impressed by Küppers' fighting retreat from Montebourg. The major
asked if he could take a closer look at the map. 'We left nothing to chance,'
said Barton, seeing Küppers' expression. He told the major, 'Before we
started out on the invasion our Intelligence service had got hold of every
detail of the German coastal defences, complete with the measures listed
in your detailed area schedules, straight from original plans.'[33] Küppers
promptly surrendered.

General Eddy tried to prevent the men of his 9th Division from looting
all the alcohol, but they had fought a hard battle and were in no mood
to relinquish their prizes. 'Okay, everybody take twenty-four hours and
get drunk,'[34] he conceded. Eddy knew there was still more fighting to
be done, and one night off would not hurt morale. To keep the chain of
command happy, Bradley was sent half a case of champagne. It was not
until 29–30 June, D plus 23, that resistance was completely subdued in the
Contentin and the Americans were able to survey the terrible damage.[35]

Behind the scenes, Rommel indulged in a private 'I told you so'
moment. All that effort fortifying the Channel ports had clearly been a
waste of time, as the Allies had simply attacked Cherbourg from the landward side. He pointedly signalled Rundstedt saying the coastal fortresses
were 'not equal to the massed operations of the enemy air force and naval
artillery. Even the strongest fortifications [at Cherbourg] were demolished
section by section.'[36]

Rommel must have felt sick to the pit of his stomach, knowing he had been right to argue that it was imperative to defeat an Allied landing on the beaches, before they were ever given the chance to develop a bridge-head. Although Hitler's meddling had not helped, it was Collins' successful build-up that had made the loss of Cherbourg a foregone conclusion. This was ultimately facilitated by Eisenhower bravely sticking to his decision to drop his airborne divisions across the base of the Cotentin.

Rundstedt's plans of conducting swift large-scale counterattacks had come to nothing in the Cotentin. None of the divisions in the area were mobile, and, lacking Luftwaffe support, were unable to concentrate their forces. Most were quickly worn down opposing the landings and then conducting penny packet counterattacks. The 77th Division, sent to help, had not been full-strength and had been forced to flee south after losing its commander.

Over on the Channel Islands, a flicker of unease passed through General von Schmettow when he heard the news. Would the Allies be encouraged by this success to tackle his formidable defences? He personally doubted it, as there was no sound strategic reason to do so. Nonetheless, his garrison needed to remain alert to the threat. Constant enemy reconnaissance flights and the proximity of the patrolling Royal Navy seemed to indicate the Allies were content to starve them out. While he was still able, Schmettow shipped out non-essential person-nel, including remaining Todt Organisation workers and concentration camp prisoners.

While the victory was good news for the Allies, Eisenhower was not buoyed by it. 'Ike is considerably less than exuberant these days,' observed Captain Butcher. 'He didn't seem to get a kick out of the fall of Cherbourg.'[37] Based on their experiences clearing Naples in 1943, the Americans had originally estimated that it could be reopened within three days. Engineer Colonel Alvin Viney, amazed by the thoroughness of the Germans, reported, 'The demolition of the port of Cherbourg is a mas-terful job, beyond a doubt the most complete, intensive and best planned demolition in history.'[38]

Initially, the recovery effort was held up. Despite the liberation of Cherbourg, German troops continued to hold out in Fort Central and Fort de l'Ouest. Frustratingly, a German battery in the far north-west of the peninsula at Cap de la Hague, where 4,000 Germans remained holed up, for a while prevented American minesweepers from entering the harbour. After it was captured, Butcher saw evidence of preparations to launch flying bombs from the peninsula against England.

Colonel Viney's assessment was correct and Eisenhower had good reason to be despondent. During a visit to Cherbourg, Captain Butcher witnessed the extensive damage:

> In the Navy yard, I saw E-boat pens, one of which was badly damaged by our own bombs, the other partly damaged by German demolition. In the latter there was an oil barge burning. The locks to the drydocks had been demolished by an explosion. Ships had been sunk at the mouth of the basin. The building in which torpedoes and mines were stored had been blown up. Many buildings in the yard were shambles.[39]

Eisenhower may have got some secret satisfaction from the wreckage of the German Navy at Cherbourg. It was E-boats based at the port that had been responsible for badly mauling Exercise Tiger near Slapton Sands. The raiders had been a constant nuisance off the southern coasts of Devon and Dorset. Their attacks were, 'Like foxes loose in a chicken coop.'[40]

After Cherbourg was secured, Americans engineers faced a supremely challenging task in rehabilitating the port's infrastructure and dealing with all the unexploded ordnance. 'The Germans had accomplished major demolitions and had planted in the harbour and its approaches a profusion and variety of mines,' noted Eisenhower.[41] The Allies needed to use the port as soon as possible, and Ike was fulsome in his praise of the clearance efforts, adding, 'The work of the minesweepers and deep-sea divers in Cherbourg Harbour was one of the dramatic and courageous incidents of the war.'[42]

Nevertheless, it would take three weeks of minesweeping operations just to clear the outer harbour, and the first supplies could not be landed until 16 July. Even then, this was achieved by DUKWs running a ferry service from vessels anchored offshore. This was a slow and far from ideal process. All the German obstacles were not removed from the harbour until the end of September.

Where Rundstedt and Rommel were concerned, the loss of Cherbourg meant that it would be impossible for them to hold on to Normandy. Once the port facilities were functioning, nothing could stop the already quite considerable Allied build-up in France. It also put an end to plans for launching a counterattack against the junction of the British and American bridgeheads, involving six panzer divisions. The reality was that three of these had not arrived in Normandy yet, and two others were already tied up fighting the British and Canadians around Caen. This left a single panzer division available, and that would be forced to act in a fire-fighting role.

'With Cherbourg in Allied hands and the Normandy bridgehead thus consolidated almost beyond dispute,' wrote Chester Wilmot, 'it seemed to von Rundstedt and Rommel that the stage was set for the second phase of the Allied plan, as they interpreted it – the landing north of the Seine.'[43] This misapprehension was testimony to the success of Allied deception plans. Rommel, upon hearing of Schlieben's capture, had signalled Rundstedt saying intelligence indicated the Allies would now conduct 'a thrust from the area north and north-west of Caen towards Paris' and 'a large-scale landing between the Somme and Le Havre'.[44] Although wholly necessary, the three-week battle for Cherbourg had been an unwanted distraction. Only now could the real battle for Normandy commence.

18

CAEN LINCHPIN

Following the D-Day landings, Eisenhower and Rundstedt both appreciated that the strategic ground lay in the east, where Montgomery's British Second Army was fighting around the city of Caen. Just to the southeast lay open tank country that could facilitate the Allies' break out from their Normandy bridgehead. After Rommel had successfully blunted Montgomery's initial advances, rather than fight a bloody frontal battle for Caen, Monty decided he would launch his main effort to the west towards Villers-Bocage and Evrecy, then south-east towards Falaise.

Montgomery committed two veteran divisions, the 51st Highland and 7th Armoured, to these flank attacks. The 51st were to push through to the 6th Airborne Division, east of Orne, and the 7th Armoured would attack to the south-west. The 51st's operation on 11 June was stalled, and two days later their assault had petered out. The 7th Armoured Division's advance was slow, but a hole in Rommel's line between Villers-Bocage and Caumont was discovered. Greeted by joyful locals, the advance elements of 7th Armoured entered Villers-Bocage on 13 June.

Rommel's defences around Caen were considerable, consisting of the 21st and 12th SS Panzer Divisions and the Panzer Lehr Division.[1] After some difficulty, the latter came into the line to the left of the 12th SS on 9 June. It had driven 90 miles from Chartres, losing eighty-nine armoured vehicles and 130 trucks to constant Allied air attacks.

Under Lieutenant-General Fritz Bayerlein, Panzer Lehr was one of the most powerfully equipped panzer divisions in the whole of France. It was also one of the few divisions at almost full strength.[2] Panzer Lehr first went into action opposite the Canadians, but then side-stepped to attack up the road towards Bayeux. The battle of Le Mesnil-Patry resulted in them halting just 3 miles from the city on 11 June. Lehr then went onto the defensive around Tilly-sur-Seulles, and as the rest of its units arrived it blocked the British XXX Corps' advance.

This forced Montgomery to shift his efforts west of Caen to the flank of Panzer Lehr and the high ground beyond Villers-Bocage. The idea of a right hook was Major-General G.W. Erskine's, commander of the 7th Armoured Division, and it had been first discussed at XXX Corps headquarters on 10 June. It was hoped this move would break up the resistance in front of the British 50th (Northumbrian) Division, and it was also hoped to encircle the now troublesome Panzer Lehr. Sited at the head of the Seulles valley, Villers-Bocage dominated the approaches to Mont Pincon 10 miles to the south, the Odon valley and Caen in the east. The road network for the whole region stemmed from the village, making it of strategic importance to both sides. Anyone controlling Villers-Bocage controlled the roads.

When 50th Division drove against Panzer Lehr, 7th Armoured Division swung to the west, driving three-quarters of a circle into the American sector, then south through the gap in the German line and eastwards behind Lehr at Villers-Bocage. Notably, the arrival of 7th Armoured Division had been delayed by bad weather. Had all its tanks and supporting infantry arrived on time, the Villers-Bocage right hook might have gone completely differently.

Spearheading the attack was 22nd Armoured Brigade, led by the 4th County of London Yeomanry (the Sharpshooters) armoured regiment, 1st and 5th Battalions Royal Tank Regiment (RTR) and half-tracked infantry of the 1st Battalion the Rifle Brigade, under Brigadier Robert 'Loony'[3] Hinde (a nickname gained whilst in North Africa). They were supported by the 8th King's Royal Irish Hussars and the 11th Hussars, followed by the Queen's Royal Regiment of 131st Infantry Brigade. Moving through the gap west of Aure on the evening of 12 June, the leading elements reached the Caumont-Villers-Bocage road 5 miles west of the town. Hinde only had 3 hours of daylight left, so rather than give the game away he halted for the night.

At 0800 hours on 13 June, a British force, spearheaded by the 4th County of London Yeomanry and A Company, 1st Battalion the Rifle Brigade, occupied the sleepy Normandy village of Villers-Bocage with the minimum of fuss. Just two surprised German soldiers sped off in a Volkswagen jeep. The British were about to be in for a rude awakening.

On the flanks, the supporting 8th and 11th Hussars were slowed up by enemy troop movements. Colin Thomson, an armoured car driver-operator with the 11th, recalled:

> My troop penetrated ... as far as Cahagnes where ... we saw a large concentration of enemy armour moving towards Villers-Bocage. Round the corner of a narrow lane came a German 8-wheel armoured car ... Our lead car gunner let go. The Jerry vehicle went up in a cloud of smoke. We heard another vehicle ... 'Please God it's not a Tiger' someone said. It turned out to be a huge self-propelled gun which we hit with everything we had, destroying it and its crew.[4]

However, it was not long before Tiger tanks were on a bloody rampage.

At about 0900 hours, Regimental Headquarters (RHQ) of the Yeomanry dismounted. Hinde ordered their commander, Lieutenant-Colonel Lord Cranley,[5] to reconnoitre the wooded road N175 to Caen and take hill Point 213 to the north-east, where the national highway led straight to German-occupied Caen. Cranley was not happy about this, especially as some German armoured cars had already been observed. They were in fact a weak scouting element from Panzer Lehr's reconnaissance battalion, and ironically the previous day had been the only unit defending the gap.

His request for more time to assess the situation was refused by Major Lever, Hinde's brigade major. So, as ordered, Cranley despatched A Squadron of the Sharpshooters to seize Point 213 less than a mile to the north-east, while A Company of the Rifle Brigade parked on the highway. This column consisted of British-built Cromwell tanks, American-supplied Honey light tanks, two degunned Observation Post tanks, Bren Gun Carriers and half-tracks.

Cranley decided to inspect these new positions for himself, and hopping into his scout car he drove off, leaving the four tanks of the RHQ in town. What he did not know was that the 2nd Panzer Division had been alerted to move from Amiens to Normandy to establish blocking positions in this sector, and that a Tiger tank battalion from the I SS Panzer Corps reserve under the leading panzer ace Lieutenant Michael Wittmann had occupied Point 213.[6] The British were outclassed from the start. The Cromwell, which had replaced 7th Armoured Division's Sherman tanks when they left Italy, was too lightly armoured and armed. In stark contrast,

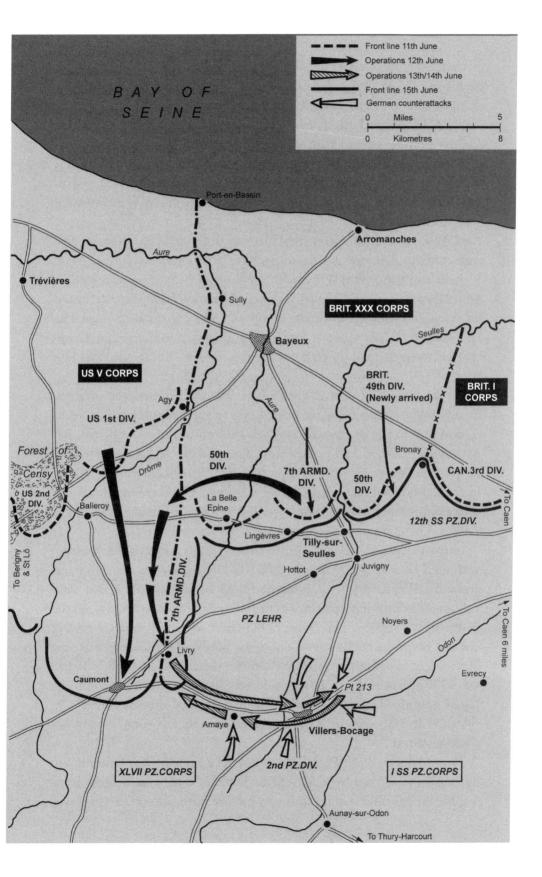

BAY OF SEINE

Front line 11th June
Operations 12th June
Operations 13th/14th June
Front line 15th June
German counterattacks

0   Miles   5
0   Kilometres   8

Port-en-Bassin

Arromanches

Trévières

Aure

Sully

BRIT. XXX CORPS

Bayeux

US V CORPS

BRIT. 49th DIV. (Newly arrived)

Seulles

BRIT. I CORPS

Agy

US 1st DIV.

Aure

Forest of Cerisy
US 2nd DIV.

Drôme

50th DIV.

7th ARMD. DIV.

Bronay

CAN.3rd DIV.

Balleroy

La Belle Epine

50th DIV.

12th SS PZ.DIV.

To Caen

To Bérigny & St Lô

Lingèvres

Tilly-sur-Seulles

7th ARMD.DIV.

Hottot

Juvigny

PZ LEHR

Noyers

Odon

To Caen 6 miles

Livry

Evrecy

Caumont

Pt 213

Amaye

Villers-Bocage

XLVII PZ.CORPS

2nd PZ.DIV.

I SS PZ.CORPS

Aunay-sur-Odon

To Thury-Harcourt

the German Tiger tank could expect to remain unharmed by the majority of Allied tanks except at point-blank range.

The 101st Heavy Tank Battalion was part of I SS Panzer Corps, which consisted of the 1st and 12th SS Panzer Divisions. The battalion, commanded by Lieutenant-Colonel von Westernhagen, had a theoretical strength of forty-five Tigers, but in fact numbered thirty-seven, less than half of which were available at Villers-Bocage. By 1 July, only eleven were fully serviceable.

At the time of the invasion, the 101st was stationed in the Beauvais area with corps headquarters at Septeuil, west of Paris. It reached Normandy on 12 June, and Lieutenant Wittman's 2nd Company found welcome cover from Allied air attack in a small wood north-east of Villers-Bocage, minus four tanks left with the workshop company under Lieutenant Stamm. The 1st Company, under Captain Mobius, was deployed to their right. Corps HQ had moved to Baron-sur-Odon between Villers-Bocage and Caen on 9 June.

On the 13th, the Germans planned to carry out maintenance, until the British column outside Villers-Bocage was spotted. Wittmann decided to reconnoitre to the north-west to see if the rumour that the British 7th Armoured Division had pushed into the left flank of Panzer Lehr was, in fact, true. With about five Tigers and one Panzer Lehr Panzer Mk IV, he fanned out and advanced on Villers-Bocage. Upon seeing the British armoured column moving east towards Point 213, Wittmann realised the vital road junction must be secured at once.

In the meantime, the British had halted on the hill past the junction with the Tilly road. At 0905 hours, the lead elements of the Sharpshooters and units of A Company had reached the base of Point 213. The main column of twenty-five vehicles stopped several hundred yards away on the hedge-lined highway, while most of the tanks, including four Cromwells and one Sherman Firefly, spread out to the north, where Cranley was now checking on them. Wittmann's gunlayer, Sergeant Balthasar Woll, who had served Wittmann well in Russia, and whose own tank was now under repair, grumbled, 'They're acting as if they've won the war already.' To which Wittmann replied, 'We're going to prove them wrong.'[7] It was not a hollow threat.

Two or three of the Tigers drove parallel to the British column, but Wittmann, to the north, decided to circle round and attack without waiting for the others. Heading from the east, he rammed aside a Cromwell blocking his way and drove into the town's high street, rue Clemenceau. In the town square, the RHQ tank crews had dismounted and were alarmed by the sight of a lumbering Tiger tank. Any 6-pdr anti-tank guns that had been deployed were useless, their shells bouncing off the Tiger's armour.

First, Cranley's tank was knocked out. Regimental second-in-command Major Carr fired point-blank at the Tiger, to no effect. Wittmann halted, took aim, and Carr's Cromwell exploded in flames, followed by the Regimental Sergeant-Major's tank. The fourth tank, under Captain Pat Dyas, reversed desperately out of the way into a garden, but Dyas and his gunner were outside their vehicle and could only watch helplessly as the Tiger drove by, presenting its thinner side armour.

Wittmann descended the slope towards the river valley of the Seulles, past some bombed-out houses. At the road junction he bumped into Major Aird's B Squadron parked on the Caumont road. Sergeant Stan Lockwood, commanding a Sherman Firefly, heard all the firing and was confronted by a scout car and its frantically waving driver. Lockwood drove round a corner to find Wittmann's Tiger 200 yards away, firing down a side street. The Firefly quickly poured four 17-pdr rounds into the Tiger, which began to burn, but its turret rotated and a shell brought half a building down on Lockwood's tank. When Lockwood emerged, the Tiger had vanished.

The battered and bruised Tiger beat a hasty retreat back up the hill, running into Dyas' Cromwell. Wittmann and his crew sustained two more hits before the Cromwell was brewed up and two of its crew killed. Dyas, with the help of a French girl, escaped to reach one of B Squadron's tanks. Lying to the left of and parallel to the highway was a narrow track, clanking up which was Wittmann's first victim, a half-track at the base of the column. This was followed by an unsuspecting Honey tank. Further up the road, a 6-pdr crew hurriedly swung their gun round, but a well-placed shell hit the Bren Carrier loaded with ammunition in front of it.

Wittmann's rampaging Tiger then proceeded to brew up the rest of the startled column, knocking out a row of Bren Carriers and half-tracks as armour-piercing shells continued to bounce off his impervious armour. British soldiers scattered in all directions, many taking shelter in the ditch behind the column. A tank tried to block Wittmann's path on the track, so he drove onto the road, crushing everything in his way.

Hinde, who had arrived to check on progress, managed to extricate his scout car and sped back to town to try to organise its defences. Wittmann withdrew to the woods to the south-east. In short succession he had reduced Cranley's advance to a shambles, destroying twenty-five vehicles single-handedly.

Frantically, Dyas made contact with Major Aird and radioed Cranley to inform him of what had happened. Cranley, in his last radio message, replied that he was also under attack from German Tiger tanks and needed help. The 8th Hussars, the divisional reconnaissance regiment, to the north advanced to help, but were engaged by Wittmann's four Tigers and suffered heavy losses. 'By the time we reached the outskirts reports spoke of extremely hard fighting there,' Colin Thomson of the 11th Hussars observed. 'We began to work up north and north-west and also to the south where, at Tracy-Bocage, the troops came under fire from 88mms.'[8]

In the early afternoon, a triumphant Wittmann, rearmed and refuelled, returned to join the rest of his forces – four Tigers, a Mark IV and possibly three other tanks, with infantry support – attacking the remnants of A Squadron and A Company trapped around Point 213. On the edge of the hill, at least two Cromwells and one Firefly were knocked out, blocking the road, while not far away in the woods on the crown of the hill, two more Cromwells were brewed-up.

The battle for Point 213 was a one-sided affair, and with the Germans now pressing around Villers-Bocage, attempts to reinforce Cranley failed. Major Aird despatched three Cromwells and a Firefly under Lieutenant Bill Cotton to try to make contact. They managed to cross the town, but were unable to get over the railway embankment and turned back to take up positions in the square.

The survivors of A Squadron were quickly overrun by Wittmann's battlegroup. Cranley and many of his men were captured, with only one making it back to town. The members of the Rifle Brigade were also mopped up. The Sharpshooters lost four killed, five wounded and seventy-six missing, while at least twenty Cromwells, four Fireflys, three Honeys, three scout cars and a half-track were destroyed. A Company lost eighty men, including three officers, and only about thirty infantry managed to escape. By late afternoon, both units had ceased to exist. This left only B Squadron precariously holding onto Villers-Bocage.

Supported by units of the 2nd Panzer Division, Wittmann now turned his attention back on Villers-Bocage. This time the British were not going to be caught out; the Sharpshooters would wreak revenge on him for the disaster he had inflicted on them. B Squadron, with four Cromwells and a Firefly, took up defensive positions around the main square, with a Queen's Regiment 6-pdr guarding the main street from a side alley. It was hoped the latter would catch the Tiger's side armour.

Wittmann, overplaying his hand, noisily re-entered Villers-Bocage, this time in strength with two Tigers (possibly including Mobius) and a Panzer IV. Rounding the bend into the high street, he drove straight into the prepared ambush. 'When the Tigers were about 1,000 yards away and were broadside to us I told 3 Troop and my gunner to fire,' recalled Lieutenant Cotton. 'The Firefly did the damage, but the 75s [75mm shells of the Cromwells] helped and must have taken a track off one which started to circle out of control.'[9]

Wittmann's tank was hit by the anti-tank gun, the following Tiger by Sergeant Bobby Bramall's Firefly, Corporal Horne's Cromwell missed and the Panzer IV had driven almost past the second Tiger when Horne drove out behind the German and blasted him. It seems a third Tiger entered town, but was also caught by B Squadron a few dozen yards from the main street at the crossroads of rue Jeanne Bacon and rue Emile Samson.

Lieutenant Cotton noted that the engagement was not all one-way, recalling 'They shot back at us, knocked the Firefly out, as its commander was hit in the head. However, at the end of a very few minutes there were three "killed" Tigers.'[10] The German crews escaped because too few British infantry remained. Later, Lieutenant Cotton, armed with an umbrella alongside Sergeant Bramall carrying blankets and petrol, walked in the pouring rain to the German tanks and set fire to them to prevent recovery.

The ordeal for the defenders was not yet over. Lieutenant-Colonel Kurt Kauffman, Operations Officer for Panzer Lehr, assembled three field guns, two 88mm anti-tank guns and some rear echleon troops, which he led in a successful attack against Villers-Bocage, while panzergrenadiers of the 2nd Panzer Division now began pushing up from the south. By 1600 hours the German attacks had been beaten off, with Bayerlein reporting the loss of six precious Tigers and several Panzer IVs.

This series of brutal engagements fought throughout 13 June rendered it impossible for Montgomery to hold onto Villers-Bocage. Brigadier Hinde's men were split in two, with one group at Villers-Bocage and another at Tracy-Bocage several miles west, while the 7th Armoured was strung out along the road from Villers-Bocage to Livry. Alarmingly, 7th Armoured's intelligence estimated that up to forty Tigers from 2nd Panzer were in the area, with which it was feared the Germans would cut the road between Villers-Bocage and Caumont, trapping B Squadron.

This estimate was inaccurate: 2nd Panzer had no Tigers, and its panzers did not begin to arrive from Paris until 18 June. Nor did the 12th SS Panzer Division have any Tiger tanks. It is doubtful that the 101st Battalion had any more than a handful in the Villers-Bocage area on 13 June.

Bayerlein, likewise, had no spare tanks – his division was being held down frontally by 50th Division – and Kauffman's ad hoc forces showed what Panzer Lehr had in the way of reserves.[11] Therefore, the 7th Armoured Division, even at this stage, was still a considerable threat to the German flank. Even so, Erskine ordered Hinde to pull back at nightfall and hold Tracy-Bocage, concentrating on Hill 174.

At about 1700 hours, while the Germans were regrouping, the British withdrew 2 miles to the west, having lost twenty-five tanks and twenty-eight armoured fighting vehicles. B Squadron was ordered to time its withdrawal to coincide with a covering barrage. Lockwood had driven his Firefly across the town square when it stalled. 'I can't start the bloody thing!' yelled the driver desperately. Disaster was averted as Sergeant Bill Moore in the following tank jumped down under small-arms fire and attached a cable to Lockwood's tank, towing him out just before the bombardment commenced. 'We felt bad about getting out, it made it seem as if it had been such a waste of time,' concluded Lockwood.[12]

The following day, XXX Corps launched a series of attacks using 50th Division against Tilly and Panzer Lehr's 901st Panzergrenadier Regiment, in the hope of forcing Lehr back to enable 7th Armoured Division to continue its own ill-fated offensive. Lieutenant-General G.C. Bucknall, Commander of XXX Corps, failed to ask Second Army for direct infantry support for 7th Armoured's beleaguered tanks. In consequence, when Bucknall was visiting 7th Armoured's tactical headquarters, he had both his escort tanks knocked out by lurking Tigers. Upon returning to his own headquarters, he concluded that Erskine's communications were in danger of being severed.

Afterwards, an American artillery 'serenade' broke up an attack by 2nd Panzer, knocking out eleven tanks, but the British tanks were still in serious danger of being cut off. The 2nd Panzer's divisional reconnaissance group, upon entering Villers-Bocage found an almost intact Sherman; its turret was removed and the vehicle was pressed into service as a much-needed recovery vehicle.

The 50th Division's failure to get forward, the arrival of 2nd Panzer, which fanned out north-west of Caumont, north of Livry and north-east of Villers-Bocage, plus the two-day delay in the British build-up, meant the 7th Armoured was in danger of being crushed. The division formed a defensive box about 1,000 yards by 700 yards, which was attacked on three sides by enemy armoured forces on 14 June. 'The 3rd and 5th Royal Horse Artillery were firing over open sights into the woods 300 yards away,' Colin Thomson recalled. 'The result was unbelievable carnage. This battle lasted until 10.30pm when Jerry decided to retire and presumably regroup.'[13]

That evening, Brigadier Hinde arrived with their orders to withdraw and provided a little light relief. Suddenly, in mid-instruction, he stared at the ground and asked, 'Anybody got a matchbox?' When Lieutenant-Colonel Carver pointed out more pressing matters, Hinde snapped, 'Don't be such a bloody fool, Mike! You can fight a battle everyday of your life, but you might not see a caterpillar like this in fifteen years!'[14] Under cover of darkness and artillery fire, the mauled brigade withdrew east of Caumont, while the RAF flattened Villers-Bocage.

The British withdrawal conceded the battle to the Germans by default and the village remained in German hands until August. The official account of the engagement rather misleadingly described the results as 'disappointing'. This led to the impression that the fighting at Villers-Bocage was of little consequence. Subsequently, this conclusion was criticised for placing 'a facile gloss over the significance of the setback to British aspirations'.[15]

Rommel, on the other hand, could not understand why Montgomery had not exploited the gap and was relieved when it was plugged. It had presented the closest thing to an open flank prior to the breakout by the Americans, but the British lost their one great opportunity, leaving the bloody slogging match with the panzers to continue.

Both XXX Corps and 7th Armoured Division failed miserably, while the Germans reacted well. The gap between the British tanks and supporting infantry had been too great, allowing the German infantry to hold up the armour. The Sharpshooters were over-confident, with poor tank-infantry cooperation and inadequate dispersion. The Tiger was a vastly superior tank to the light Cromwell, but this was no excuse for the shambles that Wittmann inflicted at Villers-Bocage.

Corps Commander Lieutenant-General G.C. Bucknall was blamed for not being flexible enough, nor committing infantry reserves to help

7th Armoured exploit its position. The failure to act while the tanks were exposed at Tracy-Bocage was also blamed on Bucknall. The consensus was that Villers-Bocage should have been held onto. General Dempsey, commanding the British Second Army, stated:

> This attack by 7th Armoured Division should have succeeded. My feeling that Bucknall and Erskine would have to go started with this failure. Early on the morning of the 12 June I went down to see Erskine – gave him his orders and told him to get moving ... If he had carried out my orders he would not have been kicked out of Villers-Bocage. But by this time 7th Armoured Division was living off its reputation and the whole handling of the battle was a disgrace.[16]

This is perhaps a little harsh. If Cranley had been allowed to be more cautious, Wittmann would not have taken 22nd Brigade so completely by surprise. In total, the brigade lost 225 men, twenty-seven tanks, fourteen half-tracks, fourteen Bren Carriers and a number of anti-tank guns.[17]

The only consolation for the British was that by 18–19 June, Panzer Lehr had lost about 100 of its 260 tanks in the fighting in the Villers-Bocage area. Bayerlein claimed this battle had weakened his division so much it was incapable of launching an armoured thrust towards the sea.[18] Wittmann's prompt action in thwarting Montgomery's plans enabled Villers-Bocage to be retaken later in the day by the Panzer Lehr kampfgruppe and units of 2nd Panzer, thus plugging the gap. A few days later he was promoted to captain.

During an attack near Cintheaux, Wittmann's luck finally ran out on 8 August. He had succeeded in destroying two Sherman tanks and immobilised a third, but was overwhelmed by five others who finished him off before he could escape. At the time of his death, Wittmann was credited with 138 armoured fighting vehicles, most of them tanks, and 132 anti-tank guns, which he had chalked up in under two years.[19] His greatest victory has to be inflicting the debacle of Villers-Bocage on the British. Through a mixture of luck and courage, Wittmann largely single-handedly halted a British armoured thrust that could have encircled Panzer Lehr or even rolled up the entire German corps front. If this had happened, the German collapse in Normandy could have been much swifter and perhaps even more catastrophic.

Wittmann's successful defensive action forced Montgomery to launch two more costly and controversial enveloping attacks around Caen. These consisted of Operation Epsom to the west on 25 June and Goodwood to the east on 18 July. In between these two, he launched Operation Charnwood, a frontal assault on 8 July, losing 3,500 casualties and eighty tanks. During Epsom, VIII Corps secured a bridge near Baron, but in the face of tough resistance from elements of the three SS panzer divisions, only managed to create a bridgehead 2½ miles wide and 1 mile deep. Goodwood made good initial progress until it ran into Rommel's in-depth positions held by infantry and armour, including Tiger tanks and elements of the two SS panzer divisions. The offensive cost 6,000 British casualties and 400 tanks, and was called off by 20 July.

At the same time the Canadians finally drove the Germans from Caen's southern suburbs. They pushed through the ruined city and penetrated the defences to the west, while Montgomery fought to linkup with them. However, as Rommel hoped his defences on the high ground to the southeast of the city successfully held the Allies. For Montgomery there was no dramatic breakthrough, just criticism of his mounting losses. Although he missed the battle, having been wounded, Rommel outfoxed his old adversary. In this instance his meticulous preparations proved far superior to Montgomery's. It would be the last time he could exert influence on German tactics and strategy in Normandy.

In the meantime, the Allied air commanders were bitterly disappointed that the city had not been taken much sooner. Tedder and Leigh-Mallory held Montgomery responsible. Quite unreasonably they had expected that Caen's airfields would be secured very shortly after the landings. Despite this, Montgomery, de Guingand and Belchem all steadfastly refused to give such guarantees. It did them no good and Caen was seen unfairly as an operational failure. The city's defence proved to be Rommel's finest moment in Normandy. Cherbourg and Caen had been taken but still there was deadlock.

19

COBRA STRIKES

D-Day and the battle for Normandy were all about timing. Following the capture of Cherbourg, General Bradley's next mission was to swing his forces south. The key to a successful outflanking manoeuvre would be getting over the River Sée at Avranches and the Sélune at Pontaubault. Rather optimistically, Montgomery wanted to schedule the US First Army's break out, codenamed Operation Cobra, for 3 July. 'We had hoped originally,' said Monty, 'to launch the operation from the line St Lô–Coutances.'[1] In the meantime, Dempsey's British Second Army would maintain its pressure on Caen. Both Bradley and Montgomery appreciated that speed was of the essence because the Germans only had limited armour facing the Americans, while eight panzer divisions were holding the British at bay.

Hitler would not continue to believe that an Allied assault led by General Patton in the Pas de Calais was possible indefinitely.[2] This deception would soon crumble once Patton arrived in Normandy to take charge of the US Third Army in early August.[3] The worry was that if Hitler permitted the redeployment of his infantry divisions from north of the Seine, this would free up Rommel's armoured divisions for a thrust to the coast.

Montgomery then wanted Lieutenant-General Hodges' US First Army to reach Alençon and Le Mans, with a subsidiary right hook to Vannes to cut off Brittany. Looking ahead, Monty proposed dropping an airborne division into the Chatres gap, between the Loire and Seine, which would trap the German Seventh Army. However, there was no way that Bradley could be ready in time, as he would first have to secure a favourable start line. This heralded the bitter battle of the hedgerows in the bocage. Thanks to the latter and the flooded marshy country courtesy of the Carentan estuary, it made advancing southward to the Périers-St Lô line very slow work.

To the west, Major-General Middleton's US VIII Corps struck la Haye-du-Puits on 3 July, but it took almost a week to secure the town. In the meantime, Major-General Collins' US VII Corps attacked south-west of Carentan, only to be counterattacked by the 2nd SS Panzer Division, which had successfully redeployed from the British sector. Montgomery was alarmed by this development, and was also concerned that Rommel might strike at the junction of Bradley and Dempsey's armies.

'If we could break into Coutances from the west coast road,' observed Bradley, 'the enemy would be forced to withdraw across the rest of the Cotentin neck for fear of being cut off by a pincer attack from St Lô.'[4]

Through the first half of July, the Americans continued to push south against determined German resistance, while the British attacked to the north and either side of Caen. Montgomery was not terribly supportive of American efforts, noting that, 'Bradley's first attempt at the break-out, made towards Coutances in early July, had failed.'[5]

Bradley's forces had reached a line running west to east from Lessay through Périers to St Lô by 17 July.[6] The eight-day battle to take St Lô cost the US 29th Infantry Division 3,000 casualties, while the 35th Division lost 2,000.[7] The town had been scheduled to be liberated on 11 June, but it was not taken until 18 July. Even then, the Germans were still shelling St Lô and still controlled the road from Lessay to Périers. In all, the Americans had fought their way some 7 miles west of Vire and 4 miles to the east.

Bradley informed Montgomery that he would not be ready to conduct Cobra until 20 July as he needed artillery ammunition and other supplies. The bloodletting had been such that Bradley also desperately needed considerable reinforcements. He was very grateful for Monty's patience. 'During these operations in the lodgement where Montgomery bossed the US First Army as part of his Army Group,' said Bradley, 'he exercised his Allied authority with wisdom, forbearance and restraint.'[8]

To keep Rommel occupied, Monty launched Operation Goodwood. This had the desired effect. 'On 15 July, the German forces facing the American west wing totalled 190 tanks and 85 infantry battalions,' noted Colonel Belchem, 'On the British-Canadian front, there were massed 645 tanks and 92 infantry battalions.'[9] In total, Bradley intended to throw six US divisions, some 70,000 men, supported by over 600 tanks, forty-three battalions of artillery and 3,000 aircraft at the heart of the German defences in Normandy.[10]

At this crucial stage, Rommel's influence on the fighting was lost after he was caught on the open road by fighter-bombers and hospitalised. In the event, Bradley did not commence Operation Cobra until 25 July. It was going to start the day before, but was cancelled at the last minute due to bad weather. Bradley and Leigh-Mallory had given Cobra the go-ahead on the assumption the weather would clear up by the time the bombers arrived over their targets – they were wrong. Unfortunately, some of the bomber attacks still went ahead on the 24th, resulting in American casualties.[11]

The plan was that in the west, VIII Corps would attack south from Lessay to take Avranches. Collins' VII Corps would strike south-west to take Coutances and south-east to Mortain. On Collins' left, the XIX Corps, backed by V Corps, was to strike toward Vire. The break-out assault was preceded at 0940 hours first by fighter-bombers and then bombers who mercilessly pounded German defensive positions over a 4-mile wide and half-a-mile deep rectangle. In order to stop the Americans, the Germans were tied to the roads, which made them sitting ducks. General Bradley was at Collins' command post to watch the bombers do their work.

Both American heavy and medium bombers rained down 4,700 tons of bombs. The blasts and resulting shockwaves reverberated for miles. Great clouds of dust rose skyward and the landscape was left covered in pock marks. Captain Stewart Reid was one of the bomber pilots flying a B-24 Liberator committed to Cobra. He and his ten-man crew were with the 493rd Bomber Group. He was not happy to find cloud over the target area, which meant dropping 4,000ft to an altitude of 12,000ft. Below them stretched the patchwork quilt of fields created by Normandy's hedgerows. Reid's bombardier, Charles W. McArthur, had to recalculate the bombing data before releasing their 2-ton bomb load.

Reid was relieved that there was little flak and no sign of the Luftwaffe. The Germans were short of anti-aircraft ammunition and had fired off most of what they had the previous day. American artillery had also targeted German anti-aircraft artillery positions. Nonetheless, five bombers were shot down and fifty-nine damaged.[12] Seeing the bombs go, McArthur remarked that 'it was a sight one does not forget'.[13]

Unfortunately, some of the bombs fell short again, inflicting severe casualties on three of the spearhead divisions.[14] Bradley had been obliged to compromise with the air commanders over the safe distance for the ground forces to be from the bombers. He wanted the troops withdrawn only 800 yards; the air commanders wanted nearly 3 miles. They then wanted 3,000 yards, and compromised at 1,200 yards. Eisenhower, who had come forward to watch the day's proceedings, was furious, stating, 'I don't believe they [the bombers] can be used in support of ground troops. I gave them the green light on this show, but this is the last one.'[15]

Some American officers were philosophical about their losses to friendly fire. 'I believe every man in the company will agree that if we have such an attack again they would want the bombing just where it was, right to our lines,' said Lieutenant Gude of the US 4th Infantry Division. 'We would rather take the ones that fall on us to get the effect on the Germans in front of us.'[16]

The raids certainly had the desired result on the German troops caught in the carpet bombing, who were either killed, wounded or left dazed and confused. 'My flak had hardly opened its mouth, when the batteries received direct hits which knocked out half the guns and silenced the rest,' recalled General Bayerlein, commander of the Panzer Lehr Division. Within an hour, he had lost communication with his men and, he said, 'All my forward tanks were knocked out.'[17]

The previous day, Bayerlein's division had weathered the air attacks quite well, suffering about 350 casualties and losing just ten armoured vehicles.[18] But on 25 July, of the 3,600 men under his command he lost 1,000 to the bombing and as many wounded.[19] The following day, Bayerlein only had fourteen tanks left and, although he was promised reinforcements, only five tanks arrived.

When General Collins' VII Corps advanced at 1100 hours, fighter-bombers and medium bombers cut a path for them. Tough resistance was met to the west, but the central column made good progress. Within two days the Germans were giving ground, and to the east the Canadians attacked again towards the main Caen–Falaise road. The latter were met by elements of four panzer divisions. The Allied front line now pivoted on Caumont.

American troops had successfully torn an irreparable hole in the German front line. Granville on the coast was taken by the VIII Corps by 31 July, and it was in Avranches at the beginning of August. It was then that General Patton's US Third Army Headquarters became operational, as did Bradley's US Twelfth Army Group, with Patton initially assuming control of just VIII Corps. The army group command elevated Bradley to the same status as Montgomery – thereby technically ending Monty's dominace.

Bradley had first got an inkling of his promotion earlier in the year, not from Eisenhower but indirectly via the British press. On 18 January, he had been hurrying from the Dorchester Hotel in London to get breakfast when he stopped to pick up a copy of the *Daily Express*. 'This won't be news to you, sir,' said the reception clerk with a smile, pointing at a head-line announcing that Eisenhower had chosen Bradley as America's answer to Montgomery.[20] Bradley had been taken aback, as this was the first he heard of it. It seemed that the newspaper had got ahead of itself. The previous day, Eisenhower had said Bradley would be the senior American commander on the ground, but this was not the same as being an army group commander. At the time, Bradley assumed Ike was just referring to the US First Army.

Patton suspected that Monty had been in no hurry to see his army operational, 'as he fears I will steal the show'.[21] He was understandably in high spirits. Patton and Colonel Paul Harkins, his deputy chief of staff, 'decided to celebrate the birthday of the Third Army with a drink. The only thing we could find was a bottle of alleged brandy ... we tried to drink this, but gagged.'[22]

While Patton was to spearhead the American breakout, his other mission was to clear the Germans from Brittainy. This was no easy task, and was to needlessly tie up two American armoured divisions. The Germans had extensively fortified the key ports, and in light of the destruction inflicted on Cherbourg, it seemed unlikely they could be wrestled from German control without serious damage. St Malo was protected by a series of coastal forts, and the old citadel had been reinforced with tons of concrete. Likewise, Brest was defended by coastal batteries, including one with four 280mm naval guns. While Patton may have liked the idea of his tanks hurtling westward, he had no desire to become bogged down in siege warfare.

Eisenhower knew from his dealings with Patton in North Africa that the man was an emotional rollercoaster, who sometimes suffered from quite terrible impulse control issues. 'Patton always lived at one extreme or another of the emotional spectrum,' wrote Ike. 'He was either at the top of his form, laughing and full of enthusiasm, or filled with remorse and despondency.'[23] However, Patton, bipolar or not, was a man who got a job done and, importantly, at speed.

   Characteristically, Patton did not hang about. He had no intention of lingering in the Avranches area, which could become a choke point in the face of determined German counterattacks. He ordered both the VIII and XV Corps to pass through the town as quickly as they could. 'It was only made possible by extremely effective use of veteran staff officers,' recalled Patton, 'and by the active part taken in it by corps and division command-ers who, on occasion, personally directed the traffic.'[24] So determined was he to keep things going that even Patton had a go at this task.

   Although Patton had a reputation for being an impetuous, if not reck-less commander, he always ensured that his decisions were backed by the latest information. Initially, Patton was not a fan of Ultra-derived intel-ligence, but that soon changed. Group Captain Frederick Winterbotham, who formed the special liaison units that shared Bletchley Park's Enigma decrypts with field headquarters, was largely responsible for this. 'Patton studied every Ultra signal and, knowing where every enemy soldier was in his path, would tread his way round or through them and find an undefended spot,' said Winterbotham.[25] Patton 'never failed to use every opportunity that Ultra gave him to bust open the enemy',[26] added the group captain approvingly.

   Field Marshal von Kluge, who had replaced von Rundstedt and also took over command of Army Group B after Rommel's wounding, tried to remain calm as information filtered through, but the situation was not encouraging. Looking at his situation maps, he noted that it was vital that Avranches and Pontaubault were secured if the Americans were to be stopped. Colonel Bacherer's jaw dropped when his chief of operations read out a signal from CinC West. 'Avranches is to be taken and held at all costs,' ordered Kluge. 'It is the keystone of our defence. On it hinges the decision in the west.' Bacherer and his battered German 77th Infantry Division had suffered heavy losses during July, having originally been north of Countances. He now had just over 1,000 men recuperating to the west of Pontaubault.[27] This was hardly adequate for what Kluge wanted.

   Nonetheless, Bacherer rounded up an improvised battle group that was supplemented by elements of the 5th Parachute Division, fourteen self-propelled guns and any stragglers he could lay his hands on. Thanks to low cloud and drizzle, Bacherer's force managed to fight its way into Avranches. However, when the weather cleared the Allied fighter-bombers appeared, all his armoured fighting vehicles were destroyed and his men were driven out by American tanks. Turning back toward Pontaubault, Bacherer ordered, 'Demolition party to blow up the Sélune bridge.'[28] The first group came under fire and the second one ran into an ambush. On the afternoon of 1 August, Major-General John 'Tiger Jack' Wood[29] drove his US 4th Armored Division over the still intact Sélune bridge at Pontaubault. His spearhead dashed forward over 30km almost to Rennes, which was held by around 2,000 Germans.[30]

'The bottleneck of the single road from Avranches to Pontaubault became a sheep-race,' reported Chester Wilmot. 'At the mouth senior officers herded units through in any order.'[31] Upon witnessing a snarl-up at Avranches, Patton leapt from his jeep and spent an hour-and-a-half sorting it out himself. 'Believe me,' said Colonel Charles Codman, Patton's long-suffering staff officer, 'those trucks got going fast and the amazed expressions on the faces of their drivers as recognition dawned were something.'[32]

Within 72 hours, Patton squeezed seven divisions – numbering some 100,000 men and 15,000 vehicles – through the bottleneck. The Luftwaffe tried to destroy the bridge at Pontaubault from 3–7 August.[33] They were met by Allied fighters and anti-aircraft guns which were protecting Patton's corridor. One bomb caused minor damage, but the rest completely missed. At Dinan, south of St Malo, the remains of Bacherer's command held up Patton's 6th Armored Division before retreating to the port. Colonel Andreas von Auloch, who was a veteran of Stalingrad, and his garrison made it clear they would not give up without a fight.

Despite his many faults, Patton was fearless. 'We have been bombed, strafed, mortared, and shelled,' said Colonel Codman. 'The General thrives on it.'[34] The previous day, heading back to his headquarters and passing the burnt and smashed remains of a German convoy, Patton had asked, 'Just look at that, Codman. Could anything be more magnificent?'[35] Patton was in his element.

War correspondent James Wellard, who was accompanying Patton's army, was caught up in the euphoria of the breakthrough. 'Those of us who were not in the fighting vanguard,' he noted, 'were carried along on a tide of emotion and champagne.' For a few days it was not entirely clear what was happening, but that was soon to change. 'The German defeat was becoming a rout, and the rout a collapse,' said Wellard. 'General Patton had effected the greatest movement of armour in history.'[36]

British Centaur IV bunker-busting tank. These were used during D-Day on 6 June 1944 by the Royal Marines Armoured Support Group on Gold, Juno and Sword beaches alongside the 'Funnies'. (Author's Collection)

Exhausted but defiant-looking commandos after the Dieppe raid in 1942. Major Pat Porteous described it as 'an absolute disaster'. The failure of Operation Jubilee convinced the Allies that when they finally opened the Second Front it would have to be across open beaches supported by artificial harbours. (National Army Museum)

Hitler's Atlantic Wall used millions of tons of concrete to build a defensive network stretching all the way from Norway to Spain. 'All this expenditure and effort was sheer waste,' said Albert Speer, the Nazi armaments minister. (US National Archives)

Many of Hitler's bunkers and emplacements were impervious to bomber and naval attack. The walls of this concrete gun emplacement behind Utah Beach at St-Marcouf were over 12ft thick. (US Coast Guard)

Field Marshal Erwin Rommel was drafted in to improve the Atlantic Wall in late 1943. Thanks to his drive and energy, he was dubbed 'a fanatic' by one of his subordinates. He became obsessed with beach obstacles and minefields. (Via Author)

One of the numerous methods the Germans devised to counter enemy landing craft was placing Teller anti-tank mines on the top of wooden posts driven in below the high tide line. (US National Archives)

Once General Montgomery was appointed ground forces commander, his first move was to modify Operation Overlord. He warned, 'The initial landing is on too narrow a front.' (Author's Collection)

Major-General Hobart's British 79th Armoured Division was responsible for specialised armour developed to support D-Day. These were affectionately dubbed the 'Funnies' and included the Armoured Vehicle Royal Engineer based on the Churchill tank. Eisenhower called them 'novel mechanical contrivances'. (Via Author)

The American Sherman was used not only as the basis for a swimming tank, known as the Duplex Drive, but also the Crab flail. 'It is doubtful if the assault force could have firmly established themselves,' said Eisenhower, 'without the assistance of these weapons.' (Author's Collection)

Churchill decided the Allies needed piers that 'float up and down with the tide'. While the Germans were busy pouring concrete to create their bunkers, the Allies were building two artificial harbours from concrete that would be towed in sections to Normandy. (Via Author)

Thanks to the work of Dr R.V. Jones, the Allies were able to wage a selective campaign to blind Hitler's coastal radars employing rocket-armed Typhoon fighter-bombers. (Author's Collection)

Other vital equipment included the Landing Ship Tank, which could simply beach itself to disgorge its cargo through the bow doors. (US Navy)

Landing craft such as this were vital for getting the troops and their supporting equipment onto the beaches. However, they offered the men and vehicles in them no protection from small-arms and shell fire. (US Navy)

While the American DUKW was well suited for transporting supplies from ship to shore, it was not designed as an assault craft. (*Portsmouth News*)

General Eisenhower, Allied Supreme Commander (left), with General Bradley, commander of the US First Army, and Major-General Collins of VII Corps. Upon being appointed, Eisenhower said his title made him sound like a 'Sultan'. (US Army Signal Corps)

During the early part of 1944, the Allies instigated their Transportation Plan as part of Operation Pointblank. This saw bombers systematically pound France's railways and marshalling yards to hamper Hitler's ability to move reinforcements. (US National Archives)

On the eve of D-Day, Eisenhower went to watch the US airborne forces depart their English airfields. He told them, 'I've done all I can, now it is up to you.' (US Army Signal Corps)

British Horsa gliders were used to help capture the Orne River and Caen Canal bridges. They managed to land with remarkable accuracy. (US Army Signal Corps)

German defences on the five Allied invasion beaches of Omaha, Utah, Gold Juno and Sword were first pounded by Allied bombers and naval gunfire. Most notably on Omaha this did not have the desired effect. (US Navy)

Both flanks of the Allied landings were secured by airborne divisions that comprised paratroops and glider-borne infantry. Gliders included the American Waco seen here. (National Museum of the US Air Force)

Men of the US 1st Infantry Division heading for Omaha Beach in a LCVP (Landing Craft, Vehicle or Personnel). (US Army Signal Corps)

Omaha proved the bloodiest of the beaches. The initial assault waves from the US 1st and 29th Infantry Divisions suffered heavy casualties and the attack was almost called off. (US Army Signal Corps)

Once ashore, construction of the Mulberry harbours became a priority in order to maintain a steady flow of supplies to the Allied armies. (Author's Collection)

An American truck being driven onto a floating pier. The American Mulberry off St Laurent was damaged beyond repair by the terrible storm in late June 1944. (US Navy)

Once the Allies had established their bridgehead in Normandy, General Bradley's US First Army had to capture the port of Cherbourg. Before it was taken, the Germans destroyed all the dock facilities. (US Army Signal Corps)

General von Schlieben surrendered Cherbourg on 26 June 1944, although resistance continued until the end of the month. He had signalled Rommel beforehand, 'Enemy superiority in material and enemy domination of the air overwhelming ... backs against the sea.' (US Army Signal Corps)

The remains of the German garrison march out of Cherbourg. Such was the damage to the port that the first supplies could not be landed until mid-July 1944 and the harbour was not cleared until the end of September. US Army Engineer Colonel Viney called it the 'best planned demolition in history'. (US Army Signal Corps)

While Bradley fought the Battle of the Hedgerows to clear the Germans from the Cotentin Peninsula, Montgomery became mired in controversy over his attempts to liberate Caen. (US National Archives)

American troops at La Haye Du Puits in the western Cotentin prior to Operation Cobra. (US National Archives)

The town of St Lô acted as the pivot for the American breakout, which took them to Avranches and beyond. This finally broke the deadlock in Normandy. (US National Archives)

Canadian (seen here) and Polish troops were instrumental in trying to close the northern shoulder of the Falaise Pocket. (National Archives of Canada)

Some 50,000 Germans were captured in the Falaise pocket, while another 10,000 lay dead on the battlefield. (US National Archives)

General Leclerc's French 2nd Armoured Division came ashore at the beginning of August 1944. Its one goal was the liberation of Paris. Although Eisenhower wanted to bypass the French capital, General Charles de Gaulle, leader of the Free French, forced his hand. (US National Archives)

The German garrison in Paris under General Choltitz was woefully inadequate, and in the face of French insurrection and the advancing Allies did not last long. Choltitz surrendered on 25 August 1944. These Army and Luftwaffe officers were captured at their headquarters in the Hotel Majestic. (US National Archives)

American sightseers watch as the French tricolour flutters over the Eiffel Tower. The liberation of Paris was inevitably seen as the culmination of D-Day and the Normandy campaign. (US National Archives)

A city in ruins. At Rouen, the Norman capital, the German rearguard held long enough for large numbers of troops to escape over the Seine, though they were forced to leave all their heavy equipment behind. (Author's Collection)

Once the Allies were across the Seine, organised German resistance had all but ended in France. (Via Author)

French civilians welcoming a Canadian convoy. The Allied victory in France was thanks to a combination of scientific and technical ingenuity and courage. Eisenhower described D-Day as a 'staggering multiplicity of decisions'. (National Archives of Canada)

At Bletchley Park, the Allied codebreakers watched in amazement as the Americans tore through the German defences with apparent ease. Selmer Norland, from Minnesota, one of the Americans assigned there, recalled, 'I remember a particular night when I was working on a message and some German unit reported that the American tank spearheads were in the outskirts of Rennes.' She informed the duty officer, and the pair examined a map of the region. 'We were astonished to find that it was almost all the way across to the Brittany peninsula.'[37] Further to the west, units of the US 6th Armored, taking parallel routes, had also reached Plouray and Rostrenen on the road to Brest. It would not be long before German forces were trapped in all the Breton ports.

Some of Patton's generals could not understand the logic of roaring off into Brittany, especially when the real threat posed by the panzers lay to the east. In particular, General Wood of the US 4th Armored could see little point in using his tanks against the German garrison at Rennes or the static German infantry divisions in Brittany. His men had been halted by resistance at Rennes airport and pushed back.

Wood, believing he could be in Chatres in two days, decided to bypass Rennes and turn south-east, but General Middleton at VIII Corps intervened. Reluctantly, a chastised Wood sent his men into the city centre. Patton and Middleton may have been anxious to press on with liberating Rennes because, on 1 August, Bletchley Park decoded a signal ordering the destruction of the city.[38] This clearly indicated that Hitler was preparing to abandon Rennes, even though it was the capital of Brittany.

The weather was hot, and General Wood stripped to his waist before unfolding maps on the grass besides his staff vehicle early on 4 August. He was trying to figure out where exactly his 13th Infantry Battalion was, and indeed the rest of his division. It was at this point that Middleton arrived. Wood was relieved, thinking he had seen sense, and gave his corps commander a hug. 'What's the matter John,' said Middleton jokingly, 'you lost your division?'[39] Wood's infantry were in Rennes, and he complained bitterly, 'We're winning this war the wrong way, we ought to be going toward Paris.'[40] Word reached Patton, who noted in his diary that day that Wood had turned east but must head for his objectives of Vannes and Lorient in south-western Brittany.[41]

In the meantime, General Hausser, in charge of Seventh Army, had given the garrison commander at Rennes permission to escape. Most of his men managed to slip through American lines, despite the presence of the US

13th Infantry. Wood, back on the move, reached Vannes on Quiberon Bay on 5 August, thereby sealing off Brittany. Two days later he was on the outskirts of the port of Lorient.

Going over Middleton's head, Wood resorted to signalling Patton, 'Have Vannes, will have Lorient this evening … Trust we can turn around and get headed in the right direction soon.'[42] Patton understandably saw this as yet more insubordination, and responded, 'You almost got tried for that.'[43] Undeterred, Wood replied, 'Someone should have been tried but it was certainly not I.'[44] Patton, who was on his best behaviour with Bradley, would not deviate from the plan to take Brittany's ports. 'I protested long, loud and violently,' said Wood. 'But No! We were forced to adhere to the original plan – with the only armor available, and ready to cut the enemy to pieces. It was one of those colossally stupid decisions of the war.'[45]

Wood, lacking infantry support, was loath to commit his tanks against the 25,000-strong German garrison at Lorient.[46] As a result, his 4th Armored Division was tied up outside the port from 6–10 August, vainly hoping the garrison would surrender. Wood was not allowed to push east again until 15 August. Brest was also denied to the Allies by the Germans. Frustrating as it was, this mattered little as Le Havre and Antwerp were now looking attainable.[47]

20

GOING FOR BROKE

Once Patton had broken out of the Normandy bridgehead, the battle reached a critical tipping point. Ideally for the exhausted German armed forces, they should have regrouped behind the Seine and held the Allies off from there. As far as Colonel Belchem was concerned, the Führer could 'have reformed his army on a strictly defensive deployment, on ground of his own choosing, in order to obtain a respite for his men and a chance to stock up for his next move'.[1] This was far too logical. Instead, Hitler insisted that Patton's breakout be cut off. Hitler would not listen to the reservations of his senior commanders, remarking, 'My generals think of nothing but retreat.'[2]

When Bradley was in a blocking position facing east at Mortain, Patton was free to overrun Brittany. Hitler misread this situation, assuming that the Americans would head west to try to seize the German-held Brittany ports, especially St Malo and Brest. This impression was reinforced by Patton's 79th Infantry Division, which was pushing in that direction. Other units were also racing south for Nantes. Bradley, now in charge of the US Twelfth Army Group, handed the US First Army over to Lieutenant-General Courtney Hodges and ordered Patton to also attack eastward into the rear of Army Group B.

Hitler, in the meantime, believed that if he broke through Hodges' positions at Mortain and took Avranches, Patton would be isolated in Brittany and the front restored. Cut off from supplies, Patton would then be helpless. 'Just look at that crazy cowboy general,' said Hitler, 'driving down to the south and into Brittany along a single road and over a single bridge with an entire army. He doesn't care about the risk, and acts as if he owned the world!'[3] Divorced from reality, Hitler thought it was Patton who would be trapped.

His generals knew better. Field Marshal von Kluge realised that if he withdrew now, his troops stood some chance of reaching the Seine intact, but this was only possible as long as the men held firm in the Caen and Caumont sectors. Instead, on 4 August, Hitler ordered Kluge to launch Operation Lüttich, a counterattack with eight or nine panzer divisions, which, he claimed, would be supported by all the Luftwaffe's reserves, including a thousand fighters.[4]

'We must strike like lightning,' Hitler instructed Kluge. 'When we reach the sea the American spearheads will be cut off.'[5] While this seemed a plausible plan on paper, Kluge simply did not have the resources to conduct such an operation. Furthermore, with the Americans sweeping eastward threatening his southern flank, and with Montgomery pressing from the north, counterattacking westward seemed like putting his head in the noose. Nonetheless, Hitler's enthusiasm for this enterprise seemed to know no limits as he added, 'We might even be able to cut off their entire beachhead.'[6] Kluge knew that this was impossible, but Hitler was adamant, ordering, 'We must wheel north like lightning and turn the entire enemy front from the rear.'[7]

Both Kluge and Hausser, the commander of the Seventh Army, knew that it was pointless to object, especially as Hitler had sent Generals Walter Warlimont and Walter Buhle as his emissaries to oversee things. In addition, after the 20 July assassination attempt on Hitler, the field marshal lived in fear that his anti-Nazi sympathies might be unmasked. 'The German generals were, of course,' said Colonel Belchem, 'fully aware that the Mortain counter-attack was a suicidal risk.'[8] For Kluge, the Führer's dictates had to be treated as sacrosanct.

Kluge understood that politically he was on borrowed time. The Gestapo, when they investigated the plot to kill Hitler, discovered documents that implicated him. He fell under further suspicion after Patton's breakout when he went missing from his headquarters. Hitler smelled a rat. The real reason for Kluge's absence was that he had become stuck at the front. His radio was destroyed, so he was unable to report back to his staff. After sheltering for several hours, he commenced the long drive back.[9] Hitler, in trying to flush out his wayward commander, sent an order stating, 'Field Marshal von Kluge is at once to extricate himself from the battle area around Avranches and conduct the battle of Normandy from the tactical headquarters of the 5th Panzer Army.'[10]

After consulting the weathermen, who warned of fog, Kluge was slightly reassured that Allied air superiority would be held at bay for a while on 7 August. Hausser knew that the weather 'would be the decisive factor'.[11] 'In spite of all past experience,' wrote Colonel Belchem, 'Hitler still did not understand that major offensive operations in war could not (in the mid-1940s) be undertaken without – at the very least – local air superiority over the battlefield.'[12] Just for good measure, Kluge therefore planned to attack on the night of 6–7 August.

One of the many problems faced by the German high command was that the Allies were intercepting their communications. If they moved their infantry divisions, the Allies knew about it; if they moved their panzers, the Allies knew. It felt as if every redeployment was greeted by Allied fighter-bombers. Bletchley Park's code breakers ensured that Eisenhower and Bradley were well informed about Lüttich. Eisenhower remarked, 'Bradley and I, aware that the German counter-attack was under preparation, carefully surveyed the situation.'[13]

Bletchley's Ultra intercepts revealed on 3 August that Hitler was planning to counterattack with at least four panzer divisions.[14] It also monitored Kluge's grumbling over the next few days that it would be difficult to disengage his armoured divisions from elsewhere in order to conduct the attack. His understandable concern was how this would affect his defences on the Caen front. Hitler had ordered numerous such counterattacks before, but they had always been derailed before they even started. Bradley nonetheless remained alert to the danger.[15]

When Eisenhower was briefed on Hitler's intentions, he acknowledged, 'His attack, if successful, would cut in behind our breakout troops and place them in a serious position.'[16] Although Ike appreciated that Hitler's Mortain counterattack was little more than an inconvenience, he knew even short-term German success would be a public relations disaster with the press, as it would be 'characterized as a lost battle'.[17]

Eisenhower and Bradley decided the best course of action was to first hold their ground and let the Germans exhaust themselves, then contain and crush them. Eisenhower had every confidence in Patton, who was 'a great leader for exploiting a mobile situation', and the 'sturdy and steady Hodges'.[18] Also, they were reassured that the air freight delivery of up to 2,000 tons of supplies a day meant they could easily resupply any units cut off.

Regardless of the Ultra warnings, fortunately for Bradley, his tanks were already well-placed to help counter the Germans. Combat Command A from the 2nd Armored Division was to the north of the planned German offensive in the Vire area, supporting the 28th and 29th Infantry Divisions.

Combat Command B was near Bareton on the southern flank. In the path of Kluge's attack was the 30th Infantry Division, flanked by elements of the 4th and 9th Infantry Divisions, supported by the 3rd Armored Division.[19]

When Kluge's headquarters issued orders for the operation, they discovered that only four panzer divisions[20] were available, with perhaps fewer than 250 tanks.[21] The situation was such that of the five panzer divisions committed against the British and Canadians, only one could be released. Similarly, only two infantry divisions were available to help.[22] Another half dozen divisions were tied down holding the northern shoulder of the German salient east of Vire.

General Hausser's orders sounded more like propaganda than a sound strategic plan. 'On the successful execution of the operation the Führer has ordered, depends the decision of the War in the West,' said Hausser, 'and with it perhaps the decision of the war itself.' His closing remark was tinged with irony, 'Only one thing counts, unceasing effort and determined will to victory.'[23] For the men who had been fighting for the past two months, they must have wondered what more was expected of them.

In the meantime, by the evening of 6 August Patton's men were roaring towards Le Mans way to the south-east, which meant that the newly arrived 9th Panzer Division had to be sent to intercept them. By this point, the Americans and British were also converging on Vire, threatening Kluge's northern flank. This greatly disrupted his preparations for the Mortain counterattack. Patton, who was dismissive of the threat, now sensed the Germans were planning something. 'Personally I think it is a German bluff to cover a withdrawal,' said Patton, 'but I stopped the 80th, French 2nd Armored and 35th [Divisions] in the vicinity of St Hilaire just in case something might happen.'[24]

Ultimately, in light of Allied air superiority, Hitler's grandiose schemes would achieve little other than dragging out the fighting in Normandy even longer. There was absolutely no chance of catching the Americans by surprise, thanks to Bletchley. Bradley, forewarned, wisely took no chances and ensured that the 18-mile front between Vire, St Pois and Mortain was well defended. To meet the threat, he deployed five infantry divisions backed by two armoured combat commands. For good measure, he then positioned three of Patton's divisions west of Mortain.

Trying to stall the Americans at Vire, Kluge was obliged to commit part of his attack force, but even this did not stop the liberation of the town. General Hausser received more bad news when General von Funck,

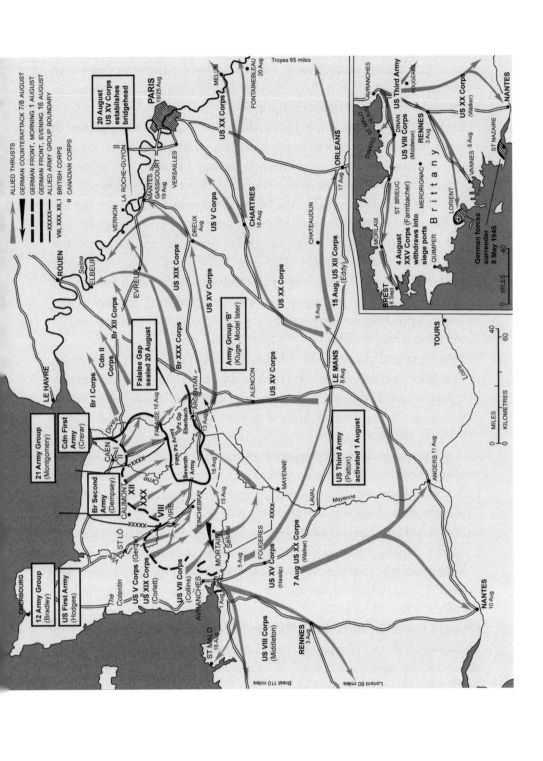

ALLIED THRUSTS
GERMAN COUNTERATTACK 7/8 AUGUST
GERMAN FRONT, MORNING 1 AUGUST
GERMAN FRONT, EVENING 16 AUGUST
XXXXX — ALLIED ARMY GROUP BOUNDARY
VIII, XXX, XII, I BRITISH CORPS
II CANADIAN CORPS

20 August
US XV Corps establishes bridgehead

PARIS
19/25 Aug

Troyes 65 miles

MELUN

FONTAINEBLEAU
20 Aug

US XX Corps

GASSICOURT
19 Aug

VERSAILLES

VERNON

LA ROCHE-GUYON

ROUEN

Seine

ELBEUF

EVREUX

DREUX
Aug

US V Corps

CHARTRES
16 Aug

ORLEANS

17 Aug

CHATEAUDUN

15 Aug, US XII Corps
(Eddy)

6 Aug

US XX Corps

TOURS

Loire

Br XII Corps

US XIX Corps

US XV Corps

Br XXX Corps

Falaise Gap sealed 20 August

Army Group 'B'
(Kluge, Model later)

US XV Corps

ALENCON

LE MANS
8 Aug

Br I Corps

Cdn II
Corps

FALAISE 16 Aug

ARGENTAN

2 Gp
Eberbach

13 Aug

MAYENNE

ANGERS 11 Aug

21 Army Group
(Montgomery)

**Cdn First
Army**
(Crerar)

CAEN

XXXXX

Orne

Fifth Pz Army

Seventh
Army

16 Aug

Dives

16 Aug

15 Aug

Mayenne

LAVAL

US Third Army
(Patton)
activated 1 August

**Br Second
Army**
(Dempsey)

XII

XXX

CAUMONT

VIII

VIRE

TINCHEBRAY

XXXX

5 Aug

Séine

MILES

KILOMETRES

XXXXX

MORTAIN

FOUGERES

US XV Corps
(Haislip)

7 Aug US XX Corps
(Walker)

LE HAVRE

CHERBOURG

12 Army Group
(Bradley)

US First Army
(Hodges)

The Cotentin

ST LO

US V Corps (Gerow)

US XIX Corps
(Corlett)

US VII Corps
(Collins)

AVRANCHES
1 Aug

ST MALO
16 Aug

RENNES
3 Aug

US VIII Corps
(Middleton)

NANTES
10 Aug

Brest 110 miles

Lorient 60 miles

4 August
XXV Corps (Farmbacher) withdraws into siege ports

ST MALO
16 Aug

DINAN

DINARD

ST BRIEUC

MORLAIX

QUIMPER

BREST
8 Sept

LORIENT

MERDRIGNAC

B r i t t a n y

VANNES
5 Aug

ST NAZAIRE

AVRANCHES

FOUGERES

US Third Army

US VIII Corps
(Middleton)

RENNES
3 Aug

US XX Corps
(Walker)

NANTES

**German forces surrender
8 May 1945**

MILES

0

KILOMETRES

0

commander of the XLVII Panzer Corps informed him at 2200 hours that delays in marshalling his forces would mean the attack could not commence until the morning. 'I must admit that this is a bad start,' replied an exasperated Hauser. 'Let us hope that the loss of time this evening can be made good by fog tomorrow morning.'[25]

Colonel von Kluge, the field marshal's son, witnessed the reality of Hitler's massed counterattack. Funck's force rolled forward with only eighty panzers. The 2nd Panzer Division managed to push 7 miles toward Avranches before it ran into elements of the US 3rd Armored Division. To the south, Funck successfully took Mortain but could not budge the US 30th Infantry Division from the high ground to the north-west and west of the town. One battalion from this division was cut off to the east, but was to hold out for five days until relieved.[26] General Collins, commander of the US VII Corps, said this was 'one of the outstanding small unit actions of World War II'.[27] According to Colonel von Gersdorff, Hausser's chief of staff, '[T]his enemy group had a very disturbing effect and constantly pinned down forces of the [2nd SS Panzer] division.'[28]

Funck's momentum was short-lived once the fog lifted. By midday, the air was full of circling American Thunderbolts and RAF Typhoon fighter-bombers, which descended with a vengeance on the German columns. To make matters worse for Funck, there was no sign of the thousand fighters that Hitler had promised. Not a single combat sortie was flown above the area between Mortain and Avranches. Allied radar ensured the Luftwaffe could not intervene. The minute the German fighters were in the air around Paris, they were promptly intercepted and prevented from reaching Mortain. The Luftwaffe's General Bülowius pledged to get at least 300 fighters in the air. 'In ceaseless sorties,' he promised Hausser, 'they will keep the skies clear above the area of operations.'[29] It was a hollow statement.

Funck had lost fifty panzers by 1300 hours,[30] and two hours later was raging, 'The activities of the fighter-bombers are almost unbearable.'[31] Caught on the open road by rocket-firing Typhoons, the 2nd Panzer Division lost 200 trucks and sixty armoured vehicles.[32] 'It is difficult to understand how the German troops withstood the intensive and continuous attacks brought to bear on them throughout the day,' recalled Colonel Belchem with some admiration.[33]

Amongst those going in for the kill was Wing Commander Charles Green, whose Typhoon pilots located 300 enemy tanks. His 184 Squadron knocked out eight panzers in a single strike, and his other squadrons soon joined in.[34] 'We turned out to stop the German counterattack at Mortain,' recalled Pilot Officer Jimmy Simpson with 193 Squadron, 'when the Germans tried to cut off the Americans and we were involved in the destruction of a lot of transport etc.'[35] There were inevitable losses as the Germans fought back. Flight Lieutenant R.G.F Lee, of 245 Squadron, was trapped for five days in his overturned Typhoon after being shot down.[36]

Back at Hausser's Seventh Army's headquarters, Colonel von Gersdorff knew exactly what was happening. '[O]ur own fighter formations had taken off from their bases in the Paris area,' he said, 'but already they were engaged in air combat or, on their approach to the attack area, were being forced away by Allied fighter formations.'[37] On the ground, Funk's forces found themselves being counterattacked by four American infantry divisions and an armoured division belonging to VII Corps. On 8 August, the US 2nd Armored Division entered the fray on the southern flank. Lüttich had been stopped in its tracks.

'The attack failed because Kluge wanted it to fail,' ranted an angry Hitler.[38] 'The armoured operation was completely wrecked exclusively by the Allied Air Forces,' lamented Kluge in response, 'supported by a highly trained ground wireless organisation.'[39] 'It was only thanks to the superiority of the enemy air force that our own well-prepared attack was checked,' complained Hausser.[40] Operation Lüttich was not well prepared, and Hausser did not know that the Ultra intercepts meant that the Allies knew his every move before he had even made them. Hitler demanded that a second pointless attack be conducted on 11 or 12 August using the newly formed Panzer Group Eberbach, that included the XLVII Panzer Corps.

Madness now began to prevail in the German camp. In the south, stretching from Domfort through Le Mans down to Angers on the Loire, Kluge had only one panzer division, an infantry division and half-a-dozen security battalions trying to hold at bay four of Patton's divisions. To the east, the Canadians had launched Operation Totalize, driving southward on Falaise. It was evident to all that a large trap was rapidly forming.

Kluge, with Hitler yelling in his ear, on the evening of 8 August ordered Hausser to redeploy the 9th Panzer from Le Mans to Mortain. Hausser, understandably flabbergasted, responded, 'The withdrawal of the 9th Panzer Division, at the moment when strong enemy tank units are thrusting into our flanks, would deal a death blow not only to Seventh Army but to the entire Wehrmacht in the West.'[41] Kluge explained he had no choice.

The Allies were content that the Mortain threat was over. 'This morning Ike phoned Bradley to learn the latest news,' wrote Captain Butcher on 9 August, 'and found that elements of Patton's Third Army had taken Le Mans, and that the four Panzer-division counter-attack intended to split the Americans at Avranches had been defeated, the enemy losing some eighty tanks to our air attack alone.'[42]

Hitler, however, was not prepared to give up. The following day, he sent a delusional signal saying, 'Objective of the attack, the sea at Avranches, to which a bold and unhesitating thrust through is to be made.'[43] This was almost immediately deciphered by Bletchley. Codebreaker John Prestwich was amazed that Hitler was trapping his army. He remembered, 'Then there came through this detailed order that four or five German armoured divisions were to go hell for leather for Avranches and this opened up the whole possibility of wiping out the cream of the German armed forces.'[44]

General Kuntzen, the corps commander on the southern flank, signalled Seventh Army at 0915 hours on 10 August in a state of panic, warning, 'The enemy has begun to push north and northeast [from Le Mans].' The implications were all too clear. He then added that there was nothing he could do, 'With my present forces, four battalions, I cannot delay this advance. We must count upon Alençon being in enemy hands tomorrow.'[45] This was terrible news, because the town was Seventh Army's main supply depot.

Feebly, Kluge requested that Panzer Group Eberbach be allowed to be 'temporarily transferred from the Mortain area' in order to 'destroy the enemy spearhead thrusting northwards'. This, he argued, 'would render possible the prosecution of the decisive offensive'.[46] This was a lie, but Kluge was desperate to save his men. Hitler, though, dithered. It mattered little, as the Americans retook Mortain and the German forces protecting Alençon were also forced back.

Thanks to Hitler's obsession with Operation Lüttich, an enormous pocket of German troops was forming, hemmed in by Mortain and Vire to the west and Falaise and Argentan further east. 'In the remote fastness of his HQ in East Prussia Hitler,' wrote war correspondent Chester Wilmot, 'was living in a world of fantasy, sustained by optimism, ignorance and his unrivalled capacity for self-delusion.'[47]

Despite the Allies' ongoing success, there was no room for complacency. It was unwise to underestimate Hitler's panzer commanders. Yet when Captain Butcher warned Eisenhower that the Germans still had around

500 tanks in the Mortain area, his boss responded, 'We've got 3,500; what are we scared of?'[48] Only now did Hitler acquiesce in allowing Kluge to withdraw, on the grounds that his attack be resumed as soon as possible.[49]

'The enemy concentrated the bulk of his available armour at Mortain,' noted Eisenhower, 'and continued his obstinate attack until 12 August.'[50] It was, however, simply too little too late, as time was rapidly running out for the Germans in Normandy. 'Their task was impossible: their losses were appalling,' observed Colonel Belchem. 'Hitler's desperate gamble had failed – and at a terrible price.'[51] At Bletchley, John Prestwich surmised that the German generals must have thought that Hitler's order was 'lunatic'. Bletchley knew when Hitler finally gave up on 16 August: '[T]he message was to say how the Germans were planning to get out of this impasse.'[52]

Eisenhower saw Hitler's actions as folly from the start, observing, '[A]t Mortain he was repulsed immediately and materially added to the severity of his own battle losses.'[53] De Guingand was perfunctory in his praise for thwarting Operation Lüttich, saying, 'The German counter-attack from Mortain towards Avranches started on the 7th [August], but was successfully held by the Americans.'[54] All eyes were now on Falaise, the choke point for Kluge's withdrawing divisions.

21

TOTAL DESTRUCTION

Now that Patton was off the leash and Montgomery was grinding his way south, the battle for Normandy was set for the final endgame. After almost three months of bitter fighting, the German front line had completely collapsed. The Allies could see their plans coming to fruition. The Canadians drove south of Caen and fought toward Falaise, while the Americans sped eastwards. A gigantic trap was rapidly forming around Fifth Panzer Army and Seventh Army. Montgomery instructed Bradley to make a long hook, so as to envelop as many German units as possible and prevent them escaping over the Seine.

Allied reconnaissance aircraft detected eastward movement by the Germans from the Mortain area through the gap between Falaise and Argentan on 12 August. It was clear they were making for the Seine ferries. General Patton had the chance to close the open 'neck' as two of his divisions had just reached Argentan, which lies south-east of Falaise. At 2130 hours that day, Major-General Haislip, commander of XV Corps, signalled Patton to inform him that he was about to capture the town. After that, Haislip was ready to push north to link up with the Canadians. In the early hours of 13 August, Patton authorised him 'to continue to push on slowly until … contact with our allies was made'.[1]

General 'Sepp' Dietrich, commanding the remains of the Fifth Panzer Army, knew that the game was up. On the morning of 13 August, he signalled Kluge's headquarters requesting 'immediate … move to the east before such movement is definitely too late'.[2] He did not mince his words, warning that if this did not happen then 'the army group will have to write off both armies'.[3] It was a stark assessment. He also warned that it would soon be possible for Allied artillery to fire on the pocket from all sides. At Army Group B, Kluge's days were numbered. Hitler had got it in his mind to replace him.

When the US 5th Armored Division burst into Seés on the Orne and then headed north for Argentan, they tightened the noose around over twenty German divisions belonging to Fifth Panzer and Seventh armies, as well as Panzer Group Eberbach. Trapped in the developing pocket were the cream of the German tank forces, including elements of seven panzer divisions.[4] The Germans, though, had certainly not given up.

When the US 5th Armored and French 2nd Armoured Divisions attempted to follow Patton's orders, they were caught by the waiting German guns positioned on the hills north of Argentan. Likewise, when 2nd Armoured sent a patrol into Argentan in the afternoon of 12 August, it beat a hasty retreat when confronted by German tanks. Although elements of three emaciated German panzer divisions had moved into place to block Haislip, they knew they could not hold for long after their mauling at Mortain. At Argentan, the Germans mustered just seventy tanks with which to fend off 300 American Shermans.

'The gap was not, however,' observed Colonel Belchem at Twenty-first Army Group Headquarters, 'closed as quickly as had been intended.'[5] The problem was that Patton and the British I Corps were approaching each other head-on. Advising the two forces on safe bomb and gun lines took time. No one wanted a repeat of the friendly fire losses incurred during Operation Cobra. 'To avoid unnecessary risks,' added Belchem, 'it was decided that Patton would halt his advance at Argentan.'[6] Reluctantly, Patton ordered Haislip to withdraw any units that were 'in the vicinity of Falaise or to the north of Argentan'.[7] This officially created the Falaise gap.

It begged the question why Bradley, as a fellow army group commander, should be taking orders from Montgomery. However, the battle for Falaise was Monty's show and he was in charge tactically. In addition, Haislip's left flank was exposed until the arrival of the US VII Corps. To complicate matters, the US XX Corps was also crowding into this area. Once Haislip had sent his 5th Armored and 79th Infantry Divisions east toward Dreux and the Seine, this greatly weakened the American forces on the southern shoulder of the Falaise Pocket.

This decision meant that the two German armies trapped in the Falaise Pocket were able to struggle eastward for another week. To the north, the

Germans held up the Canadian advance, known as Operation Tractable, for two days before they reached Falaise. Once again, heavy bombers were called in to soften the way, and once again, the bombs fell short, this time catching Canadian forces.[8] Even when Falaise had been liberated, the Germans still had a 15-mile gap through which to escape.

Hitler's position in France became completely untenable on 15 August when the Allies landed in the Riviera.[9] In strategic terms, Operation Dragoon was largely nugatory, as it had not been conducted in concert with Overlord due to shortages of amphibious transport and landing craft. Moreover, once the Allies triumphed in Normandy, Army Group G would be forced to withdraw from southern France to avoid being cut off. Additionally, the Germans had very few tanks in the region. All of Army Group G's panzers had already been drawn north to the fighting in Normandy, except for one division which was refitting after being mauled on the Eastern Front.

Kluge's attempts to liaise with his generals almost cost him his life and further incurred the displeasure of Hitler. On 15 August, he had left La Roche-Guyon heading for the pocket and promptly vanished for 12 hours.[10] Hitler convinced himself that Kluge was trying to reach the Allies in order to surrender, but was thwarted by the timely intervention of Allied fighter-bombers.[11] When a dishevelled-looking Kluge finally appeared at General Eberbach's headquarters, he explained how he had been trapped in a ditch by Allied shelling and that his radio truck had been hit by enemy aircraft.

Hitler grudgingly agreed to let his forces withdraw through the Argentan-Falaise gap on 16 August. The II SS Panzer Corps[12] was to hold the northern flank against the British and Canadians and XLVII Panzer Corps[13] was to protect the south against the Americans, while remaining divisions conducted a fighting retreat.

Eisenhower made it a point to visit his forward units, even to the point of placing himself in danger. At one stage he drove to see General Haislip's XV Corps on the southern flank. However, Haislip was far from pleased to see him, and said Ike should turn around immediately. 'We've got Nazi artillery firing on our flank and we think there's a counterattack build-ing up that just might overrun the area,' warned Haislip.[14] Eisenhower responded, saying he wanted to see how things developed and that he had every confidence that XV Corps would handle it. 'I just don't want it said that I allowed the Supreme Commander to get killed in my corps area,' grumbled Haislip. 'Now if you want to get killed, go into some other area.'[15] Eisenhower was adamant that he was staying for lunch. 'That lunch was a comedy,' recalled Ike, 'served in speeded-up, double quick-time.'[16] Panic stricken, Haislip could not get rid of the Allied Supreme Commander quick enough.

While Kluge got permission to retire beyond the Orne, his replacement, Field-Marshal Model, ordered a withdrawal behind the Dives. He also launched the II SS Panzer Corps against the British moving southward towards Trun on the eastern side of the Dives, north of the main crossing point at St Lambert. It would take three nights to get the westernmost troops over the Orne, and at least one night to complete the withdrawal over the Dives. In other words, the mouth of the pocket had to be kept open for four days at all costs. This had to be done under constant Allied artillery and fighter-bomber attack.

Patton's US Third Army and the British I Corps were slowly heading for each other, and the Falaise Pocket was steadily squeezed from all sides as the Germans valiantly held open the neck. By 17 August the pocket was just 20 miles wide by 10 miles deep, and contained about 100,000 men, remnants of some fifteen divisions with elements from at least twelve others, all frantically wanting to escape eastwards.[17] The panzer divisions managed to hold the Americans and Canadians at bay, but the vast, vulnerable columns of retreating Germans were decimated by Allied aircraft and artillery, the roads becoming choked with burnt-out vehicles which added to the chaos.

Second Lieutenant Herbert Walther of the 12th SS recalled:

My driver was burning. I had a bullet through the arm. I jumped on to a railway track and ran. They were firing down the embankment and I was hit in the leg. I made 100m, then it was as if I was hit in the back of the neck with a hammer. A bullet had gone in beneath the ear and come through the cheek. I was choking on blood.[18]

Miraculously, he survived and was taken prisoner.

Montgomery demanded the Trun-Chambois gap be closed and on 17 August insisted, 'It is absolutely essential that both armoured divisions of 2nd Canadian Corps, i.e. 4th Canadian Armoured Division and

1st Polish Armoured Division, close the gap between First Canadian and US Third Army. 1st Polish Armoured Division must thrust past Trun and Chambois at all costs and as quickly as possible.'[19] Canadian and Polish tanks were soon pushing on the Germans flanks. In the meantime, the US V Corps was instructed to fight its way to Chambois and Trun.

Free French Forces fighting alongside the Americans were given a bloody nose by rearguard units of the 9th and 116th Panzer Divisions, but Patton was driving with all speed towards the Seine. He was on the line Orleans-Chartres-Dreux, facing little or no resistance. The drive was continued, hoping to swing north to seal off the Germans trapped against the Seine. The US XV Corps, though, was held up by determined resistance as the retreating Germans fought desperate rearguard actions along the Seine. The US 79th Division from XV Corps managed to secure a bridgehead over the Seine at Mantes-Gassicourt on 19 August.

Canadian troops burst into Faliase on 16 August and three days later, supported by Sherman tanks, seized St Lambert-sur-Dives in the path of the fleeing Germans. They held out for three days, withstanding efforts by the remains of 2nd Panzer Division to dislodge them. Germans fleeing over the river came under constant fire, and at one point the Canadians called down artillery fire onto their own positions. 'Germans charred coal-black, looking like blackened tree trunks lay besides smoking vehicles,' said Canadian soldier Duncan Kyle. 'One didn't realise the obscene mess was human until it was poked at ... The road to Falaise was nauseating.'[20]

The disgraced Field Marshal von Kluge, who had fought so hard to hold the Allies at bay, stopped at Metz on 19 August and quickly scribbled Hitler a final note. He started by saying, 'When you receive these lines I shall be no more', then went on to urge the Führer to bring an end to the war.[21] Afterwards, Kluge unrolled his blanket, lay down and took cyanide. Officially, his cause of death was announced as a cerebral haemorrhage.

By 19 August, the German escape route was just 5 miles wide, though it would not be completely sealed for another two days, and the rapidly shrinking pocket measured just 7 miles by 6 miles. Under pressure from German paratroops, the Poles were forced to relinquish control of some of the roads and up to 4,000 paratroops, supported by three tanks, escaped. Outside the mouth of the pocket, II SS Panzer Corps attempted to reach the remnants of Seventh Army on 20 August, but with just twenty tanks they were unable to achieve much and the 9th SS were halted by the Poles.

Above the Falaise pocket, Allied aircraft mercilessly pounded the fleeing Germans columns. Flight Lieutenant Henry Ambrose, flying a Typhoon with 175 Squadron, said, 'They just blocked roads, stopped them moving and just clobbered them.'[22] It 'was absolute murder from the German point of view,' recalled Flying Officer George Clubley, piloting a Typhoon with 181 Squadron. The situation soon developed into a free-for-all. 'It was dangerous from our point of view because there were so many aircraft trying to get in to have a crack at all these targets,' noted Clubley. 'I went down there afterwards, it was quite horrifying.'[23]

General Heinrich von Lüttwitz, commanding 2nd Panzer Division, desperately attacked toward Canadian-held St Lambert with just fifteen tanks and found the bridge undamaged. He recalled, 'The crossing of the Dives bridge was particularly horrible, the bodies of the dead, horses and vehicles and other equipment having been hurled from the bridge into the river formed a gruesome tangled mass.'[24] Survivors from the 10th SS and 116th Panzer Divisions crossed and briefly held the encircling Allies at bay. The 116th escaped with just fifty of its vehicles remaining.

The 9th SS tried to break through again on 21 August using two massive King Tiger tanks, but these were swiftly knocked out. The Allies began to mop up the remaining Germans trapped west of the Dives, and about 18,000 men went into the 'bag' that day. The Allies found the surrounding countryside a charnel-house, the air fouled by the stench of rotting corpses, cattle and horses. 'The wreckage and confusion within the "pocket" is difficult to describe,' recalled Colonel Belchem. 'Enemy transport vehicles, guns and tanks were found packed nose to tail in a landscape of total destruction.'[25]

The war correspondent for *The Times* was aghast at the terrible destruction wrought in the Falaise Pocket. He wrote:

> For four days the rain of death poured down, and with the road blocked with blazing tanks and trucks little can have escaped it. Nothing can describe the horror of the sight in the village of St Lambert-sur-Dives, an enemy graveyard over which his troops were struggling yesterday in an effort to break through the cordon hedging them off from the seeming escape lanes to the Seine.

The correspondent observed Hitler's armoured forces were completely spent, reporting that, 'Within an area of about a square mile hundreds of tanks and armoured cars, great trucks and guns and horse-drawn wagons, lie burned and splintered in hideous disarray.'[26]

Eisehower went to see the devastation for himself. 'Forty-eight hours after the closing of the gap I was conducted through it on foot,' recorded Ike, 'to encounter scenes that could be described only by Dante. It was literally possible to walk for hundreds of yards at a time, stepping on nothing but dead and decaying flesh.'[27] He was rightly pleased with the crushing defeat of the Nazi war machine, noting, 'German command-ers concentrated particularly on saving armoured elements, and while a disappointing portion of their panzer divisions did get back across the Seine, they did so at the cost of a great proportion of their equip-ment. Eight infantry and two Panzer divisions were captured almost in their entirety.'[28]

At Falaise, Hitler lost 60,000 men – 10,000 killed and 50,000 captured. The Americans discovered in their area 540 tanks and self-propelled guns, as well as 5,000 vehicles. In the British, Canadian and Polish areas were another 344 armoured vehicles. Coningham's 2nd Tactical Air Force claimed to have destroyed or damaged 190 tanks and 2,600 vehicles during its numerous sorties over the battlefield. The Germans claimed that 40,000 troops escaped, although many of them were killed before they got over the Seine, and crucially they only took twenty-five panzers with them. In total, the II SS Panzer Corps lost 120 tanks during its counterattack at Falaise, though it managed to withdraw to fight another day.[29]

For those who escaped Falaise, they still had to contend with the Seine. The main crossing point was at Rouen, the ancient capital of Normandy. However, with the river unfordable and all the bridges down, the Germans had to rely on boats and rafts. Surviving tanks and other vehicles had to be abandoned on the dockside. A few days after the pocket was overrun, the Germans found that from the remains of the armoured divisions commit-ted to the battle, they could muster just sixty-seven tanks. The Germans had lost all their equipment in what was seen as their worst defeat since the Battle of Stalingrad.

'The battlefield of Falaise was unquestionably one of the great-est "killing grounds" of any of the war areas,' said Eisenhower. 'Roads, highways and fields were so choked with destroyed equipment and dead men and animals that passage through the area was extremely dif-ficult.'[30] Even the veteran *Daily Express* reporter Alan Moorehead was appalled by the destruction. 'Certainly this is the most awful sight that has come my way since the war began,' he wrote. 'I think I see the end of Germany here.'[31]

There seemed no denying that Falaise had paved the way for Allied victory in Western Europe. Moorehead, like Ike, toured the battlefield, visiting St Lambert. 'This was their best in weapons and men, their strongest barrier before the Rhine,' he concluded. 'It has been brushed aside, shattered to bits … I say again I think I see the end of Germany here.'[32]

22

DE GAULLE PULLS IT OFF

The goal of D-Day had always been the opening of the Second Front against Hitler's Germany and the liberation of occupied Europe, in particular France. However, the fate of the French capital proved something of a military and political headache for all concerned. 'A special problem that became acute toward the end of August,' said Eisenhower, 'was that of determining what do about Paris ... In this matter my hand was forced by the action of the Free French forces inside the city.'[1]

The liberation of Paris never loomed large in Eisenhower and Montgomery's post D-Day plans – militarily it was an irrelevance. They simply hoped that the German garrison would withdraw or, if surrounded, surrender. Winning the tough battle for Normandy was enough of a preoccupation for the Allied commanders. They had not really anticipated conducting a separate operation to secure the French capital. This was at best naive, and chose to ignore the volatile political situation in France.

Eisenhower, Bradley, Montgomery and Patton assessed that once the Allies had reached the Seine, Hitler would not be in a position to hold the French capital. In order to keep damage to a minimum, the Allies had taken steps to ensure that they did not directly bomb the city. Eisenhower's stated aim was, '[W]e wanted to avoid making Paris a battleground.'[2]

To complicate matters, Churchill and Roosevelt did not altogether trust the democratic credentials of the self-appointed Free French leader, General Charles de Gaulle. They were not keen on the idea of helping de Gaulle, whom they always viewed as a poorer and troublesome cousin, to install himself in power in Paris. If he achieved that he would inevitably be seen as the saviour of France, ensuring a subsequent ballot box victory. Nevertheless, it was unreasonable not to expect the regular Free French units to hurtle toward Paris the moment the opportunity arose. 'So when the Free French forces inside the city staged their uprising it was necessary to move rapidly to their support,'[3] acknowledged Eisenhower with an air of resignation.

Following the successful Allied landings in French North-west Africa in late 1942, de Gaulle had moved his headquarters from London to Algiers and appointed General Pierre Koenig as head of the French military mission in the British captial. Hitler's response to the landings was swift and predictable – the Wehrmacht and SS occupied France's southern Free Zone ruled from Vichy.

The US State Department was alarmed by intelligence that anti-Gaullist politicians in France were being betrayed to the Gestapo, and reported this to President Roosevelt. 'I am fed up with de Gaulle and the secret personal and political machinations,' wrote Roosevelt to Churchill in mid-1943. 'I am absolutely convinced that he has been and is now injuring our war effort and that he is a very dangerous threat to us.'[4] Unconcerned by what the British and Americans thought, de Gaulle made himself president of the French Committee of National Liberation.[5]

French security forces were employed against their fellow countrymen throughout occupied France, including the capital. Whilst no organised units of the French armed forces took action against the French Resistance, the French police and various collaborationist militias certainly did. Following the occupation of the Free Zone, Vichy approved Interior Minister Joseph Darnand's creation of the Milice Française, whose main arm was the Franc Garde consisting of 13,000 personnel.[6] They, along with the French police's 10,000-strong Groupes Mobiles de Reserve (GMR), supported Wehrmacht operations against the Resistance.[7]

Darnand sought to turn the Milice into a French Waffen-SS. Initially the Milice operated in the Vichy Zone, but its activities spread north. In Darnand's fight against the Resistance, he collaborated closely with the feared Higher SS and Police Leader for France, Paris-based Major-General Karl Oberg. In reward for his efforts against his own countrymen, in January 1944 Vichy appointed him to the post of General Secretary for the Maintenance of Order. Darnand became one of the most reviled men in France. The Milice were hated in Paris for their support of the German security forces.

By 1943, German and Milice convoys were coming under attack, and in the spring the Franc Garde first went into action against the Resistance in Haut Savoie, followed by operations in the old Occupied Zone in December. The Wehrmacht, GMR and Franc Garde then moved to liquidate a Resistance stronghold on the Glieres plateau in early 1944. Once the Allies landed in Normandy, the desire to collaborate began to wane. It disappeared altogether after Operation Dragoon when the Allies, including Free French forces, landed in southern France.

Prior to D-Day, Britain and America were loath to discuss their plans with General Koenig. This was due to well-founded concerns that information shared with Algiers would end up in Paris, and as the Resistance was heavily infiltrated by the Germans it would inevitably reach Hitler. In February 1944, de Gaulle created the French Forces of the Interior (FFI) under Koenig to unite all the various resistance groups. The national liberation committee became the Provisional Government of the French Republic. De Gaulle considered himself head of the French government, though neither Roosevelt nor Churchill recognised him as such. At the end of the month he returned to London, where he disassociated himself once more from the Allied cause by refusing to broadcast to his fellow countrymen on D-Day.

In late 1943, de Gaulle had hinted to General Jacques Leclerc, commander of the Free French 2nd Armoured Division, that the Allies might employ his division in the Normandy landings. Leclerc was a staunch Gaullist whose men were veterans of the fighting in Libya and Tunisia. In the summer of 1943, Leclerc's force became known as the 2e Division Blindee and was fully equipped along the lines of an American armoured division.[8]

Leclerc pressed for transport to Britain, causing a row with General de Lattre, who wanted Leclerc's division as part of his French First Army, which was due to land in southern France. When Leclerc's division finally moved to Britain from North Africa in April 1944, all black colonial troops were returned to France's African possessions, on the grounds they would be unable to cope in Europe. Leclerc and his men hoped they would fight alongside the British in the opening assault, but instead his division was attached to Patton's US Third Army. Both de Gaulle and Leclerc made a mental note of this snub, though in reality there had not been time to train the French for an assault role.

In preparing for the Normandy landings the Allies tried to spare Paris, but its major rail marshalling yards made its suburbs a prime target. For

2 hours on 21 April 1944, yards at St Denis and the Gare de La Chappelle were bombed and 640 civilians were killed.[9] Allied flares and German flak units lit up the night sky as the bombs fell, not only on the freight yards, but also neighbouring homes. The pro-Nazi Vichy government had a field day, with its media revelling in the brutality of the Allies. Vichy leader Marshal Petain even made a point of visiting Paris to attend mass and see the wounded.

Following D-Day, the French capital remained calm until the end of June, when Pétain's propaganda secretary Philippe Henriot was gunned down by three assailants at his official residence in the Ministry of Information on rue de Solférino.[10] 'Well that's one viper the less!'[11] remarked a jubilant Parisian news vendor.

Throughout July, Paris became increasingly restless, though the Germans largely left it to Darnand's Milice Francaise to keep order and conduct reprisals. On 20 July, the city became embroiled in the bomb plot to kill Hitler. Karl Oberg and 1,200 members of the Nazi security apparatus were briefly arrested by the plotters until it became apparent that Hitler was still alive.

From early August, Parisians made their city ungovernable, though the Resistance were under instructions from de Gaulle not to rise up until the arrival of Leclerc and his tanks. Between 10–12 August, Paris was paralysed by a rail strike, then on 15 August, 20,000 police went on strike, supported by the Communist-dominated FFI. Two days later, as shooting broke out, Vichy supporters began to flee Paris. Petain and Darnand headed to Germany, while the Germans began disarming the troublesome French police.

General Dietrich von Choltitz, the new garrison commander, was under strict orders to deny Paris to the Allies, even if it meant razing it to the ground. Hitler told him the city 'must not fall into the hands of the enemy, if it does, he must find there nothing but a field of ruins'.[12] Hitler wanted any rising in Paris crushed, as it was crushed in Warsaw.[13] Choltitz, fortunately, was a cultured man who had no intention of going down in history for torching Paris. The German armed forces were certainly in no position to assist in holding the city. Hitler had promised Choltitz two skeleton panzer divisions from Denmark, but they did not arrive.

The German garrison was weak, consisting of Brigadier Walter Brehmer's 325th Security Division, a company of tanks and some batteries of 88mm anti-aircraft guns with inexperienced teenage crews, supported by sixty aircraft. This amounted to just 5,000 men, with fewer than twenty old French light tanks and fifty guns.[14] The force was just about adequate to contain insurrection, but nothing else. There were 17,000 German administrative staff in the city, some of whom, in theory, could bear arms. Choltitz's problems were compounded by the presence of these rear echelon personnel, including the female 'Grey Mice', needing transport to safety. In addition, as Paris was the heart of the German occupation, Choltitz had to oversee the evacuation of thousands of classified files. These included personnel and payroll records, as well as the Gestapo's documentation on members of the Resistance. There was also the thorny issue of thousands of French women who had struck up relations with German soldiers and were now desperate to escape retribution.[15]

Leclerc's armour did not come ashore on Utah Beach until 1 August, and along with three American divisions formed the US XV Corps under General Haislip. The initial advance covering 70 miles in four days as far as Le Mans was fairly uneventful. Then US Third Army swung north to help trap the retreating German forces in the Falaise pocket. Unfortunately, near Argentan, Leclerc let his enthusiasm run away with him and his tanks clogged a road earmarked for petrol supplies. The chaos gave the Germans a much-needed breathing space. Tantalisingly, Leclerc and his men were just over 100 miles from the French capital.

After the loss of some of his tanks, the division successfully established a bridgehead over the River Orne. Leclerc was now assigned to the US First Army and V Corps under Major-General Gerow. The two men instantly took a dislike to each other. De Gaulle was concerned that the French Communists would liberate Paris, and got an undertaking that Leclerc could enter the city. However, at this stage Eisenhower felt it best to by-pass Paris, as once the River Seine was crossed it would lose all strategic importance.

De Gaulle was determined the city would not escape his control, and Koenig's military delegate, General Chaban (Jacques Delmas), arrived on the scene, followed by Gaullist Charles Luizet, who was to take command of the police. On 19 August, almost 2,000 police staged a general rising, but Colonel Rol (Henri Tanguy), head of 600 Communist FFI, was annoyed that they had acted without his orders and stolen his leadership's thunder. Choltitz and Brehmer made a half-hearted counterattack against the Police Prefecture building using tanks, but withdrew before things turned really ugly for the French. The FFI also liberated the Palais de Justice and Hotel de Ville, and almost 400 barricades were erected throughout the capital.

When it was suggested to Choltitz that the FFI revolt was directed at Vichy rather than his garrison, he replied, 'Perhaps. But it's my soldiers they are shooting at!'[16] A truce was agreed, but Rol's Communists did not observe it, accusing General Chaban of being a coward. His faulty intelligence indicated that the Germans had 150 Tiger tanks to hand, and he did not wish to see the lightly armed FFI slaughtered or the city's historic buildings damaged.

In the meantime, at 1030 hours on 20 August, an eager Leclerc presented himself at General Hodges' US First Army headquarters near Falaise. 'His arguments, which he presented incessantly,' recalled Hodges irritably, 'were to the effect that, roads and traffic and our plans notwithstanding, his division should run for Paris at once. He said he needed no maintenance, no equipment, and that he was up to strength – and then, a few minutes later, admitted that he needed all three.'[17]

General Bradley found himself under siege by the international press, demanding to know when the French capital would be liberated. He explained that the plan was to pinch off the city so that it would fall without a shot having to be fired, and that Paris was not to be entered until 1 September. When they asked which division would be given the honour, Bradley quipped, 'You've got enough correspondents here to do it.'[18]

Leclerc, ignoring orders, sent a reconnaissance group, consisting of twenty tanks and armoured cars, toward Paris on 21 August. A furious Gerow ordered him to recall them, but Leclerc adamantly refused. However, the Communist Resistance and French police had now forced Eisenhower's hand. 'Throughout France the Free French had been of inestimable value in the campaign,' Eisenhower recalled, knowing he could no longer ignore them in Paris. 'Information indicated that no great battle would take place and it was believed that the entry of two Allied divisions would accomplish the liberation of the city.'[19]

General Bradley prevailed on Eisenhower that they had little choice but to act or cause a diplomatic incident. Bradley signalled Hodges, who noted:

Paris since Sunday noon, he said, had been under control of the [Gaullist] Free French Forces of the Interior, which, after seizing the principal buildings of the city, had made a temporary armistice with the Germans, which was to expire Wednesday noon. General Bradley said that higher headquarters had decided that Paris could be avoided no longer, that entry of our forces was necessary in order to prevent possible heavy bloodshed among the civilian population.[20]

On 22 August, Eisenhower authorised Leclerc's division and General Barton's US 4th Infantry Division to drive on Paris the following day. Leclerc was determined to get there before Barton. His division, totalling 16,000 men equipped with 200 Sherman tanks, 650 pieces of artillery and 4,200 vehicles, converged on the city in three columns. The Americans were dismayed at the antics of the French soldiers, who treated the advance as one big party, kissing and hugging everyone en route.

Angrily, Gerow phoned Hodges to complain that the French troops were stopping at every town for a celebratory drink, with predictable results, and that they were holding up the traffic. At about 1700 hours, a light aircraft swooped over the Police Prefecture building and dropped a message. When the defenders opened it, they discovered a message from Leclerc, 'Hold on, we're coming.' While this was welcome, the question remained, when?

Upon nearing Paris, German resistance became more vigorous and Leclerc's main thrust was launched from the south, with a feint from the south-west. Outlying German defences consisted of small numbers of tanks supported by anti-tanks guns holed-up in the villages and at the crossroads. At Jouy-en-Josas, three French Shermans were lost in tank-to-tank engagements. Stiff resistance was also met at Longjumeau and Croix de Berny. German 88mm guns at Massy and Wissous accounted for more of Leclerc's tanks. Similarly, an 88mm sited in the old prison at Fresnes, blocking the Paris road, held off three Shermans. The first was knocked out, but the second destroyed the gun and the third ran over it. The French lost another four tanks to German anti-tank guns trying to outflank Fresnes. The push on Paris proved no picnic, costing Leclerc almost 300 casualties, with forty-one tanks and self-propelled guns and another eleven assorted vehicles disabled or destroyed.

On the evening of 24 August, a French patrol slipped into the captial. Three light tanks, four armoured vehicles and half-a-dozen half-tracks entered Paris through the Porte Gentilly. By nightfall, the tanks were within a few hundred yards of Choltitz's headquarters at the Meurice.

The next day, as Leclerc entered in force, cheering Parisians mobbed his tanks crossing the Seine bridges. Elements of the 2nd Armoured reached the Police Prefecture at 0830 hours. During five hours of fighting to clear the German defenders from the foreign office building on the Quai d'Orsay, another Sherman tank was lost. At the Arc de Triomphe, a French tank silenced its German counterpart at a range of 1,800m. Three Shermans were then lost after they drove onto the Place de la Concorde with their turret hatches open and each received a German grenade.

A note from 2nd Armoured was sent to Choltitz demanding he surrender or face annihilation. He refused to receive it. Instead, Choltitz went through the charade of urging his men to fight to the last. Leclerc's Shermans closed in on the Meurice, and Choltitz was captured and driven to the Prefecture to see Generals Leclerc, Barton and Chaban, as well as Luizet and Colonel Rol. The latter wanted joint signature on the surrender document with Leclerc.

Feeling he was the ranking officer, Leclerc signed on behalf of everyone else. A tired Choltitz then asked for water. 'I hope you've no idea of poisoning yourself,' asked a concerned interpreter. 'No, young man, I wouldn't do anything like that,' responded a slightly taken aback Choltitz. 'I have to take medicine for a heart ailment.'[21] His glass of water was then duly handed over.

The Communist Resistance leaders, after weeks of fighting the Germans, felt aggrieved at Leclerc, so a second document was drawn up with the signature of Colonel Rol given prominence. This was understandable, because while the liberation cost Leclerc 130 dead and 319 wounded, the FFI had suffered 1,000 dead and 1,500 wounded. De Gaulle and the Allies, however, were displeased by this act of diplomacy, which failed to acknowledge that Leclerc had been acting as a subordinate of the Allied High Command. At 0930 hours, teams of FFI and German officers went out to pass the word to the remaining German strongpoints still holding out.

De Gaulle made his official entry into the city on 26 August. Upon hearing he intended using the 2nd Armoured Division for a victory parade, Gerow ordered Leclerc to disregard this and get on with cleaning up the city. There remained 2,000 German troops in Paris and fighting was still ongoing. When de Gaulle insisted, Eisenhower had little choice but to give way. Triumphantly, de Gaulle, Leclerc, Koenig and Chaban, surrounded by French officials, walked from the Arc de Triomphe to Notre Dame, with the French 2nd Armoured Division proudly lining the route.

Afterward, Gerow ordered Leclerc to clear the Germans from the northern suburbs, but de Gaulle wanted to keep the division in Paris to counter the Communists. He then wanted the division to join the French First Army pushing up from the south of France, but instead Leclerc got his force reassigned to XV Corps moving towards Alsace.

Chaos reigned in Paris as de Gaulle manoeuvred to place himself in the ascendancy and ultimately the French Presidency. In addition to Leclerc's, Barton's and Choltitz's men, there were now 50,000 self-proclaimed FFI running about the city. Both Gerow and Koenig considered themselves temporary military governor of Paris. Gerow flew to Hodges' headquarters and demanded, 'Who in the devil is the boss in Paris? The Frenchmen are shooting at each other, each party is at each other's throat. Is Koenig the boss, is de Gaulle the boss? Am I, as the senior commander, in charge?'[22]

The Council of National Resistance wanted de Gaulle to proclaim a new Republic from the Hotel de Ville. His response was emphatic, 'The Republic has never ceased to exist … Vichy always was null and void and remains so. I myself am the president of the government of the Republic. Why should I proclaim it?'[23] On 28 August, he acted to remove the threat from the Communist Resistance as an independent force. The FFI was dissolved and those useful units were absorbed into the regular French Army. Discipline and central authority would prevail by ending the various independent militias.

De Gaulle requested thousands of American uniforms for his FFI recruits and additional military equipment with which to organise new French divisions. More worryingly, de Gaulle asked for the loan of two American divisions to help reinforce his position in Paris. Eisenhower was bemused: not even in North Africa had the Free French requested Allied troops to help impose their political authority.

Nonetheless, in response to this request, two American infantry divisions marched down the Champs Elysees on 29 August on their way to the front. Eisenhower, Gerow, Koenig and de Gaulle stood on the reviewing stand as the troops trudged past. De Gaulle left before the parade was finished, a deliberate snub that was not lost on the American generals. To make matters worse, de Gaulle's actions in liberating Paris helped prolong the war, for the delay around the city enabled a greater part of the German First Army to escape over the Rhine. The parade, though, had achieved de Gaulle's aim – a warning to the various FFI factions: look at my powerful friends. His political coup was complete. De Gaulle, not the Resistance or the Americans, would be remembered as the saviour of Paris and ultimately of France.

23

HITLER'S GREAT ESCAPE

General Hans Höcker's 17th Luftwaffe Field Division deployed between Dieppe and Le Harvre was to play a major role in the fighting at Rouen, along with elements of Brigadier Otto Baum's 2nd SS Division and General Gerhard Graf von Schwerin's 116th Panzer Division, as well as General Walter Steinmüller's 331st Infantry Division.[1] Ridiculously, as well as his coastal defence role, Höcker was supposed to be able to redeploy his entire division within 48 hours to act as reinforcements against any invasion point.[2]

Although Höcker's command had time to train prior to D-Day, they were ill-equipped, lacking transport and armed with obsolete weapons. The army was responsible for this paucity of vehicles, feeling the regular army divisions had a much better use for them. The division gained reinforcements in the shape of two rather dubious battalions of former Soviet prisoners of war.

In the case of the 16th Luftwaffe Field Division, lost at Caen, it was almost 10,000 strong, equipped with sixty artillery pieces and anti-tank guns, so it is fair to assume that Höcker's command was of a similar strength.[3] In contrast, the 91st Airlanding or Luftlande Division, lost during the early stages of the Normandy campaign, totalled no more than 8,000, equipped with 105mm mountain howitzers and captured Czech and Russian guns. Höcker's divisional fire support was provided by an artillery regiment that had only just been equipped with 1914-vintage 150mm field guns. This meant that the crews did not have time to train on their weapons.[4]

In mid-August 1944, even as part of Model's Army Group B was being overwhelmed in the Falaise pocket, to the south, Patton's US Third Army was driving all out for the Seine, forming a larger encirclement. It seemed as if Hitler's forces in Normandy were on the verge of a second bigger disaster. Unfortunately, determined resistance held up the US XV Corps as Model's retreating troops fought rearguard actions all along the Seine. After the Falaise pocket had been overrun, Model conducted a highly successful operation at Rouen to save the survivors of his exhausted and scattered command.

It was not until the first week of August, following the Allies' breakout, that Höcker's men left their prepared positions around Le Havre for the front. Mid-month they crossed the Seine below Rouen, but their shortage of vehicles meant men and equipment had to be left behind. Höcker took up position near Dreux along the Eure River on 17 August. However, within three days he was falling back toward Evreux. Combat against the Americans did not go well; at Pacy-sur-Eure, his 17th Fusilier Battalion, whilst resisting the US 5th Armored Division, was pounced on by Allied fighter-bombers.

Recuperating from the Eastern Front, the 331st Infantry Division, which had been refitting in northern France, was not ordered to the front until late July. This indicated just how unready it was, and although it numbered around 11,900 men, few of them had combat experience. Commanding officer General Steinmüller had only taken charge on 1 August.[5] During the Mortain counterattack, Fifth Panzer Army brought forward elements of the division to relieve pressure on the 1st SS Panzer Division. By 11 August, a 331st Division battle group was operating in the L'Aigle-Gráce area about 25km east of Argentan.

While the destruction of the German forces at Falaise seemed a deathblow from which Model could never recover, crucially, numerous units had escaped. On the Allies' immediate eastern flank were elements of five German infantry divisions, numbering about 32,450 men, behind whom were another nine infantry and parachute divisions.

Altogether, Hitler had about 250,000 troops and 250 panzers still west of the Seine, consisting of men outside the pocket, those who had escaped it and units from General Blaskowitz's Army Group G's area. All were streaming eastwards in headlong retreat. It was not until it was almost too late that Hitler, finally grasping the gravity of the situation, ordered all non-combatant troops in western and southern France to commence withdrawing.

For those who avoided the Allies' encirclement, they still had to cross the river. Now that the front line had vanished, much of France had become bandit country. The retreating troops were in a constant state of fear. Rumbling through villages and towns, there was the danger they would bump into enemy patrols and hostile locals or be attacked by the ever-present Allied fighter-bombers circling menacingly overhead.

On the 19th, the US XV Corps' 79th Division secured a bridgehead over the Seine north of Paris at Mantes-Gassicourt, just south of Model's headquarters at La Roche Guyon, posing an immediate threat to Fifth Panzer Army's left flank. If Patton had been instructed to exploit this with a rapid thrust north along the east bank instead of the west, certainly fewer Germans would have escaped the following battle.

Model was fully aware that he had suffered a catastrophe at Falaise, but there was no time to reflect as he had much more pressing matters. He and Generals 'Sepp' Dietrich, commanding Fifth Panzer Army, and Heinrich Eberbach, commanding Seventh Army, knew they must hold the west bank stretching north from Paris, through Rouen to the coast and Le Havre, at all costs while their fleeing forces tried to get over the river. This would provide a new line of resistance, or if it came to the worst, as seemed likely, they could withdraw behind the Somme.

Once the Falaise gap was closed, the British I Corps, under the command of the Canadian First Army, pushed along the coast to Honfleur, while on its flank the Canadian II Corps headed for the ancient city of Rouen and the Seine. In the run-up to Normandy, to prevent the Germans bringing up reinforcements, Rouen's rail yards had been heavily bombed in April 1944. The city itself suffered extensive damage, causing much ill-feeling toward the Allies amongst the civilian population.

Four American aircraft attacked the main Rouen bridge on 4 July. Two days later, twenty-two American fighter-bombers bombed Rouen, and on the 8th, six heavy bombers hit the city's marshalling yards. Subsequent attacks were also made on Hitler's V-weapon sites in the Rouen area, though poor weather resulted in the mission being called off. On 18 July, German gun positions in the city were dive-bombed, while rail traffic to the south of the city was attacked a week later.

Providing a fighting screen for the retiring forces meant no rest for the shattered panzer divisions, which Model described as little more than 'torsos'. From the shambles of Falaise, 'Sepp' Dietrich found that each of the panzer divisions averaged just 3,000 men, while each infantry division could only muster around 2,000.[6] The remains of his Fifth Panzer Army took command of the entire sector west of the Seine, ordering that Elbeuf, laying on a huge westward-facing loop in the river south of Rouen, should be held. This mission would partly fall to Höcker.

The remnants of three panzer divisions were formed into Group Schwerin, with about twenty battle-worthy tanks and assault guns between them. On the night of 23/24 August, 21st Panzer and 2nd SS Panzer Divisions moved to reinforce the eastern flank of Fifth Panzer Army, between the Seine and the Risle, in an effort to protect the crossings near Rouen. The 21st Panzer was subordinate to the 116th Panzer Division, while the 2nd SS Panzer was to hold blocking positions south and south-east of Elbeuf. By the evening of the 24th, a line had been established between Elbeuf and the Risle north of Brionne. The withdrawing 9th SS Panzer Division was also ordered to join Group Schwerin.

Model instructed Dietrich to counterattack with his panzer divisions, and a few weak panzergrenadier units with about thirty panzers which were launched into an attack that was quickly brought to a stop. This was repeated, with similar results. In the meantime, the exhausted German Seventh Army, no longer capable of directing anything, was ordered to collect all available infantry units beyond the Seine. By the 25th, as the retreat got underway, Fifth Panzer Army was able to muster just 18,000 men, forty-two tanks and assault guns and 314 guns: essentially a single panzer division.[7] These forces were pulled back to the Seine bridgehead formed by three large river loops to protect the crossings at Caudebec-en-Caux, Duclair, Elbeuf and Rouen.

Höcker's soldiers had withdrawn to Louviers, close to the junction of the Eure and Seine rivers. Falling back again, the general and his men found themselves taking cover up to twenty times every day in the face of persistent and deadly air attacks. Rallying several batteries of the 17th Artillery Regiment on 26 August, the division got over the Seine, making contact with Fifth Panzer Army and elements of the 2nd Panzer Division. They were assigned the high ground on the east bank opposite Elbeuf, covering the crossing and the way to Rouen. Some might question the wisdom of deploying an inadequate Luftwaffe field division in such a key position, but it was a matter of expediency. Also, the first echelon was to be made up of Steinmüller's infantry division, which would give a good account of itself.

Model's men did all they could to hold up the US 2nd Armored Division from attempting to cross the River Avre at Verneuil. Suffering heavy casualties, the Americans crossed upstream, swinging north toward Elbeuf. They

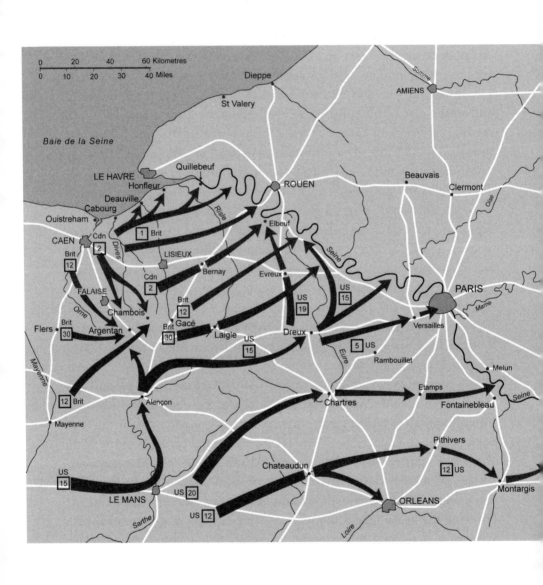

penetrated the town on 24 August, but the following morning were expelled by the 2nd SS Panzer. German resistance was so fierce that one American column attacking from the south-east was cut off for two days and nights. Further north, General Kuntzen's LXXXI Corps also found themselves at risk, necessitating moving the 9th SS Panzer Division to the Montfort area on the 25th. East of Rouen, the British 43rd (Wessex) Infantry Division crossed at Vernon and three days later the 11th Armoured Division was over and swinging northward toward Amiens and the Somme.[8]

Complete withdrawal across the Seine now became an imperative, and Model gave the order. Priority was given to their armoured vehicles, motorised transport and then horse-drawn. Model's troops made for the crossings at Elbeuf, Oissel and Rouen, which were under constant air attack. The key crossing point was at Rouen, so holding the wooded bulge in the river became vital, though with the river unfordable and with all the bridges down they had to rely on boats and rafts.

The pontoon bridge at Rouen could only take wheeled vehicles, and the bridge at Oissel, having been brought down in May, was likewise makeshift. Many surviving tanks and other vehicles that had been so painstaking coaxed eastward were abandoned on the dockside. On 25 August, bombers attacked the German transport massed on the quayside twice, with terrible results. The following day, the fires were still raging both sides of the river.

Outside Rouen, Will Fey and his comrades from the 102nd SS Heavy Panzer Battalion witnessed the fate of the surviving German equipment. 'All the panzers and artillery had to remain on the west bank of the Seine,' he said. 'They were driven out of the columns, and some were blown up. Some of the panzers that were still mobile were driven into the stream and sunk or blown up in the woods.'[9]

Some surviving Tigers reached Elbeuf on 25 August only to find the bridge down, so headed for Oissel to the north-east. There the crews found the area clogged with some 7,000 vehicles all waiting to cross. Reluctantly, the order was given for the remaining panzers to be destroyed. The 503rd Heavy Panzer Battalion lost the last of its Tigers west of the Seine near Rouen at la Bouille. There were no ferries that could take their massive weight and they had to be abandoned.

Using tanks and artillery, Schwerin's 116th Panzer Division scored a minor success at Bourgtheroulde on the 26th, briefly driving the Americans back. On the night of 26/27 August, his panzergrenadiers were deployed along the Seine loop near Moulineaux to the north and the Forêt de la Londe in the centre, with 2nd SS Panzer holding the left wing near Orival, thereby blocking off the approaches to Rouen.

The 116th Panzer and a kampfgruppe from the 2nd SS were given the task of holding the Americans at bay at Elbeuf, but on 26 August US 2nd Armored overran the town's southern outskirts. Having pinned down the Americans, the remains of Schwerin's men withdrew at midnight under the cover of fog and rain. Surviving members of the 2nd SS Panzer escaped by swimming across the river. At daybreak, the Americans mopped up resistance and handed the town over to the Canadians. The 10th SS Panzer crossed at Oissel between 25–27 August by means of two bridges they had seized, selfishly fending off attempts by other retreating units to use them until all their own troops had crossed.

A withdrawal to the three Seine loops south of Caudebec-en-Caux, south of Duclair and south of Rouen was ordered on the night of 27/28, with the 331st Infantry Division taking over the Duclair and Rouen loops and the dense forest in between. Steinmüller's command had already gained experience of conducting rearguard actions during the escape from the Falaise pocket. Supported by elements of Panzer Lehr, they had remained north of Gráce defending the Gráce-Vimoutiers road. The division had avoided being seriously mauled by the Americans, losing about 1,500 men.

At this stage, Steinmüller had the advantage that his divisional artillery was at full strength, being equipped with numerous 105mm light field howitzers and French 155mm howitzers. His anti-tank battalion also included a number of self-propelled guns and assault guns. When his guns opened up on the woods, the trees were shattered, showering the Canadians with splinters that inflicted terrible wounds.

While the Canadian 3rd Armoured Division crossed at Elbeuf, the Canadian 2nd Infantry Division pushed through Forêt de la Londe, whose wooded hills stretched northward all the way to Rouen. They suffered almost 600 casualties in three days of bitter fighting against Steinmüller's men. This was quite a remarkable performance considering the 331st Division left behind all its combat experienced officers and men, who were distributed to other local units, when it had withdrawn from the Eastern Front in March 1944.

Meanwhile, Höcker's antiquated artillery and few anti-tank guns did what they could, while enduring air attack and artillery bombardment.

However, by nightfall on 28 August, the Canadian 3rd and 4th Divisions had taken possession of the defensive positions on hills about a mile inland from Elbeuf, having put the 17th Luftwaffe Field Division to flight. The Polish 1st Armoured Division also crossed at Elbeuf on the 29th.

The survivors of 2nd Panzer Division managed to cross the Seine on 28 August. Otto Meyer, commander of the 9th SS Panzer Regiment, having survived all the fighting in Normandy, was killed on the 30th crossing at Duclair. In the early hours that day, Steinmüller, still acting as rearguard, finally pulled his men back across the river and the Canadian 3rd and 4th Armoured liberated Rouen.

Also on 30 August, Höcker for a short time set up his headquarters at La Feuillie, but with British tanks pushing on the Somme this had to be abandoned. Joining the withdrawing 331st Infantry Division, Höcker and his men continued their retreat. From the chaos he found of his two jäger regiments, they could only muster a single battalion each.[10] By this stage, the 331st had lost at least half its men.[11]

Model decided that Seventh Army would cover the withdrawal of Fifth Panzer Army toward Arras, north-east of Amiens and behind the safety of the Somme. At Amiens, 'Sepp' Dietrich was supposed to hand command of Fifth Panzer Army back to Eberbach on the afternoon of 31 August. Dietrich left early and Eberbach, commanding Seventh Army (in General Paul Hausser's absence after he was wounded), and his staff were surprised by British tanks rumbling into their midst and compelled to surrender. His chief of staff, von Gersdorff, escaped, but Fifth Panzer Army's guard company, drawn from the 116th Panzer Division, were not so lucky. Eberbach's only reserves were five Tiger tanks and they could achieve little in the face of the British 11th Armoured Division.

This drove a wedge between the German Fifteenth Army west of Amiens and Fifth Panzer Army to the east. Any hopes Model had of holding the Somme as a main line of resistance were dashed. He was now forced to retreat yet again, and the British were soon pushing on Brussels and Antwerp. In the meantime, Dietrich made his way to Model's Army Group B headquarters at Havrincourt and was briefly appointed commander of Seventh Army.

After, Falaise German armoured vehicle losses were modest considering the rapidity of the Allies' advance: only sixty panzers and 250 other armoured vehicles were left on the west bank of the Seine, and about 10,000 troops were captured. In part thanks to the rearguard action at

Rouen, there was no second Falaise pocket. Frustratingly for Eisenhower, the bulk of those German forces west of the river – well over 200,000 troops, 30,000 vehicles and 135 panzers – had escaped.

Although this was a remarkable achievement, Dietrich said that, 'From the point of view of equipment abandoned, the Seine crossing was almost as great a disaster as the Falaise pocket.'[12] According to General Blumentritt, of the 2,300 panzers and assault guns involved in the battle for Normandy, 'only 100 to 120 were brought back across the Seine'.[13] When Model reported to Hitler, he informed him that his armoured divisions only had 'five to ten tanks each'.[14] His dozen or so armoured units could only operate at regimental strength.

Throughout the campaign, mobility had always been a significant problem for the Germans. The Luftwaffe's inability to protect France's railways and roads meant that between D-Day and the flight to the Seine, the German armed forces lost 15,000 lorries.[15] Of the sixteen infantry divisions that got over the Lower Seine, Model only had the manpower to reconstitute four divisions, but was unable to equip them. He noted they 'have only a few heavy weapons and for the most part are equipped with nothing more than small arms'.[16]

The situation on the Western Front appeared irretrievable for Hitler and the Third Reich. While Model had barely 100 serviceable panzers, the Allies could muster almost 8,000.[17] It seemed as if nothing would stop their armoured juggernaut, and by 4 September they were 200 miles (320km) east of the Seine and in control of the vital port of Antwerp.

During the campaign, the panzer divisions' manpower totalled about 160,000, and while they had lost almost 62,000 men, thanks to the rearguard actions at Rouen and elsewhere, some 98,000 got away – all they needed were replacement tanks.[18] The Allies' strategic bombing campaign may have severely hampered Hitler's armaments production, but it had not brought it to a standstill, nor was it able to completely prevent equipment being shipped to the front. It was these two factors that ultimately marred the Allied victory in France.

24

NOVEL MECHANICAL CONTRIVANCES

While there were thousands of heroes on D-Day, the true architects of its success were undoubtedly men such as Jones, Hobart, Holmes, Hughes-Hallet, Morgan, Thompson and Walter. Each helped create a vast strategic and tactical puzzle that fell into place almost seamlessly for Operation Overlord. Historians delight in debating the veracity of what happened next with the Normandy campaign, but nothing can detract from the fact that D-Day proved a complete triumph of guts and ingenuity. The boffins gave the troops what they needed. D-Day was the making of victory in Western Europe – Stalin's long-awaited second front was opened by Churchill and Roosevelt as promised, and it was never defeated.

Efforts to deceive Hitler and his generals worked admirably. 'The overall contribution of the Deception Plan cannot be precisely quantified,' said Colonel Belchem, 'but there is no doubt at all that it achieved a remarkable degree of success.'[1] Hitler remained convinced until the end of July that D-Day was an elaborate ruse and the Pas de Calais was the Allies' intended invasion destination. Belchem noted, 'Hitler continued to regard the Normandy landings as a diversionary operation until it was too late to send effective reinforcements from Fifteenth Army to save Seventh Army from its fate.'[2]

'The enemy, it appears, was completely taken in by the bogus convoys and convinced that the main assault was to be in the Pas-de-Calais,' said Air Marshal Harris in praise of Bomber Command's role in D-Day. 'This, it is now known, caused a definite and vital delay in bringing up strategic reserves to Normandy.'[3]

Dr Reginald Jones' campaign to blind Hitler's radars was deemed 'extraordinarily successful'.[4] It achieved the desired results, vindicating all of his efforts. Air Chief Marshal Sir Trafford Leigh-Mallory wrote with much satisfaction, 'The enemy did not obtain the early warning of our approach that his Radar coverage should have made possible; there is every reason to suppose that Radar-controlled gunfire was interfered with; no fighter aircraft hindered our airborne operations; the enemy was confused and his troop movements were delayed.'[5] His official report concluded, 'These attacks saved the lives of countless soldiers, sailors and airmen on D-Day.'[6] 'Four years' work had proved worthwhile,' Jones recounted proudly in his memoirs, 'although I have sometimes wondered what would have happened without that after-lunch talk with Tedder.'[7]

There was no doubting that General Hobart had done his job. 'Without his "babies" or "Funnies" as they were often called,' recalled General de Guingand, 'the assault against the West [Atlantic] Wall would have been more difficult, and much more costly in lives. Even after the successful assault, his units were in continual demand.'[8] Lieutenant-Colonel Peter Young of No. 3 Commando was of the view that Hobart's armour had 'loaded the dice in favour of the British infantry'.[9]

General Eisenhower was equally fulsome in his praise of the 'Funnies':

Apart from the factor of tactical surprise, the comparatively light casualties we sustained on all beaches, except Omaha, were in large measure due to the success of the novel mechanical contrivances which we employed and to the staggering moral and material effect of the mass of armour landed in the leading waves of the assault. It is doubtful if the assault forces could have firmly established themselves without the assistance of these weapons.[10]

He was philosophical about the difficulties experienced at Omaha, 'In point of fact the resistance encountered on Omaha Beach was about the level we had feared all along the line.'[11] He seemed to bear no grudge over the key intelligence failure regarding the presence of General Kraiss' 352nd Infantry Division, noting, 'In the Omaha sector an alert enemy division, the 352nd, which prisoners stated had been in the area on manoeuvres and defence exercises, accounted for some of the intense fighting in the locality.'[12] Ike's naval aide, Captain Butcher, also propagated the myth that the division just 'happened to be in the area on manoeuvres'.[13]

This, however, was untrue as elements of the 352nd Division had arrived as early as March 1944. Monty's senior intelligence officer had warned two weeks before D-Day that it might move to the coast, but this was not promulgated to senior American commanders until three days before the landings.[14] The reality was that the 352nd's hard work almost paid off. They ensured that the Americans could not get off the beach quickly enough and almost killed the landing completely. Such an event would have vindicated Rommel's strategy.

'This congestion was chiefly due to the absence of specialised armour,' noted Chester Wilmot, 'capable of dealing with the natural obstacles and fixed defences.'[15] Wilmot was scathing of Bradley's decision not to use Hobart's armour. 'Analysis makes it clear that the American troops paid dearly for their commander's hesitation,' he said, 'to accept Montgomery's earlier offer to give them a share of Hobart's specialised armour.'[16]

Wilmot later wrote at length:

The terrible consequences of this short-sightedness were only too apparent at Omaha on D-Day. The failure of the bombardment and the non-appearance of the DD tanks left the infantry at the mercy of the strongpoints which they were required to storm. Where tanks were available, landed direct from LCTs, they proved invaluable, but they were too few and too dispersed, and they found great difficulty in manoeuvring because of the congestion of vehicles on the foreshore.

This congestion was chiefly due to the absence of specialised armour capable of dealing with the natural obstacles and fixed defences.[17]

However, an official post-war US report was quite critical of the performance of the 352nd Division, in particular highlighting its failure to conduct effective counterattacks. The assessment went on to note, 'Employed instead in close-up defense of the beach, it had made the initial assault phase harder but had not achieved a defensive success.'[18] Likewise, the command and control of the division was found wanting, 'Communications were evidently poor in the 352nd Division's sector, and no inkling had come back to [General Marks'] Corps of the scale of the landings in progress at Omaha.'[19] This seemed a little harsh in light of the firepower that was dropped on the division and the ensuing confusion caused by the landings.

Regarding German deployment, Lieutenant-Colonel Young rightly concluded, 'With the benefit of hindsight one must concede that, given Allied domination of the skies above Normandy, Rommel's plan was more realistic than Rundstedt's, however correct that may have been in theory.'[20] Nevertheless, they both underestimated the power of naval gunfire and the impact it would have in the areas adjacent to the Normandy coastline.

Of all the challenges the Allies faced, somewhat perversely, Eisenhower had taken comfort from the destruction wrought by the storm in late June:

> There was no sight in the war that so impressed me with the industrial might of America as the wreckage on the landing beaches. To any other nation the disaster would have been almost decisive; but so great was America's productive capacity that the great storm occasioned little more than a ripple in the development of our build-up.[21]

On D-Day, Eisenhower had been well served by Group Captain Stagg and his other meteorologists. He had won the crucial war of the weather. 'Supported by advice from their meteorologists the German generals decided that the invasion was no longer "immediately imminent",' said Stagg. 'Their meteorologists could foresee only continuously disturbed weather for the next ten or twelve days.'[22] This gave Rommel and the other German generals a false sense of security. Eisenhower recognised the opportunity that the forecast gap in the weather offered, and seized it. Stagg was relieved that the Germans failed to spot this, and even if they had 'their military masters could not see how the allies could use it'.[23]

If Eisenhower had not taken his momentous decision to launch Operation Overlord when he did, things could have ended in disaster. Eisenhower's next window of opportunity with low tides would have been 19 June. This would have required the green light late 17 or early 18 June. Overlord would then have coincided with the terrible storm.

Group Captain Stagg said 'two unexpected things happened' in that second window: a depression pushed north from the Mediterranean to meet a cold front sweeping south-eastwards from Iceland. From 19–22 June this created up to force 7 north-east winds. If Eisenhower had gone on 18 June, the invasion fleet would have been pulverised and he would have lost the two-week build-up period he gained between 6–18 June. Eisenhower was understandably eternally grateful to Stagg, and after seeing the devastation caused by the storm he sent the group captain a note saying, 'I thank the gods of war we went when we did.'[24] Montgomery was in full agreement, commenting, 'If we had persisted with the original D-Day of the 5th June, we might have had a disaster.'[25]

When Stagg met his German counterpart, he was amazed to learn that Major Lettau 'had failed to grasp the significance of a "weather front" which passed through the Channel early on June 5, with relatively good weather following it'.[26] Captain Butcher, who was privy to this meeting, wrote:

> The German major said they were taken completely by surprise when the Allied invasion started on the morning of June 6 – not only because of their own weather forecast but because the Allied forces went in at low tide, with all the underwater obstacles exposed, whereas the Germans assumed we would attack at high tide.[27]

Lieutenant-Colonel Young was full of praise for the speed with which the British, Americans and Canadians consolidated their beachhead. Again, this was in part thanks to the ingenuity of the boffins:

> Thanks to such imaginative devices as the Mulberry harbour and PLUTO (Pipeline Under The Ocean) the administrative build up put the Army Group on a sound footing in good time before, on 19 June, the worst storm in the Channel for more than 40 years struck the Assault Area.[28]

He also concluded that some good had come of the Dieppe raid, 'In consequence it was decided to land over the open beaches … Thus, as so often in war, the right thing happened for the wrong reason.'[29]

Despite all the ingenuity and effort that had gone into creating the Mulberries, opinion was divided over just how vital they had been. 'The Mulberry piers were criticized because eventually,' said Colonel Belchem, 'in the St Laurent sector, the Americans were landing more per day across open beaches than was the case at Arromanches, where the British harbour was repaired and utilized.'[30]

In contrast, thanks to the Mulberries, Albert Speer concluded that all their efforts fortifying the Channel ports and building the Atlantic Wall had been a complete waste of time. 'By means of a single brilliant technical idea the enemy bypassed these defences,' he said. 'Our whole plan of defence had proved irrelevant.'[31]

Rundstedt's opinion of the Atlantic Wall was understandable. He witnessed first-hand how France's Maginot Line opposite the German border had been made completely irrelevant in the face of a highly flexible and mobile attack. He reasoned, quite rightly as it transpired, that:

> The Wall was a myth, nothing in front of it, nothing behind – a mere showpiece. The best that could be hoped for was that it might hold up an attack for twenty-four hours, but any resolute assault was bound to make a breakthrough anywhere along it in a day at most. And, once through, all the rest could be taken from the rear, for it all faced out to sea and became quite useless.[32]

On the whole, protecting the flanks with the airborne operations had gone remarkably well. The Americans had secured the causeways and greatly disrupted German defences. Likewise, the British had successfully captured the bridges and denied them to the Germans. The commando linkup with 6th Airborne had gone smoothly. 'The sea crossing, dry landing, rapid break-through and intact bridges were bonus marks,' said Lord Lovat, of No. 4 Commando. 'The shock tactics had proved a complete success.'[33]

At the height of the Normandy campaign, Montgomery was lambasted for his slow progress. In reality, everything had pretty much gone to plan. Understandably, Colonel Belchem was resolute in his defence of Monty, stating categorically:

> Phase-lines never at any time had any place in Montgomery's plan. His one and only specifically dated objective was that the Allied armies should be formed up in line at the River Seine on D+90. In the event General George Patton, commanding Third US Army, arrived at the Seine well ahead of schedule – on D+75.[34]

By this stage the Allies had massed thirty-nine divisions for the push on Germany.

De Guingand was equally dismissive of criticism of Monty:

> I am afraid a lot of the controversy in respect of developments in Normandy originate from this misconception of the true significance of a phase line.

A study of the phase line map shows that Montgomery always meant to swing upon the 'Caen hinge,' and that even in the best circumstances he only intended to move this flank eastwards some ten miles in the first month.[35]

Although D-Day was the making of victory in Europe and an overarching success, clearly the battle for Normandy did not go as smoothly as some might have expected or hoped. This topic has been well trod elsewhere, and there is little point in raking over old coals.[36] Suffice to say, criticism of his handling of the battle for Caen and the closing of the Falaise pocket greatly rankled Montgomery after the war. He held General Morgan, who had worked so hard on the COSSAC plan, responsible for this state of affairs. 'He considered Eisenhower was a god,' wrote Montgomery with some bitterness; 'since I had discarded many of his plans, he placed me at the other end of the celestial ladder.'[37]

Montgomery was understandably angry there was an impression that the British and Canadians had failed to break out at Caen, and that the job had been left to the Americans. 'Morgan and those around him (the displaced strategists) lost no opportunity of trying to persuade Eisenhower that I was defensively minded and that we were unlikely to break out anywhere!' added Montgomery with rancour.[38] He also pointed the finger at the airmen who desperately wanted the airfields around Caen, as well as the Press for their treatment of Operation Goodwood.

Eisenhower, though, was generous in his assessment of Monty's leadership prior to Bradley's breakout, stating, 'Field Marshal Montgomery's tactical handling of this situation was masterly.'[39] Likewise, Bradley was generous, saying, 'Monty's primary task was to attract German troops to the British front that we might more easily secure Cherbourg and get into position for the breakout. In this diversionary mission Monty was more than successful.'[40]

Eisenhower acknowledged that the climax of the battle for Normandy was far from perfect. The closing of the Falaise pocket proved a largely insurmountable and controversial problem for the Allies. To avoid the risk of friendly fire, there had been no option but to leave the pocket open longer than it should have been. 'In aggregate considerable numbers of Germans succeeded in getting away,' admitted Ike. 'Their escape, however, meant an almost complete abandonment of their heavy equipment and was accomplished only by terrific sacrifices.'[41] What he could not have predicted was the incredible resilience of Hitler's weapons factories, which by the end of the year had replaced most of the Normandy losses.

Field Marshal von Rundstedt laid the German defeat in Normandy firmly at the feet of Hitler:

> I knew all along the German position in France was hopeless and that eventually the war would be lost. But if I had been given a free hand to conduct operations, I think I could have made the Allies pay a fearful price for their victory … But I did not have my way.[42]

After the war, the German generals refused to believe that superior Allied ingenuity and technology had defeated them. They preferred to believe that they had lost because of Allied superiority in numbers on the ground and in the air, and because of Hitler's constant meddling. They knew nothing of Bletchley Park and the role it played. Nor did they care much about the enormous scientific efforts that went into first facilitating and then sustaining the Allied bridgehead in Normandy.

The Germans fought to the last in Normandy simply because they had no other choice. Private Schulter of the 716th Infantry Division best summed up their position. 'Why did we keep going?' he asked. 'What else could we do? We were soldiers.'[43]

Hitler lost forty-three divisions by September 1944 and suffered a total loss of 450,000 men – comprising 240,000 casualties and 210,000 prisoners – as well as losing most of their equipment, including 3,500 pieces of artillery and 20,000 vehicles. The exhausted panzer divisions lost all their tanks in northern France. From an accumulated tank force of 1,804, just eighty-six remained; similarly, the independent tank battalions and assault brigades, from an accumulated strength of 458, could scrape together only forty-four vehicles.[44]

While Allied planning and preparation for D-Day was impeccable, they also benefited greatly from the Germans suffering from 'Dieppe syndrome'. Rundstedt, Rommel, Dollmann, Salmuth and Hitler simply could not conceive of the Allies landing west of the Seine: it was too far away from the Rhur. While Hitler long suspected that the Allies might threaten Normandy, in his mind such a landing would only ever be a diversion. The Pas de Calais would be their primary objective, so he could not permit German reinforcements being drawn west from the Seine to Normandy.

In the event, General Blaskowitz's forces in southern France were stripped of units instead to support the fighting in the north.

The technical innovation for D-Day was backed by outstanding intelligence. Senior codebreaker Captain Jerry Roberts was of the view that Bletchley Park played a key role in Overlord's success. 'If the D-Day landings had failed,' he wrote, 'it would likely have taken at least two years to prepare for another major assault.'[45]

Aside from the ingenuity, extensive planning and good luck that the Allies benefitted from, Eisenhower proved to be the right man for the job. On the eve of D-Day, his confidence momentarily failing him, Eisenhower had said, 'I hope to God I know what I am doing.'[46] Despite the enormous strain, the Allied Supreme Commander never buckled or shirked his responsibilities. Vice Admiral Friedrich Ruge, Rommel's chief naval advisor, said with great admiration that Eisenhower had made 'one of the truly great decisions in military history'.[47] Ike had gambled on 6 June 1944 and got it right.

79TH ARMOURED DIVISION, THE 'FUNNIES'

Major-General Sir Percy C.S. Hobart

1st Assault Brigade RE (Churchill AVRE)
5th, 6th and 42nd Assault Regiments Royal Engineers

30th Armoured Brigade (Sherman Crabs)
22nd Dragoons, 1st Lothians and Border Horse, 2nd County of London Yeomanry (Westminster Dragoons)
141st Regiment Royal Armoured Corps (Crocodiles – joined after D-Day)

Staffordshire Yeomanry (Sherman DD tanks)

DD Tank Units

Apart from the Staffordshire Yeomanry, the 79th Armoured was responsible for training all the other Sherman DD-equipped units: 1st East Riding Yeomanry (February 1944 handed its role to the Nottingham Yeomanry), 4th/7th Royal Dragoon Guards, 13th/18th Royal Hussars, Nottinghamshire Yeomanry, 6th and 10th Canadian Armoured Regiments and the 70th, 741st and 743rd US Tank Battalions.

Allocation of units

Gold Beach
British (Northumbrian) 50th Division
81st and 82nd Squadrons, 6th Assault Regt RE (AVRE)
B and C Squadrons, Westminster Dragoons (Crabs)
4th/7th Royal Dragoon Guards and Nottinghamshire Yeomanry
(DD tanks)

Juno Beach
Canadian 3rd Division
26th and 80th Squadrons, 5th Assault Regt RE (AVRE)
B Squadron, 22nd Dragoons with twelve tanks of A Squadron, Westminster
Dragoons (Crabs)
Canadian 6th and 10th Armoured Regiments (DD tanks)

Sword Beach
British 3rd Division
77th and 79th Squadrons, 5th Assault Regt RE (AVRE)
A Squadron, 22nd Dragoons (Crabs)
13th/18th Royal Hussars (DD tanks)

Utah Beach
US 4th Infantry Division
70th Tank Battalion (DD tanks)

Omaha Beach
US 1st Infantry Division
741st and 743rd Tank Battalions (DD tanks)

ROYAL MARINES ARMOURED SUPPORT GROUP

Allocation of Units

Gold Beach
1st Royal Marine Armoured Support Regiment (Centaurs)
1st Battery (A, B, C and D Troops)
2nd Battery (E, F, G and H Troops)

Juno Beach
2nd Royal Marine Armoured Support Regiment (Centaurs)
3rd Battery (J, K, L and M Troops)
4th Battery (N, O, P and Q Troops)

Sword Beach
5th Royal Marine Independent Armoured Support Battery (Centaurs)
(R, S, T and V Troops)

PRINCIPAL D-DAY TRAINING FACILITIES

British
Combined Operations Training Centre
Inverary, Western Scotland

Combined Operations Experimental Establishment
Appledore/Westward Ho!, North Devon

79th Armoured Division (A & B Training Wings)
Barafundle Bay, South Wales
Fritton Decoy, Norfolk
Kyles of Bute, Western Scotland
Linney Head, South Wales
Orford, Suffolk
Osborne Bay, Isle of Wight
Stokes Bay, Gosport, Hampshire
Studland Bay, Dorset

American
US Army Assault Training Centre
Woolacombe, North Devon

US Battle Exercise Area
Slapton Sands, South Devon

US Ordnance Experimental Station (Depot O-617)
Bideford, North Devon

FORCE MULBERRY

Rear-Admiral Mulberry/Pluto
Rear Admiral W.G. Tennant

Deputy Commander
Commander A.B. Stanford, RN

Allied Tug Control HQ
Captain E.J. Morgan, USN

Mulberry A – Omaha Beach
Captain A. Dayton Clark, USN

Force 128
US 108th Construction Battalion, 25th Naval Construction Regiment

Bombardon
Commander L.D. Ard, USNR

Phoenix
Lieutenant Commander W.M. Passmore, RN

Mulberry B – Gold Beach
Captain C.H. Petrie, RN, and Brigadier A.E.M Walter, RE

British 1st Port Construction and Repair Group
Lieutenant-Colonel S.K Gilbert

930th and 935th Port Construction and Repair Companies
969th and 970th Port Floating Equipment Companies

US 334th Harbour Craft Company
Warrant Officer John Heming

Superintending Civil Engineer
Captain J. Jellet, RNVR

Bombardon
Commander C.I. Horton, RN

Phoenix
Lieutenant Commander C.S.E Lansdown, RN

Gooseberry Force

Gooseberry 1 Commander A.B. Stanford, RN
Gooseberry 2 Commander C.R. Dennen, USN
Gooseberry 3 Lieutenant Commander A.M.D Lampen, RN
Gooseberry 4
Gooseberry 5

ALLIED ORDER OF BATTLE IN NORMANDY

6 June – 31 August 1944

British and Canadian Forces

British Twenty-First Army Group
Commander-in Chief
General Sir Bernard L. Montgomery
Chief of Staff
Major-General Sir Francis W. de Guingand

British Second Army
General Officer Commanding-in-Chief
Lieutenant-General Sir Miles C. Dempsey
Chief of Staff
Brigadier M.S. Chilton

	Landed
6th Airborne Division	D–Day
7th Armoured Division	7–12 June
11th Armoured Division	13 June
79th Armoured Division	D–Day
Guards Armoured Division	28 June

3rd Infantry Division	D-Day
(Scottish) 15th Division	14 June
(Wessex)43rd Division	24 June
(West Riding) 49th Division	D-Day
(Northumbrian) 50th Division	D-Day
(Highland)51st Division	D-Day
(Welsh) 53rd Division	27 June
(Staffordshire) 59th Division	27 June

Canadian First Army
General Officer Commanding-in-Chief
Lieutenant-General H.D.G. Crerar
Chief of Staff
Brigadier C.C. Mann

Canadian 4th Armoured Division	31 July
Polish 1st Armoured Division	31 July
Canadian 2nd Division	7 July
Canadian 3rd Division	D-Day

Independent Brigades

4 Armoured, 6 Guards Tank, 8 Armoured, 27 Armoured (DD Tanks), 31 Tank, 33 Armoured, 34 Tank, 2 Canadian Armoured, 56 Infantry, 1st and 4th Special Service Brigades. Plus the 1st and 2nd Royal Marine Armoured Support Regiments.

European Allies

Belgian 1st Infantry Brigade, Royal Netherlands Brigade and the French 3rd and 4th Parachute Battalions.

American Forces

US First Army
Commanding General
Lieutenant-General Omar Bradley

(succeeded by Lieutenant-General Courtney H. Hodges from 1 August when Bradley assumed command of the newly created US Twelfth Army Group)
Chief of Staff
Major-General William B. Keen

US Third Army (from 1 August)
Commanding General
Lieutenant-General George S. Patton, Jr.
Chief of Staff
Major General Hugh J. Gaffey

	Landed
2nd Armored Division	2 July
3rd Armored Division	9 July
4th Armored Division	28 July
5th Armored Division	2 August
6th Armored Division	28 July
7th Armored Division	14 August
2nd French Armoured Division	1st August
82nd Airborne Division	D-Day
101st Airborne Division	D-Day
1st Infantry Division	D-Day
2nd Infantry Division	8 June
4th Infantry Division	D-Day
5th Infantry Division	16 July
8th Infantry Division	8 July
9th Infantry Division	14 June
28th Infantry Division	27 July
29th Infantry Division	7 June
30th Infantry Division	15 June
35th Infantry Division	11 July
79th Infantry Division	19 June
80th Infantry Division	8 August
83rd Infantry Division	27 June
90th Infantry Division	10 June

Allied Expeditionary Air Force

Air Chief Marshal Sir Trafford Leigh-Mallory

RAF 2nd Tactical Air Force
Air Marshal Sir Arthur Coningham

No 2, 83, 84 and 85 Group
Airborne and Transport Services
No 38 and 46 Group

US 9th Air Force
Lieutenant-General Lewis Bereton
(until 7 August when replaced by Major-General Joyt Vandenberg)

IX Tactical Air Command
70, 71 and 84 Fighter Wing

XIX Tactical Air Command
100 and 303 Fighter Wing

IX Bomber Command
97, 98 and 99 Bombardment Wing

IX Troop Carrier Command
50, 52 and 53 Troop Carrier Wing

RAF Air Defence of Great Britain
No. 10, 11, 12 and 13 Group

Allied Strategic Air Force

RAF Bomber Command
Air Chief Marshal Sir Arthur Harris

No. 1, 3, 4, 5, 6, 8 and 100 Group

US 8th Air Force
Lieutenant-General James Doolittle

1st, 2nd and 3rd Bombardment Wings
VIII Fighter Command

RAF Coastal Command
No. 15, 16, 18 and 19 Group

Allied Naval Forces

Operation Neptune

Eastern Task Force
Rear Admiral Sir Phillip Vian – Flagship HMS *Scylla*

Sword Beach
Force S
Rear Admiral A.G. Talbot – HQ Ship HMS *Largs*
(Each force comprised assault, close support, gunfire support and mine-sweeper groups)

Juno Beach
Force J
Commodore G.N. Oliver – HQ Ship HMS *Hilary*

Gold Beach
Force G
Commodore C.E. Douglas-Pennant – HQ Ship HMS *Bulolo*

Western Task Force
Admiral A.G. Kirk – Flagship USS *Augusta*

Omaha Beach
Force O
Rear Admiral J.L. Hall – HQ Ship *Ancon*

Utah Beach
Force U
Rear Admiral Don P. Moon – HQ Ship *Bayfield*

1,212 major combat vessels, 4,125 landing craft and 864 merchant ships, plus 3,567 special equipment (craft, swimming tanks and trucks)

German Order of Battle in Normandy

6 June – 31 August 1944

Commander-in-Chief West
Field Marshal Gerd von Rundstedt
(until 2 July when replaced by Günther von Kluge)
Chief of Staff
General Günther Blumentritt

Army Group B (Northern France and the Low Countries)
Commander
Field Marshal Erwin Rommel
(until 17 July when wounded and succeeded by von Kluge)

Panzergruppe West
Commander
General Geyr von Schweppenburg
(until 6 July when replaced by General Heinrich Eberbach, armoured command Fifth Panzer Army and then Panzergruppe Eberbach)

	Arrived
1st SS Panzer Division	late June
2nd Panzer Division	mid June
2nd SS Panzer Division	late June
9th Panzer Division	early August
12th SS Panzer Division	7 June
17th SS Panzergrenadier Division	12 June
21st Panzer Division	in Normandy
116th Panzer Division	20 July
Panzer Lehr Division	8 June

Seventh Army
Commander
General Friedrich Dollmann

(until 28 June suicide or heart attack and replaced by SS-General Paul Hausser)

77th, 243rd, 265th 266th, 275th, 343rd, 352nd, 353rd, 709th and 716th Infantry Divisions, plus the 91st Airlanding Division and the 2nd, 3rd and 5th Parachute Divisions.

Fifteenth Army (north of the Seine)
Commander
General Hans von Salmuth

48th Infantry Division	mid-August
84th Infantry Division	by 30 July
85th Infantry Division	5 August
326th Infantry Division	by 30 July
331st Infantry Division	by 30 July
344th Infantry Division	mid-August
346th Infantry Division	by 29 June
711th Infantry Division	by 29 June
17th Luftwaffe Field Division	mid-August

Units from Army Group G (southern France)

First Army
276th Infantry Division	mid-June
708th Infantry Division	late July

Nineteenth Army
271st Infantry Division	24 July
272nd Infantry Division	24 July
277th Infantry Division	late June
338th Infantry Division	mid-August

From outside France and the Low Countries
9th SS Panzer Division (Russia)	late June
10th SS Panzer Division (Russia)	late June
2nd Parachute Division (Germany to Brittany)	mid-June
89th Infantry Division (Norway)	early August

363rd Infantry Division (Denmark)   late July
16th Luftwaffe Field Division (Netherlands)   mid-June

Independent Armoured Units
12th Fallschirm Sturmgeschütz Brigade, 101st and 102nd Heavy SS
Panzer Battalions, 206th Panzer Battalion, 217th Sturmpanzer Battalion,
4th Company, 301st Panzer Battalion (Radio-controlled), 316th
Company, 302nd Panzer Battalion (Radio-controlled), 341st and 394th
Sturmgeschütz Brigades, 503rd Heavy Panzer Battalion, 654th Heavy
Panzerjäger Battalion, 657th Panzerjäger Battalion, 902nd and 1348th
Sturmgeschütz Battalions.

NOTES & REFERENCES

Introduction: Half-Man, Half-Beast

1. The Royal Marine Armoured Support Group consisted of two regiments, each comprising two armoured support batteries, plus an independent battery, making a total of five. The 2nd Royal Marine Armoured Support Regiment was assigned to Juno Beach and the independent battery to Sword Beach. My thanks to Cobbaton Combat Collection for highlighting the little-known and unsung role of the RMASG and their Centaurs on D-Day.
2. Lewis, *D-Day as They Saw It*, p.25.
3. Ibid., p.62.
4. Ibid.
5. Ibid.
6. Arthur, *Forgotten Voices of the Second World War*, pp.313–14.
7. Ibid., p.316.
8. Lewis, *op. cit.*, p.124.
9. Ibid, p.128. The tanks responsible for this accident did not belong to the Royal Marines.
10. Bailey, *Forgotten Voices of D-Day*, p.262.
11. Warner, *The D Day Landings*, p.220.
12. Ibid., p.221.
13. Neillands and De Norman, *D-Day 1944 Voices from Normandy*, p.207.
14. Warner, *op. cit.*, p.221.
15. Ibid.
16. This was how Eisenhower described them. Thompson, *D-Day*, p.157.
17. Hills, *By Tank into Normandy*, pp.68–69.

1: Absolute Disaster

1. Trevor-Roper, *Hitler's War Directives 1939–1945*, p.171.
2. Directive No.40, dated 23 March 1942, Ref. 'Competence of Commanders in coastal areas.' Ibid.
3. Ibid., p.175.

4. Hitler first embarked on a major fixed fortification programme in the late 1930s with the Siegfried Line or Westwall. This was a massive drain on resources and ultimately proved to be a 'white elephant'. During 1936–40 around 150,000 people using 9 million tons of raw materials constructed some 17,000 bunkers.

5. British intelligence erroneously assessed the unit to be the 110th Infantry Division, which was, in fact, on the Eastern Front.

6. Interservice cooperation developing amphibious warfare techniques was masterminded by Lord Mountbatten and his British Combined Operations Headquarters. He took over this role in late 1941 and recalled, 'I went to Combined Operations Headquarters and found there were only twenty-six persons all told and not a single regular active-service officer or man among them. Before I left, this number had increased twenty-fold, all working at full pressure. The actual sailors, soldiers and airmen in Combined Operations Command increased to 50,000 trained experts.' In the autumn of 1943 he was posted to South-east Asia. Tute, *D-Day*, pp.4–5.

7. Atkin, *Dieppe 1942*, p.224.

8. See James Dorrian's *Storming St Nazaire: The Gripping Story of the Dock-Busting Raid, March, 1942* (London: Leo Cooper, 1998).

9. Canadian 14th Tank Battalion War Diary, 1941.

10. Ibid.

11. Arthur, *Forgotten Voices of the Second World War*, p.189.

12. Ibid.

13. Atkin, *op. cit.*, p.162.

14. Ibid., p.164.

15. Arthur, *op. cit.*, pp.194–95.

16. Tucker-Jones, 'Churchill's Dieppe Disaster', *Military Illustrated*, September 2008

17. Franks, *RAF Fighter Command*, p.154. This sources says that Johnson was commanding 610 Squadron and not 616 as recorded by Arthur.

18. Atkin, *op. cit.*, p.233.

19. When the smoke had cleared the Germans salvaged six Churchill Mk Is, seven Churchill Mk IIs and ten Churchill Mk IIIs. Most of these were badly damaged but one of each type was sent to the German Army Weapons Office at Kummersdorf for technical exploitation. Amongst those still functioning were *Beetle*, a Mk II formerly commanded by Lieutenant G. Drysdale, whose engine and drive train were still working, and *Blondie*, a Mk III formerly commanded by Corporal Jordan: this was photographed being driven by *panzertruppen*. They also captured seven scout cars and a truck.

20. Tucker-Jones, *op. cit.*

21. The Calgary Tank Regiment suffered thirteen dead, thirty-three wounded and 138 captured along with the loss of all their tanks. In total the Canadians lost 906 killed, the Commandos 270 killed, wounded and captured, and the Royal Navy 550 as well as losing a destroyer and numerous landing craft. The RAF lost 106 aircraft and 153 aircrew. In mopping up, the Germans took 2,195 prisoners. The Germans admitted to losing 600 casualties and forty-eight aircraft. See Atkin, *Dieppe 1942*, pp.251–54, and Perret, *For Valour*, p.272.

22. On their return to Britain the remaining Calgarys were re-equipped with Sherman tanks and became the Canadian 14th Armoured Regiment. With Canadian 1st Armoured Brigade they took part in the invasions of Sicily and Italy in 1943. They eventually joined the Canadian First Army in Holland in early 1945 where they ended the war. The unit never forgot its bloody debut at Dieppe with the Churchill tank.

23. Lovat, *March Past*, pp.268–69.

24. Young, *Commando*, p.153.

25. Arthur, *op. cit.*, p194.
26. Thanks to its thick armour the Churchill tank in various guises was later to play a highly specialised engineering role in the D-Day landings. By the end of the war, 5,640 Churchills had been built. A variant armed with the powerful 17-pdr, known as the Black Prince, was developed, though it never went into production.
27. Tute, *D-Day*, p.44.
28. These were dubbed Wolfsschlucht I & II, located at Brûly-de-Pesche, Belgium, and Margival, France.

2: Pouring Concrete

1. Belchem, *Victory in Normandy*, p.28.
2. Speer, *Inside the Third Reich*, p.274.
3. Ibid.
4. Todt held the position of three ministers; he had been in charge of road building, navigable waterways and power plants, Minister of Armaments and Munitions, and headed the construction industry along with the Todt Organisation. Ibid, p.275
5. After sulking Göring later relented and attended Todt's funeral.
6. Boyd, *Normandy in the Time of Darkness*, p.120.
7. Ibid.
8. Ibid., p.136.
9. Rankin, *Churchill's Wizards*, p.567.
10. Ibid.
11. Speer, *op. cit.*, p.433.
12. Ibid., p.440.
13. General Zeitzler noted this on 17 May 1944. However, three days earlier a doctor's report concluded that Speer was fit and healthy. Ibid, p.452.
14. Ibid., p.477. Atlantic Wall fortifications included mutually supporting strongpoints, or *Stutzpunkt* and *Wiederstandnest*, capable of housing an infantry platoon equipped with machine guns and anti-tank weapons. There were also larger fortified positions called *Verteidigungsbereich*. Whether Hitler was helped with his bunker designs is not clear, but most proved to be bomb- and shell-proof.
15. Boyd, *op. cit.*, p.186.
16. Cruickshank, *The German Occupation of the Channel Islands*, p.181.
17. Stephenson, *The Channel Islands 1941–45*, p.12.
18. This was the 213th Panzer Battalion, which arrived in late March 1942. See Michael Ginns' *German Armour in the Channel Islands 1941–1945* (Jersey: Channel Islands Occupation Society) and Werner Regenberg & Horst Scheibert's *Captured French Tanks under the German Flag* (Atglen, PA: Schiffer, 1997).
19. Cruickshank, *op. cit.*, p.203.
20. These occupation forces totalled 23,700 men, with 12,000 on Guernsey, 8,850 on Jersey and 2,850 on Alderney. Following D-Day, 28,500 Germans troops and 62,000 civilians were trapped on the islands. Stephenson, *op. cit.*, pp.50, 54.
21. Ibid., p.20.
22. This amounted to 255,000 cubic metres, compared to 244,000 cubic metres. Cruickshank, *op. cit.*, p188.
23. This amounted to 6,100,000 cubic metres, compared to 484,000 cubic metres. Ibid., pp.187–88.
24. Ibid.
25. Speer, *op. cit.*, p.477.

26. Ibid.

27. For more on this issue see Williams, *Hitler's Atlantic Wall*, p.180.

3: A Pleasant Chateau

1. Sebba, *Les Parisiennes*, p.188.

2. This nickname arose because of their light grey uniforms. These women were often employed as telephonists and radio operators. The specialist arm badge for signallers was a lightning bolt, which resulted in them also being called *Blitzmädchen* or *Blitzweiben*. Ibid, pp.114–15.

3. Unfortunately the 'Grey Mice' developed a reputation for being 'Officers' Mattresses'. Ibid., p.118.

4. This ridiculously meant that each division was expected to hold a 50-mile front, without allowing for any reserves. During the First World War, the conventional wisdom was that if a division was expecting attack it should not have a frontage of more than 3 miles! Liddell Hart, *The Other Side of the Hill*, p.382.

5. Mitcham, *Hitler's Field Marshals and their Battles*, p.289.

6. Trevor-Roper, *Hitler's War Directives 1939–1945*, p.173.

7. Tute, *D-Day*, p.52.

8. Liddell Hart, *op. cit.*, p.403.

9. Mitcham, *op. cit.*, p.290.

10. Seaton, *The German Army 1933–45*, p.220.

11. Liddell Hart, *op. cit.*, p.388.

12. Ibid., p.389.

13. Irving, *The Trail of the Fox*, p.284.

14. Ibid. – this came to pass on 1 July 1944.

15. Ibid., p.288.

16. This was according to Lieutenant-Colonel Fritz Ziegelmann, Chief of Staff, 352nd Infantry Division. Cited Zetterling, *Normandy 1944*, p.277, drawing on Ziegelmann's post-war account of his division.

17. These comprised 179 divisions on the Eastern Front, fifty-three in France and the Low Countries, twenty-six in the Balkans, twenty-two in Italy, sixteen in Scandinavia and eight in Finland, giving a grand total of 304 divisions. By June 1944 there were fifty-nine German divisions in the West, with eight in Belgium and the Netherlands. Over half of the total were static defence or training divisions. Of the remaining twenty-seven field divisions, just ten were armoured, with three in the south and one deployed near Antwerp.

18. This was achieved by the creation of a phantom British Fourth Army in Scotland, and the deception was maintained until July 1944, forcing Hitler to keep 300,000 troops in Norway. Likewise, phantom units in south-eastern England served to tie German forces north of the Seine for a considerable period after D-Day.

19. Liddell Hart, *op. cit.*, pp.383–84.

20. Ibid., p.401.

21. Ibid.

22. Irving, *op. cit.*, p.287.

23. Young, *D-Day*, p.16.

24. Liddell Hart, *op. cit.*, pp.394–95.

25. Young, *op. cit.*, p.16.

26. Ibid., p.17, & D'Este, *Eisenhower*, p.529.

27. Professor Stoebe, also spelt Stöbe, was the Luftwaffe's chief meteorologist based at their headquarters in the Luxembourg Palace, Paris. See Ryan, *The Longest Day*, pp.23, 69–70.

28. Butcher, *Three Years with Eisenhower*, p.555. After D-Day, Major Lettau was captured by American troops while attempting to get to Rennes from Paris. Once it was known who he was, his role became of great interest to his Allied counterparts. Both Lettau and Stoebe served the Luftwaffe's 3rd Air Fleet.

29. Haswell, *The Intelligence and Deception of the D-Day Landings*, p.169.

30. Wilmot, *The Struggle for Europe*, p.229.

31. The Luftwaffe and German Navy were well aware that the Allies had taken deliberate steps to hamper their weather forecasting capabilities. This first involved capturing or destroying their weather stations and then hunting down their weather ships. Those that could not be reached or were on neutral territory were subjected to electronic jamming. See Haswell, *op. cit.*, pp.167–68.

32. Mitcham, *op. cit.*, p.291.

4: The European Tour

1. Liddell Hart, *The Rommel Papers*, p.172.

2. Rommel almost certainly did not get the job because he advocated creating a defensive line north of Rome to avoid becoming trapped by the Allies' amphibious capabilities. Kesselring, in contrast, maintained a successful defence could be conducted to the south. He was to be proved right. Ibid., pp.446–47.

3. Ibid., p.436.

4. Captain Berndt was an official from Goebbels' Propaganda Ministry and attached to Rommel's staff in North Africa. He greatly admired Rommel, as did Goebbels. See Macksey, *Rommel*, pp.188–89.

5. Ibid., pp.190–91.

6. Ibid., p.189.

7. Field Marshal von Rundstedt CinC West's forces comprised Army Group B in northern France and the Low Countries, with Seventh and Fifteenth Armies, while in the south of France was Army Group G, with the First and Nineteenth Armies.

8. Speer, *Inside the Third Reich*, p.478.

9. Ibid.

10. Ibid. During this meeting Hitler had shown Rommel and Speer a self-propelled 88mm anti-aircraft gun which he claimed would provide an answer to all the Army's problems in fending off enemy aircraft. This was not a new idea and never came to fruition.

11. Irving, *The Trail of the Fox*, p.285. Historians can be notoriously bad at agreeing on dates. For example, Kaplan, *Hitler's D-Day Defences*, p.24, says that Rommel commenced his inspection on 30 November 1943.

12. Liddell Hart, *op. cit.*, p.461.

13. The German occupation forces in Denmark were convinced that an invasion might take place on the country's west coast. To counter this threat, they laid 2.2 million mines. Director Martin Zandvliet's Danish movie *Land of Mine* (2017) dramatises the terrible results of this decision when young German prisoners were made to remove 1.5 million mines after the war ended.

14. This is according to Irving, *op. cit.*, p.285, who says Rommel left Denmark on 14 December to go on leave in Bavaria. Irving causes some confusion here because, according to the *Rommel Papers*, Rommel arrived at Fontainbleau, France, on 14 December 1943; see p.461. Although *The Trail of the Fox* is extensively researched, Irving gives no explanation for the discrepancy.

15. Ibid.

16. Ibid.

17. Ibid.

18. Liddell Hart, *op. cit.*, p.461. Rommel called it 'a lovely place'. Strangely, Irving says, 'Rommel did not like it', p.286, yet he cites *The Rommel Papers* in his bibliography. Again there is no rationale for this statement.

19. Irving, *op. cit.*, p.287.

20. Eberle & Uhl, *The Hitler Book*, p.118.

21. This was previously called the Siegfried Battery, until renamed in honour of Fritz Todt, and consisted of four massive 380mm guns which could reach the British coast.

22. Eberle & Uhl, *op. cit.*, p.118.

23. Liddell Hart, *op. cit.*, p.455.

24. This force was raised from Indian troops captured in North Africa at the request of Indian nationalist leader Subbas Chandra Bose. Volunteers numbered around 2,000 at the end of 1942, with them being designated the 950th Indian Infantry Regiment. Perhaps not surprisingly, the unit never saw combat. See Jurado, *Foreign Volunteers of the Wehrmacht 1941–45*, pp.20–29.

25. Liddell Hart, *op. cit.*, p.453.

26. Ibid.

27. Ibid., p.455.

28. Ibid., p.457.

29. By the end of May 1944, the War Diary of Army Group B recorded that 4,193,167 mines had been laid on the Channel coast (2,672,000 of them on Rommel's orders). Another 1,852,820 improvised mines were under construction. There were sufficient explosives in France to produce 20 million anti-personnel mines. In addition, 517,000 foreshore obstacles had been placed on the Channel coast, of which 31,000 were fitted with mines. Just days before D-Day, Rommel was issued with a million captured shells to be fitted to the air-landing obstacles, but there was no time to install them. Ibid., pp.457–60.

30. Irving, *op. cit.*, p.293.

31. Ibid.

32. Liddell Hart, *op. cit.*, p.462.

33. These were, west to east, the 709th, 352nd, 716th and 711th Infantry Divisions deployed between Quinéville and Cabourg. They numbered 12,320, 12,734, 7,771 and 7,242 men respectively. A fifth division, the 243rd, totalling 11,529 men, was deployed in the Cherbourg area. See Zetterling, *Normandy 1944*.

34. What Rommel did not know was that the French Resistance were closely monitoring the 716th Division headquarters. One of its members, school teacher Andre Heintz, lived just across the road with his parents. He regularly gathered intelligence on German troop movements through Caen. Mayo, *D-Day Minute by Minute*, p.109.

35. Utah, Omaha, Gold, Juno and Sword.

36. Irving, *op. cit.*, p.297.

37. Ibid., p.303.

38. Liddell Hart, *op. cit.*, p.463.

5: The Fanatic

1. Irving, *The Trail of the Fox*, p.303.

2. Ibid.

3. Ibid., p.302.

4. Ibid., p.303.

5. They would have been from the 919th Grenadier Regiment, 709th Infantry Division.

6. Clark Lee, 'Rommel was Fooled about Mines: There were not enough to go round', *Southern Daily Echo*, 10 June 1944.

7. Ibid. After D-Day, Lee says this story was confirmed by US intelligence officers and him witnessing American military hospitals placed in French fields from where neither signs or mines had been removed.

8. According to Allied intelligence, there were eight concrete bunkers containing guns of 75mm or larger calibre, thirty-five pillboxes with artillery or automatic weapons, four batteries of artillery, eighteen anti-tank guns, six mortar pits, thirty-five rocket-launching sites (each with four 38mm rocket tubes) and no fewer than 85 machine-gun positions. The latter was a particular cause for concern. See Ryan, *The Longest Day*, p.155.

9. Ibid., p.99.

10. Zetterling, *Normandy 1944*, p.278.

11. There were fifteen of these running east to west, designated WN-60 to WN-74. Kaplan, *Hitler's D-Day Defences*, pp.160–61.

12. Ambrose, *D-Day*, p.274.

13. These consisted of two dachshunds called Ajax and Elbo in January 1944, and a hunting dog in May 1944. Rommel had given Ajax to his wife as a surprise, but unfortunately it was run over by a car.

14. Liddell Hart, *The Rommel Papers*, p.463.

15. Golley, *The Big Drop*, p.37.

16. Williams, *Hitler's Atlantic Wall*, p.138.

17. Zetterling, *op. cit.*, p.298. Other conflicting reports state that by D-Day the Germans had installed old 75mm guns.

18. Williams, *op. cit.*, p.139

19. Thompson, *D-Day*, p.60

20. The 91st Airlanding Division had two battalions of 105mm mountain howitzers rather than the 105mm field howitzer that did not use the same ammunition. This meant the division only had the ammunition it brought with it and could not be resupplied. Zetterling, *op. cit.*, p.239.

21. Thompson, *op. cit.*, p.60. Behind the coastline between Le Havre and Dieppe, two German divisions also created 'Rommel's Asparagus' by erecting 250,000 camouflaged stakes with barbed wire in suspected airborne drop zones. Ruffner, *Luftwaffe Field Divisions 1941–45*, p.20.

22. Rommel partly held the Luftwaffe responsible for this sorry state of affairs. Reichsmarschall Hermann Göring refused to release the II Parachute Corps or the III Flak Corps to help build the defences. In addition, although they lacked aircraft to help defend the Atlantic Wall, they still had the manpower to deploy 50,000 men in a communications role and another 300,000 deployed on the ground. This meant that there were 100 men on the ground for every one flying.

23. Thompson, *op. cit.*, p.60.

24. Zetterling, *op. cit.*, p.277.

25. Thompson, *op. cit.*, p.62.

26. Liddle, *D-Day By Those Who Were There*, p.52.

27. Ibid.

28. Carell, *Invasion – They're Coming!*, p.205.

29. Guderian, *Panzer Leader*, p.330.

30. Young, *D-Day*, p.8.

31. See Lefèvre, *Panzers in Normandy Then and Now*, p.123.

32. Its panzers were rationed to firing just five rounds per month. Ibid., p.104.

33. These were the 100th Panzer Training and Replacement Battalion stationed at Carentan and the 206th Panzer Battalion at Beaumont.
34. Liddell Hart, *op. cit.*, p.464.
35. Macksey, *Rommel*, p.207.
36. See '7 June: III Flak Corps Moving up to Normandy', by General der Flak Wolfgang Pickert, in Isby (ed), *Fighting in Normandy*, p.49.
37. There has been some confusion as to whether Rommel departed on 4 or 5 June 1944. Army Group B's War Diary recorded him leaving at 0700 hours on the 4th. Ryan, *op. cit.*, p.35.
38. This included two panzer divisions, a flak corps, a rocket launcher brigade and the mining of the Bay of Seine. Rommel felt it was vital to move these additional units forward before they were detected by Allied fighter-bombers. He planned to see Hitler at Berchtesgaden the day after his wife's birthday celebrations. He was not destined to see either. Liddell Hart, *op. cit.*, p.470.
39. Ibid.
40. For some reason Rommel's visit to Hitler was kept secret. Only Hitler's adjutant, Major-General Rudolf Schmundt, knew; all the other senior staff officers were unaware that Rommel was headed for Germany. Ryan, *op. cit.*, p.35.

6: Get Monty

1. For more on the detailed development of COSSAC's plans see George Bruce's *Second Front Now! The Road to D-Day* (London: Macdonald and Jane's, 1979).
2. Ibid., p.104.
3. Ibid., p.115.
4. Ibid., p.109.
5. Tute, *D-Day*, p.35.
6. During 1942–43, the British and Americans had come up with competing plans. The British conceived landings, dubbed Sledgehammer, either side of Normandy's Cotentin peninsula. The Americans suggested landings, dubbed Roundup, in the Calais and Dieppe areas.
7. Morgan, *Overture to Overlord*, p.165.
8. Belchem, *Victory in Europe*, p.16. Monty thought very highly of David Belchem and used him as a stand-in Chief of Staff whenever de Guingand was sick, a role he had filled admirably in North Africa. See Montgomery, *The Memoirs*, pp.204–05.
9. A major problem was caused by the availability of sufficient landing craft to support operations in Europe, the Mediterranean and the Pacific. Also, Churchill did not want to redeploy more divisions than necessary from Italy. For further reading on this issue see Tucker-Jones, *Operation Dragoon: The Liberation of Southern France 1944* (Barnsley: Pen & Sword, 2009).
10. D'Este, *Decision in Normandy*, p.57.
11. Montgomery, *The Memoirs*, p.210.
12. 'First Impressions of Operation "Overlord" made at the request of the Prime Minister by General Montgomery', Appendix 'A', marked Most Secret, 1 January 1944, cited Montgomery, *op. cit.*, p.210.
13. Ibid.
14. Eisenhower correspondence to Sir Ismay, 3 December 1960.
15. Alexander, *The Alexander Memoirs 1940–1945*, p.42.
16. Eisenhower, *At Ease*, p.268. His title was Supreme Commander Allied Expeditionary Force.
17. Montgomery, *op. cit.*, p.213.

18. Ike was referring to Hitler's V-1 flying bomb and V-2 rocket which were being deployed to the Pas de Calais region. Eisenhower, *op. cit.*, p.273.
19. de Guingand, *Operation Victory*, p.342.
20. Belchem, *op. cit.*, p.47.
21. Ibid., p.54.
22. de Guingand, *op. cit.*, p.357.
23. Ibid., p.356.
24. Montgomery, *op. cit.*, p.223.
25. de Guingand, *op. cit.*, p.358.
26. Belchem says that Monty compounded the issue. 'Because this troublesome "forecast" map subsequently appeared in Montgomery's book *Normandy to the Baltic* – complete with the phase-lines which, through an oversight, were not removed prior to publication as had been the intention – it has unfortunately misled many conscientious students of the Normandy campaign.' Belchem, *op. cit.*, p.54. Likewise, de Guingand's book *Operation Victory*, first published in January 1947, included the phase line map, see p.359
27. This was dubbed the Transportation Plan.
28. Harris, *Bomber Offensive*, p.197.
29. This was dubbed the Oil Plan.
30. Butcher, *Three Years with Eisenhower*, p.427.
31. Ibid.
32. Irving, *The War Between the Generals*, p.81.
33. Notably in his wartime memoir *Bomber Offensive*, published just two years after the war ended, Harris makes just the briefest of references to Leigh-Mallory and Spaatz, on p.215.
34. Eisenhower, *At Ease*, p.265.
35. Ibid., p.272.
36. Irving, *op. cit.*, p.84.
37. Butcher, *op. cit.*, p.440.
38. de Guingand, *op. cit.*, p.346.
39. Belchem, *op. cit.*, p.30.
40. Eisenhower, *Crusade in Europe*, p.261.
41. Wilmot, *The Struggle for Europe*, p.195. Wilmot gives the impression that this was an accident. However, examination of strike photograph A.C.I.U. Neg.No. 59615 'Sympathetic Detonation of Mines on Under-Water Obstacles Benerville', which shows fourteen such explosions, suggests that this was probably deliberate. The bomb blast was some considerable distance from the sympathetic detonations and yet the photograph caught the incident very precisely, providing an intelligence windfall. See AIR 401959 – Photographic Intelligence for D-Day, Under Water Obstacles Normandy Coast, p.62.
42. Belchem, *op. cit.*, p.31.
43. Ibid., p.37.
44. Ibid., p.38.
45. Ibid.

7: Weird & Wonderful

1. These principally comprised the Sherman Duplex Drive (DD) swimming tank, the Churchill Armoured Vehicle Royal Engineers (AVRE) tank and the Sherman Crab flail tank. Other vehicles included bridgelayers, bulldozers and flamethrowers.
2. Hobart started his career in the Royal Engineers, seeing action in the First World War. In 1923, he transferred to the Tank Corps and a decade later rose to the post of

Inspector of the Royal Tank Corps. In 1937, he was appointed Director of Military Training, a post he did not really want because the establishment was on the whole unreceptive to the tank.

3. This observation was made by Alan Herbert. Hamilton, *The Making of a General 1887–1942*, p.199.

4. This became the famous 7th Armoured Division that was also to fight in Italy and Normandy.

5. Schofield, *Wavell: Soldier & Statesman*, p.134.

6. Ibid., pp.134–35. Officers such as Major-General Nigel Duncan, who served under Hobart, felt he was treated 'unjustly'. However, even after the war General Wavell stuck to his decision to sack Hobart.

7. Churchill had been alerted to Hobart's plight by an article by Captain Liddell Hart which complained that forward-thinking armour enthusiasts such as Hobart were being wasted. Churchill had met Hobart in 1936 when he was a brigadier in command of the Tank Brigade. See Martin Gilbert, *Churchill A Life*, p.564. According to Barrie Pitt in *Churchill and the Generals*, Hobart saw the Prime Minister before he was summoned by Dill, so he must have made a good impression.

8. Forty, *7th Armoured Division*, p.9.

9. From its creation in 1942, the British 79th Armoured Division was a regular armoured unit, but the following year, with the impending invasion of Nazi-occupied France, it was earmarked for this key specialised role. In fact its task was so secret that the existence of the division was not publicly acknowledged until after the Rhine crossing in March 1945. Even then, specifications of some of the vehicles, such as the DD tank, were withheld until September 1945.

10. Futter, *The Funnies*, p.6.

11. de Guingand, *Operation Victory*, pp.352–53.

12. Macrae, *Winston Churchill's Toyshop*, p.127.

13. Futter, *op. cit.*, p.viii.

14. The British Valentine tank was first developed for this role, but was superseded by the American Sherman. For a fuller account see David Fletcher's *Swimming Shermans: Sherman DD amphibious tank of World War II* (Oxford: Osprey, 2006).

15. Eisenhower, *Crusade in Europe*, p.259.

16. The tank was pushed through the water by two propellers and kept buoyant by collapsible canvas screens.

17. Lewis, *D-Day as they Saw It*, p.16.

18. This was the submariners' Davis Escape Apparatus. It proved too large for tank hatches and was replaced by the specially designed Amphibious Tank Escape Apparatus.

19. Lewis, *op. cit.*, p.17.

20. Warner, *The D-Day Landings*, p.135.

21. Hills, *By Tank into Normandy*, p.61.

22. Ibid., p.57.

23. Bailey, *Forgotten Voices of D-Day*, p.37.

24. Hills, *op. cit.*, p.61.

25. Bailey, *op, cit.*, p.37.

26. Hills, *op. cit.*, p.60.

27. The fatalities were from the 4th/7th Dragoon Guards. Fletcher, *op. cit.*, p.14. According to Second Lieutenant Stuart Hills' information, there were reportedly 30,000 DD tank training launchings conducted, with just one fatality.

28. Hills, *op. cit.*, p.62.

29. Chamberlain and Ellis, *British and American Tanks of World War Two*, p.61. Futter's *'The Funnies'*, p.78, says over 600 Valentines were converted by 1944.

30. Bailey, *op. cit.*, p.37.

31. Duncan, *79th Armoured Division*, p.16.

32. Ibid., pp.18–19. The Sherman DD tank consisted of steel decking around the hull, upon which a screen could be raised by thirty-six air tubes and secured by hinged struts. Importantly, the front screen could be lowered to facilitate firing. The Duplex Drive i.e. propeller and tracks could manage 4–5 knots, and although the low silhouette in the water enabled an element of tactical surprise on D-Day, they had a nasty habit of capsizing in rough water.

33. Warner, *op. cit.*, p.135.

34. Highly respected tank historian David Fletcher poses the question whether there was a shortage of DD tanks, and concludes there was. See Fletcher, *Swimming Shermans*, p.17.

35. Frayn Turner, *Invasion '44*, p.33, and Wilmot, *The Struggle for Europe*, p.182.

36. This meant that each DD regiment retained a squadron of regular Shermans that would have to be delivered by landing craft. Fletcher reports a requirement for 693 DD tanks in the second half of 1943, pp.14–15.

37. In the DD tank regiments, the 3-ton lorries were replaced with the amphibious 6x6 DUKW, which were veterans of the campaigns in the Mediterranean. The prototype was built around the cab over engine six-wheel-drive military truck GMC, with the addition of a watertight hull and a propeller. However, it was not an armoured vehicle, and at 7.5 tons managed just 6.4mph in water or a respectable 55mph on land. The DUKW rode the waves well, its bilge pumps meant it could be kept free of water and for ship-to-shore stores ferrying it was ideal. Less glamorously, the division was also equipped with armoured bulldozers, largely the American Caterpillar Tractor Company's D.8, protected by armoured superstructure and engine cover.

38. Wilmot, *op. cit.*, p.182. Wilmot was to take part in D-Day, flying in with the British 6th Airborne Division.

39. Fletcher, *op. cit.*, p.17.

40. Ibid., p.18.

41. Frayn Turner, *op. cit.*, p.33, and Wilmot, *op. cit.*, p.182. On 6 June 1944, the Americans committed about ninety DD tanks, the British eighty and the Canadians seventy, giving a total of 245. Duncan, *79th Armoured Division*, p.48. Fletcher says at the end of June 1944, the British and Canadians had a total of 326 DD tanks.

42. Duncan, *op. cit.*, p.18.

43. This was 27th Armoured Brigade.

44. These were the 1st Hussars (Canadian 6th Armoured Regiment), Fort Garry Horse (Canadian 10th Armoured Regiment) and the US 70th, 741st and 743rd Tank Battalions.

45. Kahn, *D-Day Assault*, p.153.

46. Ibid., p.152.

47. Arthur, *op. cit.*, p.285. Some of these, nicknamed the 'Bobbin', were also fitted with a carpet layer for crossing soft clay and sand. Other variants included the ARK (Armoured Ramp Carrier), the mine-clearing Bullshorn Plough (which was only used on the Normandy beaches) and the SBG (Small Box Girder) Assault Bridge. All these vehicles were operated by the 5th and 6th Assault Regiments Royal Engineers (ARE).

48. Bailey, *op. cit.*, p.33.

49. Ibid.

50. Arthur, *op. cit.*, p.286.

51. This organisation was Military Intelligence Research or Ministry of Defence I, headed by Brigadier Millis Jefferis, whose task was to design special weapons for irregular warfare. Macrae, *op. cit.*, p.127.

52. The Sherman Crab was designed to clear defended minefields and barbed wire. It consisted of a Sherman V (M4A4) gun tank fitted with a rotating flail, driven by the main drive shaft, with an effective depth of about 5in. Three regiments of the 79th were equipped with Crabs: the 22nd Dragoons, 1st Lothian and Border Yeomanry and the Westminster Dragoons.

53. Bailey, *op. cit.*, p.30. There is some discrepancy between Arthur and Bailey regarding Hammerton's details. The former cites a Major Ian Hammerton, 2nd County of London Yeomanry, Royal Armoured Corps, while the latter refers to him as Lieutenant Ian Hammerton, 22nd Dragoons. To further confuse matters, Peter Liddle in *D-Day by Those Who Were There*, pp.168–70, lists a Captain Ian Hammerton, 22nd Dragoons.

54. Duncan, *op. cit.*, p.19.

55. Ibid., p.1.

56. Macrae, *op. cit.*, p.127.

57. Ibid., p.128.

58. Lieutenant-Commander Hugh Irwin commanded the 591 Landing Craft Assault (Heavy Rocket) Flotilla. Arthur, *op. cit.*, p.305.

59. Warner, *op. cit.*, p.114.

60. Ibid., p.115.

61. de Guingand, *Operation Victory*, p.366.

62. Chalfont, *Montgomery of Alamein*, p.233. Interestingly, Monty makes no mention of Hobart or his role in the Normandy landings in his memoirs. In his *A Concise History of Warfare*, he briefly refers to the 'Funnies', but not Hobart. Likewise, Monty's official biographer, Nigel Hamilton, has nothing to say about Monty's relationship with Hobart other than that he married Betty, his sister. Alistair Horne and David Montgomery's *The Lonely Leader: Monty 1944–45* barely references Hobart either. Rightly or wrongly, this seems to imply that there was ill-feeling between the two men. It is likely that Hobart held Monty responsible for not acting sooner to save his sister, who died of blood poisoning following the amputation of an infected leg.

63. Wilmot, *op. cit.*, p.265. General Hobart's account was given to Chester Wilmot on 10 November 1946.

64. Butcher, *Three Years with Eisenhower*, p.413.

65. Ibid.

66. Eisenhower, *Crusade in Europe*, p.260.

67. Wilmot, *op. cit.*, p.265.

68. de Guingand, *op. cit.*, p.354.

69. Warner, *op. cit.*, p.153.

8: Send the Engineers

1. The beach at Westward Ho! was deemed to be too exposed for the cable, so Watermouth Cove was used instead. From there they practiced filling fuel tankers using the pipeline.

2. The base facilities for HMS Appledore were at Fremington and Ilfracombe.

3. Rommel's engineers had come up with three main types of beach obstacle. The first was called Element C, which looked like iron gates with a mine or shell on the top; these were placed at low tide so when the sea came in they were covered. Behind them were steel anti-tank hedgehogs and wooden stakes driven into the sand with mines on them.

4. Keith May Briggs, Oral History, Imperial War Museum, File 2, 20 June 1996 – www.iwm.org.uk/collections/item/object/80016162. Edited highlights of this interview were also published in Bailey, *Forgotten Voices of Normandy*, pp.217–18, 233.

5. Ibid.

6. Ryan, *The Longest Day*, p.177.

7. Ibid., pp.177–78. Sergeant Briggs was assigned to the teams dealing with obstacles on Juno Beach, while Sergeant Jones was deployed to Gold.

8. Ibid., p.177.

9. While the topography is completely different in the Pacific, North Africa and Italy offered some similarities to Northern Europe. A good introduction to this subject is Gordon Rottman's *US World War II Amphibious Tactics: Mediterranean & European Theaters* (Oxford: Osprey, 2006)

10. This conference ran from 24 May to 23 June 1943; Khan, *D-Day Assault*, pp.74–75.

11. The Assault Training Centre comprised ten training areas spread across North Devon, with the main focus at Braunton Burrows and Saunton Sands. These areas provided 8,000 yards of open beaches, with another 4,000 yards of estuary beaches. Extensive assault exercise areas were also established in South Devon around the Slapton Sands area.

    According to ATC historian Richard Bass, the centre and Slapton were completely separate entities. Paul Thompson, as commandant of the ATC, had no jurisdiction or influence over the Slapton Battle Exercise area, which seems to have been administered by the US Navy and US First Army based in Bristol. Troops, including engineers, learned nothing new at Slapton, but merely put into practice what Thompson's training had taught them. For Fabius I in May 1944, Paul Thompson, then commanding 6th Engineer Special Brigade, used Slapton as a rehearsal for their Omaha Beach plan.

12. Stephen Ambrose recounts that Colonel Thompson broke the ATC training down into four phases. First, individual training on the obstacle course; second, team training for the wire cutters and demolition men; third, company exercise; and fourth, battalion exercises. *D-Day*, p.137.

13. Bass, *The Spirits of the Sand*, pp.89–90. By far the worst pre-D-Day loss of lives occurred on a dress rehearsal off the English south coast with Operation Tiger during 26–28 April 1944. German motor torpedo boats sank two vessels and damaged another, resulting in 749 dead and 300 wounded. See Ambrose, *D-Day*, pp.139–40, and Mark Khan's *D-Day Assault: The Second World War Assault Training Exercises at Slapton Sands* (Barnsley: Pen & Sword Military, 2014).

14. Ambrose, *op. cit.*, p.137.

15. Bass, *Clear the Way!*, p.19.

16. Ibid., p.24.

17. Ibid.

18. Ibid., p.19.

19. Ibid.

20. Between 1 October 1943 and 31 January 1944, the ATC hosted 805 official visitors. These included a Russian delegation headed by Major General Sharapov. Bass, *Spirits of the Sand*, p.95.

21. The depot consisted of the US 33rd Ordnance Bomb Disposal Unit, 72nd Ordnance Battalion, 107th Ordnance Medium Maintenance Company and a supporting medical unit. See The *GI's in Bideford*, www.bidefordheritage.co.uk/life-in-bideford-during-ww2/gis-in-bideford.

22. 'Compound 219', *The Royal Pioneer*, No. 40, September 1954.

23. Ibid.
24. This was either at Instow, Saunton Sands or Woolacombe, which were the locations of extensive pre-D-Day training. Behind Saunton Sands in Braunton Burrows was the heart of the US Army's Assault Training centre facilities.
25. *Compound 219, op. cit.*
26. European Theater Operation records show that between 8 December 1943 and 8 July 1944, 3,570 personnel were trained as inspectors and instructors.
27. Arthur, *Forgotten Voices of the Second World War*, p.285.
28. Lewis, *D-Day as they Saw It*, p.33.
29. Bailey, *Forgotten Voices of D-Day*, p.71.
30. Arthur, *op. cit.*, p.285.
31. Bailey, *op. cit.*, p.71.
32. Lewis, *op. cit.*, p.15.
33. WW2 US Medical Research Centre – www.med-dept.com/unit-histories/313th-station-hospital/. The hospital was busy during the first three months of 1944 with 1,676 admissions, with an average daily population of about around 265 patients.
34. These were 1st Engineer Special Brigade (ESB), assigned to support the US 4th Infantry Division at Utah, 5 ESB with the 1st Infantry Division on the eastern half of Omaha and 6 ESB with the 29th Infantry Division on the western half of Omaha. Rottman, *US World War II Amphibious Tactics*, p.17.
35. Ambrose, *op. cit.*, p.144.
36. Ibid., p.143.
37. Khan, *D-Day Assault*, p.151.
38. Butcher, *Three Years with Eisenhower*, p.452.
39. D'Este, *Eisenhower*, p.515, and Ambrose, *D-Day*, p.139.
40. Highly respected American historian Carlo D'Este, in his masterly biography of Eisenhower, has no time for allegations that Ike covered up the German attack on Exercise Tiger. He accused the conspiracy theorists of 'an unseemly feeding frenzy'. See *Eisenhower*, pp.516, 782.

9: A Nice Lunch

1. The joint Naval and Military Club was founded in 1862 and purchased Cambridge House on Piccadilly three years later. It became known as the 'In and Out' Club because of its entrance and exit signs. Following the First World War, the club also leased the adjoining hotel, 42 Half Moon Street; it moved to 4 St James's Square in 1999.
2. Arthur, *Forgotten Voices of the Second World War*, p.283.
3. Ibid.
4. Ibid.
5. Walter and Tennant answered to Major-General Donald McMullen, Director of Transportation in the War Office, and his directorate called Transportation 5, responsible for port engineering. Walter's opposite number from the Royal Navy was Captain C.H. Petrie.
6. Tute, *D-Day*, p.72.
7. Arthur, *op cit.*, p.281.
8. Ibid., p.283.
9. Butcher, *Three Years with Eisenhower*, p.475.

10. This MI5 section was B1a, which had responsibility for detecting enemy spies and then turning them into double agents. This process had been completed by 1943 with the Double-Cross System.

11. Bailey, *Forgotten Voices of D-Day*, p.15.

12. Ibid.

13. Arthur, *op. cit.*, p.286.

14. Butcher, *op. cit.*, p.448.

15. Tute, *D-Day*, p.73.

16. Bailey, *op. cit.*, pp.9–11.

17. Belchem, *Victory in Normandy*, p.15.

18. Ibid.

19. Arthur, *The Silent Day*, p.70.

20. Ibid., p.67.

21. Ibid., p.29.

22. Muirhead Bone served as a war artist in the First World War, and during the Second World War was a member of the War Artists' Advisory Committee and a full-time artist for the Ministry of Information – his speciality was Admiralty subjects.

23. Collier, *The Warcos*, p.161.

24. Bone's finished work was called 'Building a caisson for Mulberry Harbour', see Thompson, *Victory in Europe*, p.1 plate section.

25. Arthur, *Forgotten Voices of the Second World War*, pp.282–83.

26. Butcher, *op. cit.*, p.448.

27. Arthur, *The Silent Day*, p.43.

28. Hartcup, *Code Name Mulberry*, p.103.

29. Mulberry B, to be deployed off Gold Beach, was under the direction of Brigadier Walter and Captain C.H. Petrie, RN, while Mulberry A, off Omaha Beach, was the responsibility of Captain A. Dayton Clark, USN.

30. Hartcup, *op. cit.*, p.103.

31. Warner, *The D Day Landings*, p.78.

32. Ibid., p.79.

10: Blinding the Enemy

1. 198 along with 609 Squadron constituted 123 Wing based at Thorney Island, Sussex, part of No 84 Group serving with the British 2nd Tactical Air Force. For a complete order of battle of Allied air force units involved in Operation Overlord, see Humphrey Wynn and Susan Young, *Prelude to Overlord* (Shrewsbury: Airlife, 1983).

2. Codenamed 'Chimney' by the British, this was a long-range early warning radar, with height-locating capabilities.

3. Franks, *Typhoon Attack*, p.73.

4. Jones, *Most Secret War*, p.400.

5. German radars not only gave warning of Allied bomber raids, they also monitored Allied shipping in the English Channel and North Sea. German maritime radars were used to direct E-boat attacks on Allied convoys.
Disaster had befallen the Royal Navy on the night of 23/24 October 1943. A light cruiser and six destroyers had been sent to catch a German merchant ship heading from Brest for the Channel. This was clearly a case of using a sledgehammer to crack a nut, and the hunters soon became the hunted. Deploying to the west of the Channel Islands, beyond the range of the German coastal batteries, they were detected by German radar. E-boats sank the cruiser and disabled one of the destroyers, with the

loss of 503 officers and ratings. A subsequent enquiry concluded the operation had been poorly planned. See Cruikshank, *The German Occupation of the Channel Islands*, pp.246–47.

6. By comparison, in 1940 Britain had eighteen large Chain Home radar stations covering the southern and eastern coast stretching from the Isle of Wight to Scotland. These could detect aircraft out to 100–180 miles up to 18,000ft. Below 3,000ft was covered by the Chain Home Low stations. However, while British radar of the time was good at tracking targets over the sea, it was not so efficient over land. See Levine, *Forgotten Voices of the Blitz and the Battle of Britain*, pp.139–41.

7. Jones, *op. cit.*, p.401. Jones' unit and the Central Interpretation Unit had over the years supported what were quaintly dubbed 'Rhubarb' operations. Although there was no operational requirement, Jones ensured that Fighter Command gathered detailed intelligence on German coastal radar stations, which included reconnaissance photos and maps. Rhubarb grows best in the dark, though it is not clear if the Germans or the RAF were being kept ignorant of the extent of Jones' intelligence-gathering against the enemy's coastal radars.

8. Franks, *op. cit.*, p.73.

9. 198 Squadron's attack may have been assessed by 35 Reconnaissance Wing, also part of 84 Group, which flew Spitfire and American-supplied Mustang recon aircraft from Gatwick, Surrey.

10. Jones, *op. cit.*, p.405.

11. Ibid.

12. Clifford, *Crusader*, p.94.

13. Major Manus, on the Planning Staff for the Dieppe raid, had given the order on the misapprehension that Jones was taking part in Operation Jubilee.

14. Irving, *The Rise and Fall of the Luftwaffe*, p.210.

15. Ibid., p.212.

16. Ibid., p.213.

17. On 12 August 1940, the Luftwaffe tried to silence the radar stations at Folkstone, Pevensey, Rye and Ventnor. Only the latter, on the Isle of Wight, remained off-air for three weeks; the others were back up and operating within a few hours. The following day, the Luftwaffe's massed assault went horribly wrong. See Collier, *Eagle Day: The Battle of Britain*, pp.28, 41.

18. This was according to Ernest Clark, who worked as a wireless operator at one of the radar stations. See Levine, *op. cit.*, p.257.

19. For example, on 18 August 1940 the Poling Chain Home and Chain Home Low radar stations were attacked by thirty-one German Stuka dive-bombers. They dropped a total of eighty bombs and hit only one Chain Home receiving mast, taking off the top. The Germans completely missed the Low installation. None of the radar staff were harmed. The radar was fixed within three days. Ibid., p.266.

20. Jones, *op. cit.*, p.405.

21. The Fécamp spoof fleet was to be created by the Lancaster bombers of 617 Squadron, 5 Group, and the Boulogne fleet by the Stirling bombers of 218 Squadron, 3 Group. They operated from Woodhall Spa, Lincolnshire, and Woolfox Lodge, Rutland, respectively.

22. Arthur, *Forgotten Voices of the Second World War*, p.288.

23. Mandrel was designed to jam the Freya defence radar. Ibid., p.290.

24. By this stage all German agents in Britain were under MI5's control. The key ones for feeding misinformation were Roman Garby-Czerniawski, codenamed, Brutus and Juan Pujol Garcia Garbo. Bailey, *Forgotten Voices of D-Day*, p.14.

25. These two plans were known as Fortitude South and Fortitude North. See Christopher Andrew, *The Defence of the Realm: The Authorized History of MI5* (London: Allen Lane, 2009).

26. Brutus claimed he was on the Allied Mission to the HQ of the non-existent phantom US 1st Army Group. Ibid., p.299.

27. Roberts, *Lorenz*, p.53.

28. Ibid., p.131.

29. 84 Group's targets included installations at Abbevile, Berck, Boulogne, Caen-Douvres, Cap d'Antifer, Cap Gris Nez, Cap de la Hague, Dieppe, Fécamp, Fruges-Predefin, Le Havre and St Valery en Caux. The sortie against Fécamp was presumably diversionary, with no intention of hitting the radar.

30. This testimony was given by a German PoW captured after the landings. Wynn & Young, *op. cit.*, p.116.

31. Squadron Leader Niblett was killed on 2 June 1944 by flak when attacking a radar near Dieppe. Franks, *op. cit.*, p.106.

32. Jones, *op. cit.*, p.406.

33. Ibid., p.407.

34. Ibid.

35. This raid involved twenty-eight Typhoons which delivered ninety-six rockets and 7 tons of bombs. Most of the latter were delayed-action, intended to go off after the landings had started.

36. Bailey, *Forgotten Voices of D-Day*, pp.17–18.

37. *London Gazette*, 2 January 1947.

38. Belchem, *Victory in Normandy*, p.58.

39. Jones, *op. cit.*, p.409.

40. Harris, *Bomber Offensive*, p.205.

41. Ibid.

11: The Weatherman

1. Tute, *D-Day*, p.110.

2. Butcher, *Three Years with Eisenhower*, p.473.

3. According to Eisenhower, these estimated losses equated to 50 per cent of the paratroops and 70 per cent of the gliders. Eisenhower, *Crusade in Europe*, p.270.

4. Ibid., p.271.

5. Butcher, *op. cit.*, p.62.

6. Eisenhower, *op. cit.*, p.273.

7. Montgomery, *The Memoirs*, p.248.

8. Hamilton, *Monty: Master of the Battlefield 1942–1944*, pp.606–07.

9. Ibid., p.607.

10. Eisenhower, *op. cit.*, p.274.

11. de Guingand, *Operation Victory*, p.373, quoting Alan Moorehead's book *Eclipse*.

12. Tute, *op. cit.*, p.112.

13. Haswell, *The Intelligence and Deception of the D-Day Landings*, p.166.

14. Eisenhower, *op. cit.*, p.275.

15. Stagg, *Forecast for Overlord*, p.116.

16. Ibid., p.118.

17. de Guingand, *op. cit.*, p.374.

18. Eisenhower, *op. cit.*, p.275.

19. Ambrose, *D-Day*, p.189, citing an Eisenhower interview with Walter Cronkite, held by the Eisenhower Center at the University of New Orleans. Ike makes no reference to this expression in *Crusade in Europe*. Over the years there has been some debate regarding the exact wording he actually used. For example, Chester Wilmot quotes

Eisenhower as saying, 'OK. We'll go.' See *The Struggle for Europe*, p.226. Carlo D'Este, in his superb biography *Eisenhower*, opts for the latter, p.526. De Guingand, in an interview with reporter Alan Moorehead, recalled Ike simply saying, 'We will sail tomorrow.' See *Operation Victory*, p.374. Ultimately it mattered little; what was important was his historic decision.

20. Montgomery, *op. cit.*, p.249.
21. Stagg, *op. cit.*, p.119.
22. Jones, *Most Secret War*, p.409.
23. Tute, *op. cit.*, p.146.
24. Ibid.
25. Thompson, *D-Day*, p.72.
26. Liddell Hart, *The Other Side of the Hill*, pp.404–05. The Seventh Army's records refuted this as they claimed the alarm was sent out at 0130 hours.
27. Ibid., p.405.
28. Ibid. Crucially, the I SS Panzer Corps would not be released until 1600 hours on 6 June, by which time it was way too late for it to intervene.
29. Ibid., p.407.

12: Broken Cricket

1. Eisenhower, *Crusade in Europe*, p.277.
2. Butcher, *Three Years with Eisenhower*, p.482.
3. Eisenhower, *At Ease*, p.287.
4. Eisenhower, *Crusade in Europe*, p.277.
5. Ambrose, *D-Day*, p.193.
6. Irving, *The War Between the Generals*, pp.144–45. Summersby was also Ike's mistress.
7. Eisenhower, *op. cit.*, p.277.
8. Robert Barr was accompanied by Stanley Birch of Reuters, Merrill 'Red' Mueller of NBC and Ned Roberts of Associated Press. They had unparalleled access on the night of D-Day. Barr said they were 'the four most privileged war correspondents in the world'. Collier, *The Warcos*, p.155.
9. Ambrose, *op. cit.*, p.195; Collier, *op. cit.*, p.155; and Ryan, *The Longest Day*, p.86.
10. Ryan, op cit, p.54.
11. Ambrose, *Band of Brothers*, p.66.
12. Ibid., p.67.
13. Tute, *D-Day*, p.155.
14. For D-Day, Royal Navy radio intercepts of Kriegsmarine, or German Naval, communications were conducted at Bletchley Park. This was the first and only time that messages were actually picked up there. Once intercepted, within 30 minutes the decrypt could be sent to the invasion fleet's escorts alerting them of imminent danger. See Smith, *Station X*, p.178.
15. Sebag-Montefiore, *Enigma*, p.345.
16. Ibid., p.346.
17. Ibid.
18. Ambrose, *D-Day*, p.198.
19. Lewis, *D-Day As They Saw It*, p.68.
20. Ambrose, *op. cit.*, p.199.
21. Lewis, *op. cit.*, p.81.
22. Ibid, p.80. The 82nd Airborne also used a password, see Ryan, *The Longest Day*, p.117. Likewise, the 101st used 'Flash' and the countersign 'Thunder', Ambrose, *Band*

of Brothers, p.74. The British 1st Airborne Division employed a similar system with 'Punch', to which the response was 'Judy', Bickers, *Air War Normandy*, p.26.

23. Ryan, *op. cit.*, p.118.
24. Tute, *op. cit.*, p.157.
25. Ambrose, *op. cit.*, p.72.
26. Ibid., p.74.
27. Carell, *Invasion – They're Coming!*, p.16.
28. Lewis, *op. cit.*, p.85.
29. Ambrose, *D-Day*, p.217.
30. Ibid.
31. The German 6th Parachute Regiment numbered 3,500–4,500 men, but only had seventy trucks, many of which lacked spare parts. Zetterling, *Normandy 1944*, pp.164–65.
32. Carrel, *op. cit.*, p.71.
33. Ryan, *op. cit.*, p.98.
34. Ambrose, *D-Day*, p.220. Technology assisted the American airborne landings. The pathfinders' role was to plant the Eureka and Rebecca radar navigational beacons and mark the drop zones. Nonetheless, the 82nd ended up with 4,000 men unaccounted for and 60 per cent of their equipment went stray, Collier, *The Warcos*, p.163.
35. Ambrose, *op. cit.*, p.221.
36. Lewis, *op. cit.*, p.84.
37. McAuliffe was in command of the 101st's artillery, and later became famous for his defence of Bastogne in the winter of 1944, while Ewell commanded the 3rd Battalion, 501st Parachute Infantry Regiment.
38. While Winters became famous in military circles for employing so few men in this successful operation, he subsequently came to greater prominence thanks to Stephen Ambrose's book *Band of Brothers* and the excellent HBO series of the same name. See *Band of Brothers*, pp.78–85.
39. The 1st Battalion, 506th, had 195 men with which to storm the battery at Holdy. Winters later remarked, 'With that many E Co. men, I could have taken Berlin!" Ibid., p.86.
40. Eisenhower, *Crusade in Europe*, p.271.
41. Harris, *Bomber Offensive*, p.206.
42. Ibid., p.207.
43. Jones, *Most Secret War*, p.411.
44. Ibid.
45. Patch, *The Last Fighting Tommy*, p.181. Slightly differently worded versions of Harry Patch's memories of D-Day are also given in Max Arthur's *The Last Post*, p.132, and Arthur's *The Silent Day*, p.180; the general sentiment, though, remains the same.
46. Ibid.

13: Orne Bound

1. This unit was part of 5th Parachute Brigade, and along with 3 Parachute and 6th Air Landing Brigades formed the British 6th Airborne Division.
2. Bailey, *Forgotten Voices of D-Day*, p.114.
3. Johnson and Dunphie, *Brightly Shone the Dawn*, p.28.
4. Ibid., p.30.
5. Bailey, *op. cit.*, p.114.

6. Captain Alexander Morrison was Officer Commanding No.5 Flight Glider Pilot Regiment, comprising four officers and forty sergeant or staff sergeant pilots. This unit could carry an entire battalion. Morrison, *Silent Invader*, p.23.
7. Ibid., p.22
8. The 711th Infantry Division's ration strength at the beginning of May 1944 was 7,242 men. Zetterling, *Normandy 1944*, p.295.
9. Ibid., pp.298–99.
10. Ibid.
11. Johnson and Dunphie, *op. cit.*, p.31.
12. Lovat, *March Past*, p.325.
13. Ibid.
14. Bickers, *Air War Normandy*, p.24.
15. Lewis, *D-Day as They Saw It*, p.67.
16. Morison, *op. cit.*, p.30.
17. Bailey, *op. cit.*, pp.117–18.
18. Ibid., p.123.
19. Ibid., p.124.
20. Ibid., p.127.
21. Richard Todd later became an actor and film star. He appeared in the movie version of Cornelius Ryan's *The Longest Day* in 1960. Liddle, *D-Day By Those Who Were There*, p.78.
22. Bailey, *op. cit.*, p.134.
23. Bastable, *Voices from D-Day*, p.208.
24. Liddle, *op. cit.*, p.67.
25. Some accounts say that the armoured vehicles were half-tracks and not tanks.
26. Liddle, *op. cit.*, p.78.
27. Bastable, *op. cit.*, p.208.
28. Bailey, *op. cit.*, p.156.
29. Ryan, *The Longest Day*, p.97.
30. Ibid., p.100.
31. The Merville battery was built not far from the coast, which made it difficult for pilots to target. Having crossed the Channel and being greeted by heavy flak, they only had seconds to drop their bombs.
32. Meslin's network was eventually betrayed. For a detailed account of the French Resistance's extensive intelligence-gathering efforts in support of D-Day see Richard Collier's *Ten Thousand Eyes* (London: Dutton, 1958).
33. Liddle, *op. cit.*, p.76.
34. Bickers, *op. cit.*, pp.24–26.
35. Liddle, *op. cit.*, p.74.
36. Ibid., p.75.
37. For a fuller account of this operation see John Golley's *The Big Drop: The Guns of Merville, June 1944* (London: Jane's, 1982).
38. Although 9 Para damaged the guns, the Germans subsequently repaired several of them. The Merville battery was retaken on 8 June by 3 Commando Royal Marines.
39. Bailey, *op. cit.*, p.176.
40. Belchem, *Victory in Normandy*, p.76.
41. de Guingand, *Operation Victory*, p.387.
42. Lovat, *op. cit.*, p.322.
43. This was the Chateau de Bénouville. The director of the maternity hospital, Madame Vion, was a senior figure in the local Resistance. Clark, *Orne Bridgehead*, p.62.
44. Lovat, *op. cit.*, p.322.

14: Ashore with the 'Funnies'

1. Warner, *The D Day Landings*, p.121.
2. Duncan, *79th Armoured Division*, p.22.
3. Bailey, *Forgotten Voices of D-Day*, p.249.
4. Ryan, *The Longest Day*, p.177.
5. Ibid., p.178.
6. Warner, *op. cit.*, p.115.
7. Hills, *By Tank into Normandy*, p.77.
8. Warner, *op. cit.*, p.142.
9. Hills, *op. cit.*, p.78.
10. Warner, *op. cit.*, pp.121–22.
11. Hills, *op. cit.*, p.83.
12. Warner, *op. cit.*, pp.151–52.
13. Belchem, *Victory in Normandy*, p.102.
14. Ibid., p.103.
15. Bailey, *op. cit.*, p.95.
16. Ibid.
17. Keith May Briggs, Oral History, Imperial War Museum, 20 June 1996 – www.iwm.org.uk/collections/item/object/80016162.
18. Ibid. and Bailey, *op. cit.*, p.218.
19. Ibid., p.218.
20. Ibid.
21. Warner, *op. cit.*, p.96.
22. Bailey, *op. cit.*, p.233.
23. For this act he and two of his team were awarded the Distinguished Service Medal. Briggs' DSM and his other medals were donated to the North Devon Maritime Museum.
24. Arthur, *Forgotten Voices of the Second World War*, p.314.
25. 'Obituary: Deceased War Hero Patrick Churchill', *Oxford Mail*, 12 July 2018.
26. Bastable, *Voices From D-Day*, p.181.
27. Thompson, *Victory in Europe*, p.50.
28. Ibid., p.51.
29. Warner, *op. cit.*, p.136.
30. Bailey, *op. cit.*, p.195.
31. Warner, *op. cit.*, p.139.
32. Ibid., p.140.
33. Ibid.
34. Bailey, *op. cit.*, p.196.
35. Warner, *op. cit.*, p.155.
36. Ibid., p.136.
37. Ibid.
38. Ibid.
39. Ibid., p.138.
40. Ibid., p.147.
41. Bailey, *op. cit.*, p.211.
42. Warner, *op. cit.*, p.148.
43. Ibid., p.140.
44. Young, *D-Day*, p.52.
45. Ibid., p.53.
46. Belchem, *op. cit.*, p.108.

47. Warner, *op. cit.*, p.149.
48. Ibid., p.141.
49. Ibid., pp.149–50. After the Normandy landings, the 79th Armoured Division was equipped with additional specialised armoured fighting vehicles including the AVRE Log Carpet Device, AVRE Skid Bailey Bridge, Crocodile flame-thrower, Kangaroo APC, Buffalo tracked landing vehicle (both the LVT.2 and LVT.4), Terrapin 8x8 amphibious truck, Churchill Jumbo bridge and Centaur tank dozer. Other miscellaneous vehicles included the bizarrely named Conger, Rodent and 3in Snake mine clearing devices and the Onion and Goat mechanical charge placers.
50. Duncan, *op. cit.*, p.25.
51. Ibid.
52. Ibid.

15: Touch & Go

1. Thompson was appointed commander of 6th Engineer Special Brigade on 18 January 1944. He ensured that 1,600 of his men passed through the Assault Training Centre. Bass, *Spirits of the Sand*, pp.106–08.
2. Ryan, *The Longest Day*, p.161.
3. Young, *D-Day*, p.34.
4. The Omaha naval bombardment included two battleships, three cruisers and eight destroyers that fired 3,500 rounds. US Army artillery, firing from landing craft, expended 9,000 rounds, while nine rocket craft deluged the beach with 21,500 rockets. Some 400 bombers also attacked the shore defences. Accuracy was clearly a problem. See Howarth, *Dawn of D-Day*, pp.138, 140.
5. Bass, *Clear the Way!*, p.33.
6. Ibid.
7. Allied bombers, unable to see the beaches, unloaded 13,000 bombs 3 miles inland, completely missing the 352nd Division's emplacements.
8. Ryan, *op. cit.*, p.156.
9. Thompson, *D-Day*, p.117.
10. Ambrose, *D-Day*, p.380.
11. Bass, *Brigades of Neptune*, p.124.
12. Ambrose, *op. cit.*, p.380.
13. Ryan, *op. cit.*, p.165.
14. Ibid.
15. Rottman, *US World War II Amphibious Tactics*, p.62.
16. Ambrose, *op. cit.*, p.274.
17. A total of thirteen DUKWs were lost in the opening phase. Bass, *Brigades of Neptune*, p.129.
18. Thompson, *op. cit.*, p.113.
19. Irving, *The War Between the Generals*, p.149.
20. Bass, *op. cit.*, p.148.
21. Ibid.
22. Ambrose, *op. cit.*, p.379.
23. Bass, *Clear the Way!*, p.46.
24. Wilmot, *The Struggle for Europe*, p.265.
25. Ibid., p.266.
26. Ryan, *op. cit.*, p.191.
27. Tute, *D-Day*, p.230.

28. Ryan, *op. cit.*, p.191.
29. Ibid. This was the 9,500-strong German 346th Infantry Division which had deployed to Le Havre in late January 1944.
30. Carell, *Invasion – They're Coming!*, p.98.
31. Ibid., p.97.
32. Wilmot, *op. cit.*, p.266.
33. Ryan, *op. cit.*, p.167.
34. Irving, *op. cit.*, p.155.
35. According to Tute, *D-Day*, p.230, these were Landing Craft Tank 30 and Landing Craft Infantry (Large) 544. However, Neillands and De Norman, *D-Day 1944*, p.198, state they were both LCTs.
36. Ibid.
37. Ryan, *op. cit.*, p.217.
38. See Lieutenant-Colonel Fritz Ziegelmann, '352nd Infantry Division on 7 June 1944', in Isby (ed.), *Fighting in Normandy*, p.31.
39. These consisted of eight heavy field guns deployed on the right flank and six light field guns in the centre; the left flank had no artillery at all. See 'Progress of the Combat Day, 9 June: 352nd Infantry Division', by Lieutenant-Colonel Fritz Ziegelmann, Ibid., pp.84, 88.
40. Bass, *Brigades of Neptune*, p.136.
41. Thompson, *op. cit.*, p.106.
42. Duncan, *79th Armoured Division*, p.48. Fletcher, *Swimming Shermans*, p.22, says twenty-eight tanks from two DD companies were launched, with the loss of one tank.
43. Ryan, *op. cit.*, p.159.
44. Bailey, *Forgotten Voices of D-Day*, p.289.
45. Ibid., p.286.
46. These consisted of six dead and fifty-two wounded. Bass, *Brigades of Neptune*, p.138.
47. Ibid., p.147.
48. Ryan, *op. cit.*, p.168.
49. Ibid., p.170.
50. Ibid., p.212.
51. These were the US 8th and 22nd Infantry Regiments. Quite remarkably, Barton's command suffered far greater losses prior to D-Day; it lost nearly twenty times as many men during training as it did on 6 June 1944. Ambrose, *op. cit.*, p.292.
52. Roosevelt was awarded the Congressional Medal of Honor for his role in making Utah a complete success. He was appointed the commander of the US 90th Infantry Division on 12 July but never took up his post as he suffered a fatal heart attack that very evening.
53. Eisenhower, *Crusade in Europe*, p.286.
54. Belchem, *Victory in Normandy*, p.96.

16: Smashing the Mulberries

1. Belchem, *Victory in Normandy*, p.16.
2. Warner, *The D Day Landings*, p.116.
3. Ambrose, *D-Day*, p.566.
4. Neillands, *The Battle of Normandy 1944*, p.145.
5. Arthur, *Forgotten Voices of the Second World War*, p.323.
6. Tute, *D-Day*, p.73.
7. 'Urgent Warning to Fishermen', *Southern Daily Echo*, 9 June 1944.

8. Hartcup, *Code Name Mulberry*, p.115.

9. Butcher, *Three Years with Eisenhower*, p.497.

10. 'D-Day: A Second Opinion: A Medical Report of the Morning's Battle', by Dr J.H. Patterson, RAMC, Medical Officer of No. 4 Commando. Lovat, *March Past*, p.377.

11. Butcher, *op. cit.*, p.506.

12. These were LCT (Armoured) (No. 2273, 2301, 2402 and 2428) lost during Neptune, while Landing Ship (Infantry) *Empire Broadsword* (4,285 tons) was sunk by a mine off Normandy on 2 July 1944. The LSTs continued to support operations, and by the end of September 1944 they had brought 41,035 wounded men back across the English Channel.

13. Butcher, *op. cit.*, p.506.

14. Neillands, *op. cit.*, p.147.

15. Thornton, *The Liberation of Paris*, p.111.

16. Aron, *De Gaulle Before Paris*, p.67.

17. Ibid., p.67.

18. Ibid., p.68.

19. Ibid.

20. Montgomery adopted the route of least resistance and let Coulet get on with it, establishing his headquarters in Bayeux. Monty refers to him as M. Coulet, and on occasion dealt with him regarding allegations of looting by British troops. Coulet reassured him that there were no grounds for such complaints, though Monty remained unconvinced. Montgomery, *Memoirs*, p.264.

21. Harris, *Bomber Offensive*, p.209.

22. Ibid., p.206.

23. At Boulogne, twenty-eight vessels were sunk and others damaged. At Le Havre, they sank or damaged over sixty vessels. In total, 130 German naval and auxiliary craft were reportedly neutralised by Bomber Command. In the light of the accuracy of battle damage assessments based on photo reconnaissance, these figures were no doubt on the optimistic side. Ibid., p.210.

24. Belfield and Essame, *The Battle for Normandy*, p.102, and Essame, *Normandy Bridgehead*, p.76. These two books are very similar in places, with the first published in 1965 and the second five years later.

25. Ibid.

26. Neillands, *op. cit.*, p.145.

27. Steven Zaloga records that the Luftwaffe had thirteen major airbases in the Paris area. The main one was Villacoublay, 6km to the south-west of the city. See Zaloga, *Liberation of Paris 1944*, p.27.

28. These consisted of the 2nd Panzer Division, which deployed to the Caumont area, 352nd Infantry Division south of Carentan and the 3rd Parachute Division on Bradley's western flank.

29. Belfield and Essame, *op. cit.*, p.103.

30. Belchem, *Victory in Normandy*, p.181–2.

31. Thompson, *Victory in Europe*, p.96.

32. The Whales formed the quays over which the LSTs could unload their cargo. Butcher, *op. cit.*, p.506.

33. Ibid., p.508.

34. Eisenhower, *Crusade in Europe*, p.286.

35. Ibid.

36. Neillands, *op. cit.*, p.145.

37. Belfield and Essame, *op. cit.*, p.104.

38. Butcher, *op. cit.*, p.529.

17: Cherbourg Captured

1. Cruikshank, *The German Occupation of the Channel Islands*, p.260.
2. 'Mass Landings: Germans Fear Loss of Cherbourg', *Southern Daily Echo*, 9 June 1944.
3. Liddell Hart, *The Rommel Papers*, p.84.
4. Ibid., p.83.
5. As of 1 May 1944, the 243rd Infantry Division had a strength of 11,529. See Zetterling, *Normandy 1944*, pp.242–44.
6. These comprised StuG III assault guns and Marder tank destroyers. Ibid.
7. They only amounted to three battalions of infantry. Ibid., p.230.
8. Bernage, *The Battle for the Contentin Peninsula*, p.27.
9. Gorse Hill is at La Pernelle.
10. This type of tactic served the Japanese well in Burma and Malaya in 1942, when they swiftly unhinged British defences.
11. Carell, *Invasion – They're Coming!*, p.192.
12. Ibid., pp.194–95.
13. Wilmot, *The Struggle for Europe*, p.325.
14. Collier, *The Warcos*, p.169.
15. For a detailed account of the fighting in the Cotentin see Georges Bernage's *The Battle for the Cotentin Peninsula: 9–19 June 1944* (Barnsley: Pen & Sword, 2018).
16. Carell, *op. cit.*, p.196.
17. Ibid.
18. Ibid., p.199.
19. Wilmot, *op. cit.*, p.329.
20. Carell, *op. cit.*, p.197.
21. Hastings, *Overlord*, p.165.
22. Essame, *Normandy Bridgehead*, p.83.
23. Wilmot, *op. cit.*, p.330.
24. Liddell Hart, *op. cit.*, p.492. Rommel wrote this to his wife on 24 June 1944, just as the battle for Cherbourg was reaching its climax.
25. Carell, *op. cit.*, p.206.
26. Hastings, *op. cit.*, pp.163–64.
27. Neillands, *The Battle of Normandy 1944*, p.160.
28. Butcher, *Three Years with Eisenhower*, p.511.
29. Carell, *op. cit.*, p.203.
30. Ibid., p.212.
31. Neillands, *op. cit.*, p.150.
32. Haswell, *The Intelligence of the D-Day Landings*, p.183, and Carell, *op. cit.*, p.224.
33. Carell, *op. cit.*, p.226.
34. Hastings, *op. cit.*, p.165.
35. According to Chester Wilmot, total German losses in the Cotentin were over 50,000, including 4,000 dead and 39,042 prisoners. American losses amounted to 22,101: 2,811 killed, 13,546 wounded and 5,744 missing or captured. See *The Struggle for Europe*, p.331
36. Ibid, p.332, quoting from the Weekly Report of Army Group B, 26 June 1944 (*Tempelhof Papers*).
37. Butcher, *op. cit.*, p.512.
38. Essame, *op. cit.*, p.83.
39. Butcher, *op. cit.*, p.515.
40. D'Este, *Eisenhower*, p.515.
41. Eisenhower, *Crusade in Europe*, p.287.
42. Ibid.

43. Wilmot, *op. cit.*, p.332.
44. Ibid., p.333.

18: Caen Lynchpin

1. The 21st Panzer Division was equipped with a large number of modified old French tanks, but also had almost 100 powerful Panzer Mk IVs. The 12th SS was even better armed, with ninety-one Panzer IVs, forty-eight Panthers and ten Jagdpanzers.
2. In June 1944, Panzer Lehr had over 180 Panzer IVs and Panther tanks, as well as at least thirty-one assault guns.
3. Wilmot, *The Struggle for Europe*, p.309.
4. From a regimental account supplied to author.
5. Also spelt Cranleigh.
6. Wittmann was an established tank ace. In July 1941, as a corporal, he had been awarded the Iron Cross II Class while commanding an assault gun in the Balkans in the Leibstandarte SS Adolf Hitler Division, and in September had gained the Iron Cross I Class on the Eastern Front. By December 1942 he had become a 2nd lieutenant and the following year was given command of a Tiger I in the 13th Company of the Leibstandarte's SS Panzer Regiment. When he reached lieutenant on 20 January 1944 his kills stood at 117 vehicles. In April he took command of the 2nd Company of the 101st Heavy SS Panzer Battalion. He was promoted to captain for his actions at Villers-Bocage.
7. Carell, *Invasion – They're Coming!*, p.177.
8. From a regimental account supplied to author.
9. Ibid.
10. Ibid.
11. The 316th Panzer Company (Fkl) attached to Panzer Lehr had six Tigers, but only half were serviceable, and nine StuG assault guns instead of its theoretical fourteen.
12. Hastings, *Overlord*, p.133.
13. Author, *op. cit.*
14. Hastings, *op. cit.*, pp.134–35.
15. D'Este, *Decision in Normandy*, p.195.
16. Ibid., p.196, and Hastings, *op. cit.*, pp.135–36. Both cite a Dempsey interview with reporter Chester Wilmot. Diplomatically, Wilmot did not publish this in his book *The Struggle for Europe.* These notes are now held with the Liddell Hart papers, King's College, London.
17. Carell, *op. cit.*, p.180, and Hastings, *op. cit.*, p.133.
18. By 1 August 1944, Panzer Lehr had just twenty-seven tanks.
19. Lucas and Barker, *The Killing Ground*, p.110.

19: Cobra Strikes

1. Montgomery, *The Memoirs*, p.258.
2. The Germans still believed well into July 1944 that Patton's fictitious First United States Army Group, or FUSAG, was poised in south-eastern England to strike the Pas de Calais and attack the German Fifteenth Army. See Smith, *Station X*, pp.172, 177.
3. Although Patton arrived in Normandy on 6 July 1944, his US Third Army did not become operational until 1 August. It first had to be shipped from England amidst great secrecy. Hodges took over First Army then.
4. Daugherty, *The Battle of the Hedgerows*, p.121.

5. Montgomery, *op. cit.*, p.257.
6. Bradley employed twelve divisions in these operations and they suffered 40,000 casualties, the equivalent to two full infantry divisions. Carafano, *After D-Day*, p.71, and Essame, *Normandy Bridgehead*, p.158. From 6 June to 17 July, the Germans lost a total of 100,000 men. In the St Lô–Cotentin area, the German 243rd Infantry Division lost over 8,000, as did the 352nd, while Panzer Lehr lost some 3,140. Daugherty, *op. cit.*, p.209, and Essame, *op. cit.*, p.159.
7. Daugherty, *op. cit.*, p.194.
8. Some 25,000 infantry had to be requested from the US. Essame, *op. cit.*, p.159.
9. Belchem, *Victory in Normandy*, p.155.
10. Carafano, *op. cit.*, p.11.
11. The US 30th Infantry Division lost twenty-five men killed and 131 wounded to friendly fire. See Zaloga, *Operation Cobra 1944*, p.37. Carafano lists total US losses as twenty-nine dead and 145 wounded, *op. cit.*, p.17.
12. Carafano, *op. cit.*, p.112.
13. Ibid.
14. The US 4th, 9th and 30th Infantry Divisions were all hit by Allied bombs. Total losses suffered by the US VII Corps were 108 dead and 472 wounded. Ibid., p.115.
15. Ibid., p.185.
16. Ibid., p.117.
17. Wilmot, *The Struggle for Europe*, p.391.
18. Zaloga, *op. cit.*, p.40.
19. Ibid.
20. Lewis, *D-Day as They Saw It*, p.4
21. D'Este, *Patton A Genius for War*, p.614.
22. Rohmer, *Patton's Gap*, p.166.
23. Eisenhower, *At Ease*, p.270.
24. Rohmer, *op. cit.*, p.166.
25. Kerrigan, *How Bletchley Park Won World War II*, p.212.
26. Ibid.
27. Zetterling, *Normandy 1944*, p.230.
28. Carell, *Invasion – They're Coming!*, p.276.
29. Wood gained his nickname partly as a result of standing up to Patton. He was also known as 'P', for Professor, for tutoring other cadets when at West Point. D'Este, *op. cit.*, pp.631, 911.
30. Weigley, *Eisenhower's Lieutenants*, p.177.
31. Wilmot, *op. cit.*, p.399.
32. Rohmer, *op. cit.*, p.167.
33. There is some confusion over which bridge was attacked by the Luftwaffe. Paul Carell says it was the one at Pontaubault (over the Sélune); see *Invasion – They're Coming!*, p.277. However, Chester Wilmot says it was the bridge at Avranches (which crosses the Sée); see *The Struggle for Europe*, p.399.
34. Rohmer, *op. cit.*, p.189.
35. Ibid.
36. Ibid., p.188.
37. Smith, *op. cit.*, pp.181–82.
38. Kerrigan, *op. cit.*, p.213.
39. Hastings, *Overlord*, p.282.
40. Ibid.
41. D'Este, *op. cit.*, p.911.

42. Zaloga, *op. cit.*, p.57.
43. D'Este, *op. cit.*, p.631.
44. Ibid.
45. Hastings, *op. cit.*, p.282.
46. The garrison was well equipped, with 197 pieces of artillery and eighty anti-tank guns. Zaloga, *Operation Cobra 1944*, p.56
47. St Malo was captured on 14 August 1944 after a week of street fighting; the defenders of the old citadel held out for another three days, while the Germans on the Ile de Cézembre off St Malo resisted until 2 September. Brest did not fall to the Americans until 19 September. The garrisons at Lorient and St Nazaire remained under siege until the very end of the war.

20: Going for Broke

1. Belchem, *Victory in Normandy*, p.168.
2. Tute, *D-Day*, p.247.
3. Carell, *Invasion – They're Coming!*, p.278.
4. Wilmot, *The Struggle for Europe*, p.401.
5. Smith, *Station X*, p.182.
6. Ibid.
7. Ibid.
8. Belchem, *op. cit.*, p.168.
9. This account of events was given to Basil Liddell Hart by General Blumentritt, Field Marshal von Kluge's Chief of Staff. Liddell Hart, *The Other Side of the Hill*, p.414
10. Ibid., p.415. This was according to Blumentritt's recollection. Confusingly, General Speidel, Rommel's Chief of Staff who was also interviewed by Liddell Hart, claimed the order was dated 12 August and instructed von Kluge to leave the Falaise pocket. However, it seems unlikely that Blumentritt would have got Avranches and Falaise mixed up. To add to the confusion, Mitcham, in *Hitler's Field Marshals and their Battles*, p.309, claims von Kluge went missing on 15 August.
11. Isby, *Fighting the Breakout*, p.150.
12. Belchem, *op. cit.*, p.168.
13. Eisenhower, *Crusade in Europe*, p.301.
14. Weigley, *Eisenhower's Lieutenants*, p.192. There is some debate quite when Hitler's orders were intercepted by Bletchley. Richard Rohmer, in *Patton's Gap*, quotes 2 August 1944 on p.178.
15. Steven Smith, in *2nd Armored Division*, p.37, writes, 'Through Ultra intercepts, Bradley learned of the German plan with just hours to spare.' This is quite possible, as Eisenhower was at Bradley's command post on 6 August 1944. Also, the following day Patton recorded in his diary, 'We got a rumour last night from a secret source that several panzer divisions will attack west.' Rohmer, *op. cit.*, p.179. Steven Zaloga states that, 'The Ultra decrypt formed the basis for an alert at 1700 on 6 August.' *Operation Cobra 1944*, p.69. However, it was a combination of Ultra, luck, airpower and German mistakes that all helped to ensure that Bradley triumphed at Mortain.
16. Eisenhower, *op. cit.*, p.301.
17. Ibid., p.302.
18. Ibid.
19. Smith, *2nd Armored Division*, p.37.
20. These were the 1st SS, 2nd, 2nd SS, 10th SS and 116th Panzer Divisions.

21. Wilmot, *op. cit.*, p.401.
22. These were the German 84th and 363rd Infantry Divisions.
23. Rohmer, *op. cit.*, p.181.
24. Weigley, *op. cit.*, p.195.
25. Ibid., p.402.
26. The 2nd Battalion, 120th Infantry Regiment, US 30th Infantry Division, held Hill 317, suffering 300 dead or wounded. Crucially, possession of this 1,030ft peak gave American artillery spotters an ideal vantage point. The battalion was awarded a presidential unit citation, and the four company commanders each received the Distinguished Service Cross for valour. D'Este, *Eisenhower*, p.787.
27. Ibid., p.568.
28. Isby, *op. cit.*, p.128.
29. Carell, *op. cit.*, p.283.
30. Mitcham, *op. cit.*, p307. According to Carell, the Germans opened their attack with 120 tanks; *Invasion – They're Coming!*, p.280.
31. Wilmot, *op. cit.*, p.402.
32. Ibid., p.404.
33. Belchem, *op. cit.*, p.169.
34. Franks, *Typhoon Attack*, p.147.
35. Ibid.
36. Ibid., p.146.
37. Isby, *op. cit.*, p.128.
38. Mitcham, *op. cit.*, p309.
39. Franks, *op. cit.*, p.146.
40. Isby, *op. cit.*, p.151.
41. Wilmot, *op. cit.*, p.404.
42. Butcher, *Three Years with Eisenhower*, p.547. Eisenhower had set up his HQ in France near Tournières and Maisons, which was codenamed Shellburst, on 7 August 1944.
43. Smith, *Station X*, p.182.
44. Ibid., pp.181–82.
45. Wilmot, *op. cit.*, p.415.
46. Ibid., p.416.
47. Ibid., pp.416–17.
48. Butcher, *op. cit.*, p.549.
49. Hitler had signalled, 'The purpose of resuming the offensive westward to the sea, after a success against the American 15th Army Corps, must be adhered to.' This was slavishly repeated by Kluge to his army commanders at 0730 hours on 12 August. Wilmot, *op. cit.*, p.416.
50. Eisenhower, *op. cit.*, p.303.
51. Belchem, *op. cit.*, p.169.
52. Smith, *op. cit.*, p.183.
53. Eisenhower, *op. cit.*, p.303.
54. de Guingand, *Operation Victory*, p.406.

21: Total Destruction

1. Rohmer, *Patton's Gap*, p.196.
2. Ibid., p.197.
3. Ibid., p.196. Dietrich was referring to the Fifth Panzer and Seventh Armies.

4. The 9th, 21st, 116th, 2nd SS, 9th SS, 10th SS and 12th SS Panzer Divisions. By then, 116th Panzer was down to only fifteen tanks, 1st SS had just nineteen, the 10th SS eight and 12th SS about twenty. The 116th Panzer Division tried to hold up the Americans, but the Germans lost 100 panzers that day. At Falaise, 1st SS was on its last legs, and similarly 12th SS only had fifteen tanks left.

5. Belchem, *Victory in Normandy*, p.170.

6. Ibid., p.172.

7. Rohmer, *op. cit.*, p.197.

8. The 12th Field Regiment, Royal Canadian Artillery, suffered twenty-one killed and forty-six wounded. The Royal Regiment of Canada lost six dead and fifty-two missing. Ibid., p.200.

9. By the end of August, the Free French Forces had liberated Toulon and Marseilles, capturing 37,000 German troops and putting Hitler's Army Group G to flight.

10. Mitcham, *Hitler's Field Marshals and their Battles*, p.309. There is some confusion when this incident occurred; see previous chapter note 9.

11. There is no evidence to support the allegation that Kluge was attempting to surrender to the Allies.

12. The II SS Panzer Corps consisted of four panzer divisions: the 2nd SS, 9th SS, 12th SS and 21st.

13. The XLVII Panzer Corps comprised just two panzer divisions, the 2nd and 116th.

14. Eisenhower, *At Ease*, p.289.

15. Ibid.

16. Ibid.

17. Tucker-Jones, *Falaise: the Flawed Victory*, p.158.

18. Lewis, *D-Day as They Saw It*, p.271.

19. Tucker-Jones, *op. cit.*, p.160.

20. Ibid., p.156.

21. Mitcham, *op. cit.*, p.312.

22. Franks, *Typhoon Attack*, p.146.

23. Ibid., p.147.

24. Tucker-Jones, *op. cit.*, p.168.

25. Belchem, *op. cit.*, p.172.

26. Lewis, *op. cit.*, p.270.

27. Eisenhower, *Crusade in Europe*, p.306.

28. Ibid.

29. Lucas and Barker, *The Killing Ground*, pp.159–60, and Tucker-Jones, *op. cit.*, p.174.

30. Eisenhower, *op. cit.*, p.306.

31. Collier, *The Warcos*, p.170.

32. Ibid.

22: De Gaulle Pulls It Off

1. Eisenhower, *Crusade in Europe*, p.323. Ike wisely avoided commenting on the complex political machinations that were going on in liberated and occupied France to secure dominance once the Germans had been driven out. President Roosevelt, in contrast, made little secret of his complete distaste for de Gaulle. The latter returned the compliment, disliking both the Americans and the British.

2. Ibid.

3. Ibid., p.325

4. Irving, *The War Between the Generals*, p.134

5. The extent of de Gaulle's popularity was exposed on 21 April 1943 when there was an attempt on his life. The Wellington bomber flying him to Glasgow was sabotaged at Hendon airfield. Luckily for de Gaulle, the pilot detected the elevator controls had been cut just before take-off and aborted the flight. At the time, the incident was hushed up and blamed on German intelligence. De Gaulle never flew by plane in Britain again.

6. Jurado, *Resistance Warfare 1940–45*, p.22.

7. Ibid., p.19.

8. The French 2nd Armoured Division included two tank regiments, the 501e Chars de Combat and the 1er Regiment de Marche de Spahis Marocains, equipped with Sherman medium and Honey light tanks, armoured cars, self-propelled guns and towed artillery.

9. Thornton, *The Liberation of Paris*, p.107.

10. The plan had been to kidnap the anti-Semitic Henriot, but he resisted and was shot by Charles Gonard, codenamed Morlot. Henriot's daily broadcasts on Radio Paris so enraged the Free French that they called via the BBC for his assassination. Cobb, *Eleven Days in August*, pp.15–16.

11. Thornton, *op. cit.*, p.113.

12. Zaloga, *Liberation of Paris 1944*, p.67; Thornton, *op. cit.*, p.164; Cobb, *op. cit.*, p.233; and Keegan, *Six Armies in Normandy*, p.292. The wording of this order varies enormously and there is confusion as to when it was sent; both 22 and 23 August are cited, depending on the source.

13. The Polish resistance launched a national uprising to coincide with the arrival of Soviet forces from the east in the summer of 1944. The result was 'Burza', the rising in Warsaw, which started in anticipation of the Red Army crossing the River Vistula after the spectacular success of Operation Bagration. Unfortunately, Soviet help did not come soon enough and the Warsaw rising was brutally dealt with by the Waffen-SS. The Polish Home Army secured most of Warsaw by 4 August, although, lacking heavy weapons and ammunition, it was unable to consolidate its three main defensive enclaves within the city. The Germans counterattacked on 10 August, and four days later the Home Army had been divided into six enclaves. The desperate Poles held out for two months before surrendering on 5 October.

14. For a detailed assessment of the German garrison in Paris see Steven Zaloga's *Liberation of Paris 1944*, pp.25–28.

15. Even by mid-1943, around 80,000 French women were claiming support from the German authorities for children resulting from relationships with German soldiers. Likewise, the prostitutes in the French capital's 200 brothels faced an uncertain future, especially those premises reserved for German officers. Sebba, *Les Parisiennes*, pp.122, 167.

16. Thornton, *op. cit.*, p.161.

17. Irving, *op. cit.*, p.253.

18. Ibid.

19. Eisenhower, *op. cit.*, p.325.

20. Irving, *op. cit.*, p.254.

21. Thornton, *op. cit.*, p.193.

22. Irving, *op. cit.*, p.254.

23. Lacoutre, *De Gaulle: The Rebel, 1890–1944*, p.575.

23: Hitler's Great Escape

1. Of the five Luftwaffe field divisions manning the Atlantic Wall, only the 16th and 17th played prominent roles in the Normandy campaign. The 16th LFD was overwhelmed during Montgomery's Goodwood offensive in mid-July 1944, and the survivors were used to replenish 21st Panzer and create the 16th Infantry Division. See Ruffner, *Luftwaffe Field Divisions 1941–45*, pp.19–33.
2. Ibid., p.20.
3. Zetterling, *Normandy 1944*, p.226. Typically, a Luftwaffe field division on the Eastern Front had just over 6,000 men, though its actual fighting strength was half that. The divisional anti-tank battalion was equipped with 50mm and 75mm guns. Its heaviest anti-aircraft weapons were 20mm and 88mm flak guns.
4. Ruffner, *op. cit.*, p.22.
5. The division's principal combat units consisted of Grenadier Regiments 557, 558 and 559, Artillery Regiment 331 and Panzerjäger Battalion 331. Zetterling, *op. cit.*, p.267.
6. Tucker-Jones, *Falaise: the Flawed Victory*, p.177.
7. Ibid., p.178.
8. For more on this operation see Ken Ford's *Assault Crossing: The River Seine 1944* (Newton Abbot: David & Charles, 1988).
9. Tucker-Jones, *op. cit.*, pp.178–79.
10. Ruffner, *op. cit.*, p.22.
11. Zetterling, *op. cit.*, p.269. By the end of August 1944, the 331st Infantry Division was estimated to have a strength of around 6,000 men. This meant it had lost about 4,000; however, casualties were only listed until 22 August, and these numbered 1,500.
12. Wilmot, *The Struggle for Europe*, p.434.
13. Ibid.
14. Ibid.
15. In June, July and August 1944, the German Army lost 34,614 lorries, of which only 15,278 were replaced. Ibid., p.460.
16. Ibid., p.434.
17. Tucker-Jones, *op. cit.*, p.184.
18. Ibid., p.216–17.

24: Novel Mechanical Contrivances

1. Belchem, *Victory in Normandy*, p.57.
2. Ibid.
3. Harris, *Bomber Offensive*, p.207.
4. Air Chief Marshal Sir Trafford Leigh-Mallory, C-in-C, Allied Expeditionary Air Force, Official Despatch, *London Gazette*, 2 January 1947, cited Jones, *Most Secret War*, p.412.
5. Ibid.
6. Ibid.
7. Ibid., pp.411–12.
8. The West Wall is normally used to signify the German Siegfried Line built to defend Germany's western frontier, but in this context de Guingand meant the Atlantic Wall. De Guingand, *Operation Victory*, pp.352–53.
9. Young, *D-Day*, p.61.
10. Thompson, *D-Day*, p.157.
11. Eisenhower, *Crusade in Europe*, p.278.
12. Ibid.
13. Butcher, *Three Years with Eisenhower*, p.491.

14. Brigadier E.T. Williams, *21st Army Group Weekly Neptune Intelligence Review*, 3 June 1944, cited by Haswell, *The Intelligence and Deception of the D-Day Landings*, p.145.

15. Wilmot, *The Struggle for Europe*, p.265.

16. Thompson, *op. cit.*, pp.157–58.

17. Wilmot, *op. cit.*, p.265.

18. *Omaha Beachhead*, Department of the US Army, Historical Division, cited Kaplan, *Hitler's D-Day Defences*, p.164.

19. Ibid., p.172

20. Young, *op. cit.*, p.8.

21. Eisenhower, *op. cit.*, pp.286–87.

22. Stagg, *Forecast For Overlord*, p.125.

23. Ibid.

24. Ibid.

25. Montgomery, *The Memoirs*, p.249.

26. Butcher, *op. cit.*, p.555. Unfortunately, Stagg does not reference this meeting with Major Lettau in his book *Forecast For Overlord*.

27. Ibid.

28. Young, *op. cit.*, p.61.

29. Young, *Commando*, p.153.

30. Belchem, *op. cit.*, p.182.

31. Speer, *Inside the Third Reich*, p.477.

32. Tute, *D-Day*, pp.50–51.

33. Lovat, *March Past*, p.323.

34. Belchem, *op. cit.*, pp.54–55.

35. de Guingand, *op. cit.*, pp.358–60.

36. For example see Carlo D'Este's excellent *Decision in Normandy* and David Irving's *The War Between the Generals*. Nor did Montgomery hold back with criticism of his colleagues in his post-war memoirs.

37. Montgomery, *op. cit.*, p.256.

38. Ibid.

39. Essame, *Normandy Bridgehead*, p.158.

40. Ibid.

41. Eisenhower, *op. cit.*, p.305.

42. Mitcham, *Hitler's Field Marshals and their Battles*, p.291.

43. Lewis, *D-Day as They Saw It*, p.267.

44. These panzer losses are based on research conducted for *Falaise: the Flawed Victory*.

45. Roberts, *Lorenz*, p.18.

46. Arthur, *The Silent Day*, p.159.

47. D'Este, *Eisenhower*, p.529.

BIBLIOGRAPHY

Ambrose, Stephen E., *Band of Brothers* (London: Simon & Schuster, 2001/2017)

Ambrose, Stephen E., *Citizen Soldiers* (New York: Simon & Schuster, 1997/London: Pocket Books, 2002)

Ambrose, Stephen E., *D-Day* (New York: Simon & Schuster, 1994/London: Pocket Books, 2002)

Ambrose, Stephen E., *Pegasus Bridge* (London: Pocket Books, 2003)

Ambrose, Stephen E., *The Victors: The Men of World War II* (New York: Simon & Schuster, 1998/London: Pocket Books, 2004)

Aron, Robert, *De Gaulle Before Paris: The Liberation of France June–August 1944* (London: Putnam, 1962). First published as *Histoire de la Libération de la France* in 1959, translated from French by Humphrey Hare

Arthur, Max, *Forgotten Voices of the Second World War* (London: Ebury Press, 2004)

Arthur, Max, *The Silent Day: A Landmark Oral History of D-Day on the Home Front* (London: Hodder & Stoughton, 2014)

Atkin, Ronald, *Dieppe 1942: The Jubilee Disaster* (London: Macmillan, 1980)

Badsey, Stephen, *Normandy 1944: Allied landings and breakout* (Oxford: Opsrey, 1990)

Bailey, Roderick, *Forgotten Voices of D-Day* (London: Ebury, 2010)

Bass, Richard T., *Brigades of Neptune: A History of the US Army Engineer Special Brigades* (Brighton: Menin House, 2014)

Bass, Richard T., *Clear the Way! A History of the 146th Engineer Combat Battalion from Normandy to Berlin* (Brighton: Menin House, 2014)

Bass, Richard T., *Spirits of the Sand: The Story of the United States Army Assault Training Centre in North Devon* (Brighton: Menin House, 2014)

Bastable, Jonathan, *Voices From D-Day* (Barnsley: Greenhill/Pen & Sword, 2018). First published as *Tales From the Front Line: D-Day* (Newton Abbot: David & Charles, 2011)

Baverstock, Kevin, *Breaking the Panzers: The Bloody Battle for Rauray Normandy, 1 July 1944* (Stroud: Sutton, 2002)

Beevor, Antony, *D-Day: The Battle for Normandy* (London: Penguin, 2012)

Belchem, Major-General David, *Victory in Normandy* (London: Chatto & Windus, 1981)

Belfield, Eversley and Essame, H. *The Battle for Normandy* (London: B.T. Batsford, 1965/London: Pan, 1983)

Bernage, Georges, *The Battle for the Cotentin Peninsula: 9–19 June 1944* (Barnsley: Pen & Sword, 2018).

Bickers, Richard Townshend, *Air War Normandy* (London: Leo Cooper, 1994/Barnsley: Pen & Sword Aviation, 2015)

Boyd, Douglas, *Normandy in the Time of Darkness: Everyday Life and Death in the French Channel Ports 1940–45* (Hersham: Ian Allan, 2013)

Breuer, William B., *Death of a Nazi Army: The Falaise Pocket* (New York: Stein & Day, 1985)

Bruce, George, *Second Front Now! The Road to D-day* (London: Macdonald & Jane's, 1979)

Buckingham, William F., *D-Day: The First 72 Hours* (Stroud: Tempus, 2004)

Butcher, Captain Harry, *Three Years with Eisenhower* (London: William Heinemann, 1946)

Carafano, James Jay, *After D-Day: Operation Cobra and the Normandy Breakout* (London: Lynne Rienner, 2000)

Carell, Paul, translated from German by E. Osers, *Invasion – They're Coming!* (London: George G. Harrap, 1962/London: Corgi, 1963; first published in German by Gerhard Stalling Verlag, 1960)

Carruthers, Bob and Trew, Simon, *The Normandy Battles* (London: Cassell & Co, 2000)

Cawthorne, Nigel, *Fighting them on the Beaches: The D-Day Landings June 6, 1944* (London: Arcturus, 2002/2017)

Chalfont, Alun, *Montgomery of Alamein* (London: Weidenfeld & Nicolson, 1976)

Clark, Lloyd, *Battle Zone Normandy: Orne Bridgehead* (Stroud: Sutton, 2004)

Clark, Lloyd and Hart, Dr Stephen, *The Drive on Caen: Northern France 7 June – 9 July 1944* (London: Ministry of Defence, 2004)

Cobb, Matthew, *Eleven Days in August: The Liberation of Paris in 1944* (London: Simon & Schuster, 2014)

Collet, J.M. (ed.), translated from French to English by Major D. Kelly, *Arromanches 44: The Normandy Invasion* (Brussels: JM Collet, 1984)

Collier, Richard, *Ten Thousand Eyes* (London: Dutton & Co, 1958; republished New York: Lyons Press, 2001)

Collier, Richard, *The Warcos: The War Correspondents of World War Two* (London: Weidenfeld and Nicolson, 1989)

Daglish, Ian, *Operation Bluecoat. The British Armoured Breakout* (Barnsley: Leo Cooper, 2003)

Daglish, Ian, *Operation Goodwood: The Great Tank Charge July 1944* (Barnsley: Pen & Sword Military, 2004)

Daugherty, Leo, *The Battle for the Hedgerows: Bradley's First Army in Normandy, June–July 1944* (Shepperton: Ian Allan, 2001)

De Guingand, Major General Sir Francis, *Operation Victory* (London: Hodder & Stoughton, 1947)

Delaforce, Patrick, *Churchill's Desert Rats: From Normandy to Berlin with the 7th Armoured Division* (Stroud: Alan Sutton, 1994; republished London: Chancellor Press, 1999/2001)

Delaforce, Patrick, *Monty's Iron Sides: From the Normandy Beaches to Bremen with the 3rd Division* (Stroud: Alan Sutton, 1995; republished London: Chancellor Press, 1999)

Delaforce, Patrick, *The Polar Bears: Monty's Left Flank, From Normandy to the Relief of Holland with 49th Division* (Stroud: Sutton, 1995/2003)

D'Este, Carlo *Decision in Normandy* (London: Collins, 1983/London: Pan, 1984)

D'Este, Carlo, *Eisenhower* (London: Weidenfeld & Nicolson, 2003)

D'Este, Carlo, *Patton: A Genius for War* (New York: Harper Perennial, 1996)

Doherty, Richard, *Normandy 1944: The Road to Victory* (Staplehurst: Spellmount, 2004)

Duncan, Major-General Nigel, *79th Armoured Division: Hobo's Funnies* (Windsor: Profile, 1972)

Eisenhower, Dwight D., *At Ease: Stories I Tell to Friends* (London: Robert Hale, 1968)

Eisenhower, Dwight D, *Crusade in Europe* (London: William Heinemann, 1948)

Essame, Major-General H., *Normandy Bridgehead* (London: Macdonald, 1971)

Fletcher, David, *Swimming Shermans: Sherman DD amphibious tank of World War II* (Oxford: Osprey, 2006)

Ford, Ken, *Falaise 1944: Death of an army* (Oxford: Osprey, 2005)

Forty, George, *7th Armoured Division: The 'Desert Rats'* (Hersham: Ian Allan, 2003)

Forty, Simon, *Normandy 1944: The Battle for the Hedgerows* (Barnsley: Pen & Sword, 2018)

Franks, Norman, *Typhoon Attack* (London: William Kimber, 1984; republished updated and amended, London: Grub Street, 2003)

Frayn Turner, John, *Invasion '44: The Full Story of D-Day* (London: George G. Harrap, 1959; Shrewsbury: Airlife, 2002)

Futter, Geoffery W., *The Funnies: The 79th Armoured Division and its specialised equipment* (Hemel Hempstead: Bellona, 1974)

Gilbert, Martin, *Churchill: A Life* (London: Pimlico, 2000)

Golley, John, *The Big Drop: The Guns of Merville, June 1944* (London: Jane's, 1982)

Gregory, Barry and Batchelor, John, *Airborne Warfare 1941–1945* (London: Phoebus, 1979)

Hamilton, Nigel, *Monty: Master of the Battlefield 1942–1944* (London: Hamish Hamilton, 1983)

Hart, Stephen, *Battle Zone Normandy: Road to Falaise* (Stroud: Sutton, 2004)

Hart, Stephen, *The Final Battle for Normandy: Northern France 9 July – 30 August 1944* (London: Ministry of Defence, 2005)

Hartcup, Guy, *Code Name Mulberry: The Planning, Building & Operation of the Normandy Harbours* (Newton Abbot: David & Charles, 1977; republished Barnsley: Pen & Sword Military, 2006)

Hastings, Max, *Finest Years: Churchill as Warlord 1940–45* (London: Harper Press, 2009)

Hastings, Max, *Overlord: D-Day and the Battle for Normandy* (London: Michael Joseph, 1984)

Haswell, Jock, *The Intelligence and Deception of the D-Day Landings* (London: B.T. Batsford, 1979)

Hills, Stuart, *By Tank into Normandy* (London: Cassell, 2003)

Hogg, Ian V., *Fortress: A History of Military Defence* (London: Macdonald & Jane's, 1975)

Holmes, Richard, *D-Day 6 June 1944: from the invasion to the liberation of Paris* (London: Carlton, 2014)

Horne, Alistair, with Montgomery, David, *The Lonely Leader: Monty 1944–1945* (London: Macmillan, 1994; London: Pan, 1995)

Horrocks, Lieutenant-General Sir Brian, *A Full Life* (London: Collins, 1960)

Horrocks, Sir Brian, with Belfield, Eversley and Essame, Major-General H., *Corps Commander.* (London: Sidgwick & Jackson, 1977; London: Magnum, 1978)

Howarth, David, *Dawn of D-Day* (London: Companion, 1959)

Humble, Richard, *Hitler's Generals* (London: Arthur Barker, 1973; St Albans: Panther, 1976)

Hunt, Eric, *Mont Pinçon: August 1944* (Barnsley: Leo Cooper, 2003)

Hunt, Robert and Mason, David, *Camera at War: The Normandy Campaign* (London: Leo Cooper, 1976)

Irving, David, *The Trail of the Fox: The Life of Field-Marshal Erwin Rommel* (London: Weidenfeld and Nicolson, 1977)

Irving, David, *The War Between the Generals* (London: Allen Lane, 1981)

Isby, David C. (ed.), *Fighting in Normandy: The German Army From D-Day to Villers-Bocage* (London: Greenhill Books, 2001; republished Barnsley: Frontline Books, 2016)

Isby, David C. (ed.) *Fighting the Breakout: The German Army in Normandy from 'Cobra' to the Falaise Gap* (London: Greenhill Books, 2004)

Johnson, Garry and Dunphie, Christopher, *Brightly Shone the Dawn: Some Experiences of the Invasion of Normandy* (London: Frederick Warne, 1980)

Jurado, Carlos Caballero, *Resistance Warfare 1940–45* (London: Osprey, 1985)

Kaplan, Philip, *Hitler's D-Day Defences* (Barnsley: Pen & Sword Military, 2017)

Keegan, John, *Six Armies in Normandy* (London: Jonathan Cape, 1982; Harmondsworth: Penguin, 1983)

Kerrigan, Michael, *How Bletchley Park Won World War II* (London: Amber, 2018)

Khan, Mark, *D-Day Assault: The Second World War Assault Training Exercises at Slapton Sands* (Barnsley: Pen & Sword Military, 2014)

Laffin, John, *Raiders: Elite Forces Attacks* (Stroud: Sutton, 1999; London: Chancellor Press, 2000)

Latawski, Paul, *Battle Zone Normandy: Falaise Pocket* (Stroud: Stutton, 2004)

Lefèvre, Eric, translated from French by Roy Cooke and edited by Andrew Holmwood, *Panzers in Normandy Then and Now* (London: After the Battle, 1983)

Lewis, Jon E. (ed.), *D-Day As They Saw It* (London: Robinson, 2004)

Liddell Hart, B.H., *The Other Side of the Hill* (London: Cassel, 1948; London: Pan, 1983)

Liddell Hart, B.H., *The Rommel Papers* (London: Collins, 1953)

Liddle, Peter, *D-Day By Those Who Were There* (Barnsley: Pen & Sword, 2004/2018)

Lovat, Lord, *March Past: A Memoir* (London: Weidenfeld and Nicolson, 1978)

Lucas, James and Barker, James, *The Killing Ground: The Battle of the Falaise Gap, August 1944* (London: B.T. Batsford, 1978)

MacDonald, Charles, *By Air to Battle* (London: Macdonald & Co, 1970)

Macksey, Kenneth, *Rommel: Battles and Campaigns* (London: Arms and Armour Press, 1979)

Macrae, Stuart, *Winston Churchill's Toyshop* (Stroud: Amberley, 2012; first published 1971)

Mayo, Jonathan, *D-Day Minute By Minute* (London: Short Books, 2015)

McKee, Alexander, *Caen: Anvil of Victory* (London: Souvenir Press, 1964)

Miller, Robert A., *August 1944: The Campaign for France* (Novato, CA: Presidio, 1996)

Mitcham Jr, Samuel W., *Hitler's Field Marshals and their Battles* (London: William Heinemann, 1988)

Montgomery, Bernard Law, *The Memoirs of Field Marshal Montgomery* (London: Collins, 1958)

Morgan, Lieutenant-General Sir Frederick, *Overture to Overlord* (London: Hodder and Stoughton, 1950)

Morrison, Alexander, *Silent Invader: A Glider Pilot's Story of the Invasion of Europe in World War II* (Shrewsbury: Airlife, 2002)

Naval Historical Branch, *Operation Neptune: The Normandy Invasion D-Day 6 June 1944*

Neillands, Robin, *The Battle of Normandy 1944* (London: Cassel, 2003)

Neillands, Robin, *The Desert Rats: 7th Armoured Division 1940–45* (London: Weidenfeld & Nicolson, 1991; London: Aurum Press, 2005)

Neillands, Robin, *The Raiders: The Army Commandos 1940–1946* (London: Weidenfeld & Nicolson, 1989; London: Fontana, 1990)

Neillands, Robin and De Norman, Roderick, *D-Day 1944: Voices from Normandy* (London: Weidenfeld & Nicolson, 1993; London: Cassell, 2001)

Patch, Harry and Van Emden, Richard, *The Last Fighting Tommy: The Life of Harry Patch, Last Veteran of the Trenches, 1898–2009* (London: Bloomsbury, 2007)

Province, Charles M., *Patton's Third Army* (New York: Hippocrene, 1992)

Ramsey, Winston G. (ed.), 'The Battle of the Falaise Pocket', *After the Battle* (London: Battle of Britain Prints, No. 8, 1975)

Rankin, Nicolas, *Churchill's Wizards: The British Genius for Deception 1914–1945* (London: Faber and Faber, 2009)

Reit, Seymour, *Masquerade: The Amazing Camouflage Deceptions of World War II* (London: Robert Hale, 1979)

Reynolds, Michael, *Monty and Patton: Two Paths to Victory* (Stroud: Spellmount, 2005)

Rogers, Joseph and David, *D-Day Beach Force* (Stroud: Spellmount, 2012)

Rohmer, Major-General Richard, *Patton's Gap: An Account of the Battle of Normandy 1944* (London: Arms and Armour Press, 1981)

Rottman, Gordon L., *US World War II Amphibious Tactics: Mediterranean & European Theaters* (Oxford: Osprey, 2006)

Ruffner, Kevin Conley, *Luftwaffe Field Divisions 1941–45* (Oxford: Osprey, 1990)

Ryan, Cornelius, *The Longest Day* (London: Victor Gollanz, 1960; 12th Impression, 1982)

Saunders, Tim, *Hill 112: Battles of the Odon – 1944* (Barnsley: Leo Cooper, 2001)

Schofield, Victoria, *Wavell: Soldier & Statesman* (London: John Murray, 2006)

Sebag-Montefiore, Hugh, *Enigma: The Battle for the Code* (London: Weidenfeld & Nicolson, 2001)

Sebba, Anne, *Les Parisiennes: How the Women of Paris Lived, Loved and Died in the 1940s* (London: Weidenfeld & Nicolson, 2017)

Speer, Albert, translated from German by Richard and Clara Winston, *Inside the Third Reich* (London: Phoenix, 1997)

Stafford, David, *Ten Days to D-Day: Countdown to the Liberation of Europe* (London: Little Brown, 2003; London: Abacus, 2004)

Stagg, J.M., *Forecast for Overlord* (London: Ian Allan, 1971)

Stephenson, Charles, *The Channel Islands 1941–45: Hitler's Impregnable Fortress* (Oxford: Osprey, 2006)

Thompson, Julian, *The Imperial War Museum Book of Victory in Europe* (London: Sidgwick & Jackson, 1994)

Thompson, R.W., *D-Day: Spearhead of Invasion* (London: Macdonald, 1968)

Thornton, Willis, *The Liberation of Paris* (London: Rupert Hart-Davis, 1963)

Tout, Ken, *A Fine Night for Tanks: The Road to Falaise* (Stroud: Sutton, 1998)

Tout, Ken, *Roads to Falaise: 'Cobra' & 'Goodwood' Reassessed* (Stroud: Sutton, 2002)

Tout, Ken, *The Bloody Battle for Tilly: Normandy 1944* (Stroud: Sutton, 2000)

Tucker-Jones, Anthony, *Armoured Warfare in the Battle for Normandy* (Barnsley: Pen & Sword Military, 2012)

Tucker-Jones, Anthony, *Falaise: The Flawed Victory: The Destruction of Panzergruppe West, August 1944* (Barnsley: Pen & Sword Military, 2008)

Tucker-Jones, Anthony, *Operation Dragoon: The Liberation of Southern France 1944* (Barnsley: Pen & Sword Military, 2009)

Tute, Warren, Costello, John and Hughes, Terry, *D-Day* (London: Pan, 1975)

Vickers, Philip, *Das Reich: 2nd SS Panzer Division Das Reich – Drive to Normandy, June 1944* (Barnsley: Leo Cooper, 2000)

Warner, Philip, *The D Day Landings* (London: William Kimber, 1980)

Weigley, Russel F., *Eisenhower's Lieutenants* (London: Sidgwick & Jackson, 1981)

Whiting, Charles, *'44: In Combat on the Western Front from Normandy to the Ardennes* (London: Century, 1984)

Williams, Andrew, *D-Day to Berlin* (London: Hodder & Stoughton, 2004)

Williams, Paul, *Hitler's Atlantic Wall: Normandy* (Barnsley: Pen & Sword Military, 2013)

Willmott, H.P., *June 1944* (Poole: Blandford Press, 1984)

Wilmot, Chester, *The Struggle for Europe* (London: Collins, 1952)

Winters, Major Dick, *Beyond Band of Brothers* (New York: Penguin, 2006; London: Ebury, 2008)

Wynn, Humphrey and Young, Susan, *Prelude to Overlord* (Shrewsbury: Airlife, 1983)

Young, Brigadier Peter, *Commando* (London: Macdonald & Co, 1970)

Young, Brigadier Peter, *D-Day* (London: Bison, 1981)

Zaloga, Steven J., *Liberation of Paris 1944: Patton's race for the Seine* (Oxford: Osprey, 2008)

Zaloga, Steven J., *Operation Cobra 1944: Breakout from Normandy* (Oxford: Osprey, 2001)

Zetterling, Niklas, *Normandy 1944: German Military Organization, Combat Power and Organizational Effectiveness* (Winnipeg: JJ Fedorowicz, 2000)

ACKNOWLEDGEMENTS

For the fortieth anniversary of the D-Day Landings, I interviewed Dan Chadwick, a director of museum services, about the then brand new Portsmouth D-Day Museum. It had been specially built to house the Overlord Embroidery, which was produced in the late 1960s and struggled to find a suitable home. I was given a guided tour before the official opening and it proved an inspiration, as did Dan's enthusiasm for the project. Ever since, I have been in awe of the simply immense logistical, military and technical achievements of Operation Overlord.

Like all writers, I greatly benefitted from those who have gone before. D-Day remains an inordinately popular subject with readers and publishers alike. There is certainly no shortage of reference material covering the many aspects of the landings, as the not inconsiderable bibliography for this book testifies. Historians past and present who proved a particular inspiration include Stephen Ambrose, Carlo D'Este, Richard Holmes, Robin Neillands, Peter Young and last but by no means least Cornelius Ryan, who really started it all with his *The Longest Day*, first published in 1960. It was the work of the late Brigadier Peter Young, whom I had the privilege of meeting during his Sealed Knot days, that originally set me on the path to becoming a historian.

While researching a book is essentially a one-man task, there is nonetheless an element of teamwork, especially with a topic as vast as D-Day and the subsequent Normandy campaign. I am therefore grateful to Richard Bass, author, battlefield guide and historian, for sharing his extensive research on American preparations in North Devon and subsequent experiences on D-Day. This greatly helped clarify the very differing approaches adopted by the American and British assault forces.

Likewise, I am indebted to Atlantic Wall experts Richard Drew and John Flaherty, Neil Worth and the friends of the Assault Training Center, Patricia Knowles of the Upottery Airfield Heritage Trust, Jane Swindail at North Devon Maritime Museum, Rob Palmer of Britishmilitaryhistory. co.uk, Preston Isaac of the Cobbaton Combat Collection and Andrew Whitmarsh of the D-Day Story (formerly Portsmouth D-Day Museum).

Also my gratitude to those who helped source research material, too numerous to list, though a special mention must go to Katie Eaton, who assisted over and above the call of duty, and Lorenzo Cerri, purveyor of second-hand and out of print books. At THP my thanks to commissioning editor Amy Rigg, project editor Alex Waite, copy editor Tony Walton and designer Katie Beard. Finally, thanks to my wife Amelia, who as always provided a valuable confidant on all matters military and editorial.

INDEX